DISCOVER *your* INNER *Strength*

CUTTING EDGE GROWTH STRATEGIES
FROM THE INDUSTRY'S LEADING EXPERTS

INSIGHT PUBLISHING
SEVIERVILLE, TENNESSEE

TABLE OF CONTENTS

A Message from David Wright, President, International Speakers Network v

Attitude: The Key to Your Inner Strength ....

by Johnna Johnson 1

Attitude is Everything ....

by Dr. Kenneth Blanchard 15

Living a Strategic Life: The Seven C's of Success ....

by Dr. Howard M. Knoff 31

Happiness and Ultimate Wealth: The Power of Inner Strength ....

by Dr. Neera Puri 51

Character Strengths ....

by Tana Sherwood 67

Discovering The Secret to Your Sales Power ....

by Lee Knapp 87

A Values-Based Approach ....

by Dr. Stephen Covey 101

The SENSE of Humor ....

by Juli Burney 115

Little Courage – Big Rewards ....

by Sharon Jenks, CPBA 129

Has Your Vision Become an Illusion? ....

by Lyle R. Johnson 141

Using Strategy to Discover Your Inner Strength ....

by Brian Tracy 161

Bully Free at Work ....

by Valerie Cade 173

An Internet Pioneer ....

      by Hillary S. Bressler...185

Moving Beyond Fear...

      by Sharon Moist...197

Retirement with Attitude: How Boomers Reinvent the Wheel ....

      by Kim Kirmmse Toth...209

Who Gets Your Best? ....

      by JoAn Majors..221

Recognizing Your Rainbows ....

      by Karen Phillips 235

The Third Entity..

      by Faith Fuller, PhD, PCC & Marita Fridjhon, MSW, PCC 253

Learning Orientation to Learn, Innovate and Succeed.................................

      by Dr. Margaret Martinez...273

Strength Through Negotiation: The Basics ....

      by Laura Leezer 285

Purposeful Living..

      by Philip Guy Rochford 295

The Choice of Inner Strength ....

      by Jodi Fraser...315

Inner Strength: *The Key to Your Career Success* ....

      by Allison Timberlake...333

Discovery Comes with Action! ....

      by Monica J. Griffith 347

Practical Health and Wellness: Creating Balance...

      by Luanne Pennesi...365

The interviews found in this book are conducted by David E. Wright, President of International Speakers Network & Insight Publishing

A Message from the Publisher

I've faced many challenges in my life and I know what it means to struggle. I sure wish I'd had this book during those times. We handpicked some of the most successful people we know who have had to learn how to discover their inner strength. The authors I interviewed for this book have the experience and knowledge that will help everyone learn a little more about this vital component for success—inner strength.

This book is custom designed for those who want to increase their skills and knowledge. Self-development is vital to success. One author made this poignant observation: "Self-development tends to fall to the bottom of the priority list for most people and they are not the only ones to suffer for this choice. Their family suffers. Their coworkers suffer. Their employees suffer. All of the crucial relationships in their life suffer because they are not being the absolute best they could truly be."

If you strive for excellence and want valuable information about how some of the most successful people in business today have found their inner strength and achieved success, this book is the resource you need. People who want to hone their skills to cope with life's challenges will learn from what these authors have to say. I know that I did and I believe you will too.

—**David E. Wright**

Chapter One

Attitude: The Key to Your Inner Strength

An Interview With…

Johnna Johnson

David Wright (Wright)

Today we're talking with international speaker and trainer, author, and success coach, Johnna Johnson, who passionately inspires organizations, teams, and individuals to "Just Jump" out of their comfort zone and into their true potential. Her programs, products, and coaching programs provide uncommon inspiration, education, and tools to help professionals build the confidence and courage they need to take their results to an entirely new level. Professionals around the world value her essential elements of excellence: Ambition, Attitude, and Action. She received her bachelor's degree in Communication with an emphasis in Training and Development from Boise State University where she also teaches as adjunct faculty. Her articles have been featured in journals, forums, and columns around the world and her voice has been broadcast on television and radio waves from California to New York.

Johnna, welcome to *Discover Your Inner Strength*.

Johnna Johnson (Johnson)

Thank you, David! I am delighted to be with you today and honored to have been asked to participate in the *Discover Your Inner Strength* book.

Wright

In discussing ways to discover our inner strength, you have identified the key to discovering our inner strength, and it is about attitude. Why do you think attitude is a part of our inner strength?

Johnson

Our inner strength—the very core of who we are—comes from how we feel and how we think about *everything* in our lives, which is our attitude. Our attitude drives *everything* about us as human beings—our beliefs, attitudes, actions, and, most importantly, our results! For decades, we've heard "attitude is everything" and indeed, that is correct.

Wright

So, Johnna, if "attitude is everything," what *is* attitude and how do you define it?

Johnson

There are many different ideas that come to mind when people think about the term "attitude." I personally favor Merriam-Webster's definition: *"A feeling or position about something or someone. Of the mind."* So essentially, David, attitude is how we think and how we feel about every aspect of our lives and it's all in our very own mind. It's how we *choose* to feel about something or someone.

Wright

So are you saying that attitude is a choice?

Johnson

Absolutely! Attitude is 100 percent a personal choice. It's not always an *easy* choice, but it is always a *simple* choice. Our choice of attitude is simple because we only have two basic options: positive (attitude) or negative (attitude). Win or lose. Success or failure. Will or won't. Abundance or scarcity. Fear or Faith. Can or can't, and the list goes on and on.

We choose how we look at others, our experiences, and ourselves. We choose to live in fear or choose to focus on faith. We choose to see our current circumstances from a place of scarcity or abundance. We choose if we will or won't. It's very, very simple when you think about it that way. The hard part is deciding which option you want to choose—it is a choice!

We can influence essentially anything in this world, but the only thing we can truly control is our thoughts and actions. We control how we think about things. We have absolute control over our attitude. The beauty of attitude is that positive thoughts and negative thoughts cannot occupy your mind at the exact same time, so you get to choose positive or negative.

For example, you can't think about how much you want to succeed as an entrepreneur—how liberating it's going to be, and how victorious you are envisioning yourself—while at the exact same time fear that you're not going to be able to make it happen, especially in economic downturns. With unemployment rates skyrocketing and no immediate end in sight, are you going to *choose* to merely survive your circumstances, or are you going to choose to figure out what it will take to thrive? So, yes, David, attitude is an absolute choice.

Wright

How do our attitudes affect our lives?

Johnson

I'll use a recent, global example. At the age of eleven, Michael Phelps set his sights on a *single* Olympic gold medal. Twelve years later, the Baltimore, Maryland native became the most decorated Olympian of all time, taking home a record eight gold medals in the 2008 Summer Olympics. In his latest book *No Limits: The Will to Succeed,* Phelps shares, "The single most important factor in anything we do, and particularly in this endeavor [winning eight gold medals] was this: what is your attitude? You have to have the right mental attitude. You're going to be an Olympic champion in attitude long before there's a gold medal around your neck."

Phelps' attitude has and continues to affect him in numerous ways: physically (imagine downing ten thousand calories a day and still having a physique like his), financially (wouldn't you love to have a hundred million dollars in endorsements), socially (have you ever been on the front of a Wheaties box or hosted *Saturday Night Live?*), legendary (what would you feel like if you were the most decorated Olympian of all time?), and globally (when is the last time you broke any world records?). Yes, he's has and continues to work very hard for what he has earned and it all starts with his attitude.

From street sweepers and CEOs to stay-at-home moms and Olympic champions, the single most important factor in success is attitude. Your attitude will make or break you. It determines your success at all different levels.

I want to share with everybody who is reading this chapter about how important programming our minds for success is because what we put in and what we get out is exactly the same thing—garbage in, garbage out. It's about making you or breaking you. Your attitude can make the big jobs, it can make the great relationships, and it can make your financial future. You can either feel that you really deserve your promotion or not, or that you'll never amount to anything or that you'll succeed.

Wright

I'm a simple guy. Will you tell me two or three things that have the biggest affect on our attitude?

Johnson

There are *numerous* things that affect your attitude, from your past experiences and current circumstances to future hopes and dreams to your environment and the weather to the media. However, you've asked for only two or three! I can tell you, without hesitation, the three top things that have the biggest affect on your attitude are these:

    1.   Programming (your constant thoughts and feelings)

2. Passion (being passionate about what you do)
3. People (surrounding yourself with the right people)

Your personal programming (self-talk) is the number one contributor to your attitude. Your self-talk (what you say to yourself all day long) is essentially programming your mind. Simply put, your mind doesn't distinguish between fact or fiction, it just acts on what you program it to do. How are you programming your mind every day? Do you start the day with thoughts that exude excitement, gratitude, and faith, or do you wake up resentful, angry, and full of fear? Positive or negative?

The second most powerful thing that affects your attitude is passion—making sure that you are passionate about what you are doing day in and day out, with your family, with your career, and with your finances. Whatever you're doing, you have to be passionate about it! Passion creates momentum, excitement, joy, and incredible results.

The third most influential element in creating your attitude (and ultimately your results) is the people you associate with. Our friends, family, colleagues, partners, clients, and customers are very influential. The question is: are they influencing you in the right direction? Do the people you spend most of your time with believe in you, love you, support you, guide you, mentor you, and coach you in the courageous and exciting direction of achieving all of your wildest dreams and aspirations?

Again, there are many things that affect our attitude, but the top three things that are most important are: programming your mind for success, being passionate about what you do in life, and surrounding yourself with dynamic people who believe in you!

Wright

If programming our mind for success is so critical, will you give us some ideas on how we can do that?

Johnson

Most importantly, you must recognize how programming directly affects your results. Programming creates your beliefs. Your beliefs create your attitude. Your attitude creates your actions and your actions create your results.

Let's go back to my friend Michael Phelps who said, "You have to train the mind just like you train the body." Programming (self-talk) is what you put into your mind throughout your day. Do you wake up full of hope, excitement, and confidence feeling as though you can take on the world? Do you anticipate great challenges and opportunities? You start to believe those things because your programming creates your beliefs. When you start to believe those things, do you have a positive attitude or a negative attitude? You have a positive attitude, right? If you have a negative attitude about your business, about your colleagues, about your industry, about the economy, you're going to take actions that represent that attitude. As a result, if you have a negative attitude, you're going to be taking negative actions. Then we wonder why we create the negative results that we do.

Six months ago, I had a very successful financial planner and business owner on the West Coast contact me in hopes I could help her. With the financial crisis at its peak, she was losing money, clients, and hope. She was considering closing her doors after seventeen fruitful years. It was devastating. Her once abundant and deserving attitude quickly, and understandably, shifted to pure survival, fear, and ultimate panic. She was "a train wreck" in her mind. Waking up every day with a fear-stricken paralysis, it was very easy for her, her business partner, and her staff to believe that there was no hope and it was time to jump ship.

I embraced this client and we got to work immediately. She thought we should be working on business strategies. I *knew* we should be working on her (and her staff's) programming and beliefs, first and foremost. I believed in her and she trusted me.

We immediately got clear on what needed to happen within the next ninety days in order for her to experience the results she envisioned (and was desperate to attain). Then, based on my recommendation, she and her assistant created affirmations and power statements (programming techniques) and posted them all through out their office. So, when fear crept up, they could immediately replace their detrimental thoughts and feelings with positive ones.

I challenged Laura to envision what it would look and *feel* like *when* (not *if*) she met her ninety-day goals. I reminded her that feelings create our actions. We must feel success. She was so relived and excited—*and a little hesitant about my methods I was sharing with her.* Her plan was clear, her focus realigned, and she could see the light at the end of the tunnel—*though it was very faint.*

I flew back home and in less than a week I received an unexpected call from Laura. "Are you sitting down, Johnna?" I was actually standing up but slowly sat down with interest. "Yes, I'm sitting down now," I replied.

"Johnna," she said, "we just reached our ninety-day goal in *nine* days!"

That single moment in time will be one of my most prized of all time. Laura had made a *simple* shift in her programming. Her programming and commitment to visualizing and feeling that success created her fighting, whatever-it-takes attitude. Her courageous attitude inspired her to take brave actions and her actions created unprecedented results in record time! Laura represents the hero that lives in every single one of us. It all begins with programming your mind for superhero success!

I know so many of you reading this right now can relate! If you believe that it's over, it's impossible to turn things around, and you are in pure survival mode, what types of actions do you take? I can guarantee that you will take actions based on your beliefs. As a result of the actions you take, you will create the results of your beliefs. Hopeless/Fearful actions = Hopeless/Fearful results. On the contrary, exciting, courageous, and innovative actions = exciting, courageous, and innovative results—every time!

Wright

Monumental results, Johnna!

Let's talk about the second thing you mentioned that contributes to attitude—passion. This might be a problem for some of our readers. What would you recommend for those readers who are stuck in a passionless career?

Johnson

David, I speak to hundreds of people every week all over the country. I ask those in the audience if they are passionate about what they do day in and day out. In an audience of three hundred people, I would be shocked if I got five people to raise their hand! It is devastating to see how many people are spending eight, ten, twelve, fourteen, or sixteen hours a day (not to mention a lifetime) doing something that they're not passionate about. Passion equals success. Passion equals momentum. Passion equals joy. And when you have momentum and joy and excitement and enthusiasm, you have what it takes to achieve anything! On the contrary, without passion you can't do a great job—at anything.

For those who are stuck in a passionless situation, I'd love to share a few ideas on how to recreate the passion you once had or how to make a decision to live with more passion. First, think about what got you into your career/relationship/situation in the first place. What was it that inspired you to open the doors of your new business? Think about what you were passionate about before and rekindle that passion. Whether it includes delegating tasks, projects, or decisions that you *aren't* passionate about or adding things to your life, list projects that you *are* passionate about. Take action today to live with more passion!

Making a decision to leave people, things, or careers that you aren't passionate about can be very intimidating. In fact, most people would rather stay in their "comfort zone" than "jump" into unfamiliar territory and take courageous action toward a more passionate life. In order to make changes in your life, you must get clear on what you want, why you want it, and then feel the fear and "Just Jump!" Each time you jump, you build the courage and confidence to do it again and again.

For more strategies and techniques on jumping out of your comfort zone, I encourage you to invest in my book, *Just Jump: How to Build the Confidence and Courage You Need to Just Jump Out of Your Comfort Zone and Into Your True Potential,* which is available on our Web site, www.JohnnaJohnson.com.

Wright

If surrounding ourselves with other dynamic people is so essential, will you share with our readers how we can move forward in creating our thriving inner and outer circles?

Johnson

This is vital for success in your life and it's all about surrounding yourself with the right people. We all have our inner and outer circles. Your inner circle is comprised of people like spouses, siblings, children, friends, family, colleagues, etc.—people you're very, very close to, and are very intimate with in terms of your knowledge and your relationships, your fears and your challenges, your hopes and your dreams. We need an inner circle of people who are absolutely interested, supportive, and encouraging in what we're doing and where we're going.

I have a great example. When my son, Tyler, was just two years old, I remember making a huge business decision. I was feeling on top of the world and I wanted to share the exciting news but I couldn't get in touch with anyone. I happened to be home that day, and my son was home with me, so I called out to my son, "Tyler, Tyler come in here, please!" As he ran into the kitchen and crawled up onto the barstool, I felt a bit awkward getting ready to discuss business with a two-year-old. I grabbed his precious little hands and put them in mine. I looked at his crystal blue eyes and, as he gazed back into my eyes, I said, "Tyler, I am about to embark on the most incredible journey of my life!" I will never forget what he said to me, "Mommy, can I go too?"

Those are the people we must surround ourselves with—people, who love us, support us, encourage us, and who want to go with us on our journey to success, no matter where it leads. If the people in your inner circle are a far cry from loving, supporting, and encouraging, you need to make some big decisions. Perhaps you need to limit your time with them or end those relationships.

Your outer circle is comprised of other experts who are going to help you achieve what you want in life and partner with you to get you where you're destined to go and where you're focused on going. For example, you might have a business coach who helps you get through your business plans so you can increase or grow your business. You might have a personal trainer to help you achieve your fitness goals. You might have a financial planner to help you realize all of your financial dreams. Whether it's a marketing director, a publisher, or a fitness trainer, there are all kinds of experts who are willing to help you get you to where you're going. If you need a Web site, get a Web site designer. Don't spend all the time and trouble to learn it on your own if you're not passionate about that. So build up those outer circles made up of individuals who are going to be passionate about getting you to where you're going in your life.

To experience your full potential, you've got to rely on and partner with other people to help you get you to where you're going because you just simply cannot do it all on your own. If you have huge, audacious goals, you have to surround yourself with experts who love and are passionate about what they do and, most importantly, who believe in *you*.

Wright

Is it possible to create, maintain, and protect a thriving attitude?

Johnson

Not only is it possible, it is imperative! The first thing you need to do is to create it. Based on everything we've discussed so far, you need to make your choices wisely. Are you going to choose to create a successful, dynamic, exciting, and joyful life? You can also consider the things that affect your attitude most—waking up late, incomplete housework, children who don't listen, employees who take advantage of you, relationships that aren't working, a lack of finances in your bank account, or career burnout. If some of these things make it difficult for you to stay focused on the positive, abundant, and joyful things in life, start taking actions to resolve your discord with them.

There are many different things you can do to *maintain* a thriving attitude. If you create it, you have to make sure that you maintain it! Just like a house—if you invest the time, energy, and money into building a house, you have to maintain it and protect it from the weather, elements, wear and tear, etc. Maintain and protect your attitude by ensuring your self-talk is positive. Create power thoughts or affirmations that you can visualize every day. (For more on my affirmation CDs, visit JohnnaJohnson.com.)

Cancel out your negative thoughts that aren't working for you and replace them with positive ones. For example: Imagine a dream position being posted in your organization. If you were selected for the promotion, you'd be in heaven! However, your programming immediately reverts to, "There is no way I am qualified for the position. I'll never get it!" Recognize that these negative thoughts will get you absolutely nowhere. If that's what you program your mind to act upon, you start to believe it. If you believe you are way out of your league for the new position, what kind of an attitude can you imagine you have? (Hint: negative, insecure, resentful, fearful.) And with an attitude like that, what kinds of actions do you take? Do you apply for the position? No. Then, consider the results you would have created in this scenario. Negative ones! Programming creates beliefs. Beliefs create attitudes. Attitudes create actions and those actions create your results.

On August 8, 2008, in Beijing, China, Michael Phelps programmed his mind for success. He programmed each of his events in his mind down the very last hundredth of a second. With years of programming and visualizing each and every move, he believed winning eight gold medals was within his grasp. Believing in the incredible opportunities, he created a "Gold Medal Attitude." When you believe it, you achieve it because you take courageous actions that create the results you have always dreamed of.

Protect your most powerful asset you choose to create—your attitude—by surrounding yourself with people, things, and places that keep you focused on the positive aspects of your life.

Wright

Is there any way we can self-identify a negative attitude?

Johnson

If you're not creating the results that you desire, it's a great opportunity for you to look inward and to identify your current programming patterns. How are you programming yourself for success? What are you doing to sabotage your efforts? Assess the types of people you are surrounding yourself with—as we know, "Birds of a feather, flock together!" If those you spend your time with are focused on fear, scarcity, what's not working in their lives, etc., your energy, efforts, and results are most likely focused in the wrong direction.

Wright

After we've determined we have a negative attitude that isn't working for us, how do we give ourselves an attitude adjustment?

Johnson

If you're feeling fearful, hopeless, anxious guilty, unappreciated, or resentful it's a good indicator that you need an attitude adjustment. Think about how you feel about the economy. Think about how you feel about your business. Think about how you feel about your clients.

I was coaching a small business owner who kept referring to a "problem client." After a few of these detrimental references, I recommended that he change his mindset from "problem" to "challenging." No one likes a problem, but many of us love a challenge. It's just a simple change of perspective. After a few "challenging" references, he then began simply referring to his client by name and the anxiety and frustration went away.

It's not always easy but it is always simple. Resolve to think positively. Instead of thoughts like, "I can't afford to pay my bills this month," replace them with thoughts like, "I do whatever it takes to pay my bills on time each and every month." Then, visualize the experience of what if will feel like once they are paid! Doesn't it feel great? It's simply a matter of being aware of what your attitude is and how you feel about it. Then make sure that you take the appropriate measures to adjust your attitude in accordance with your desires.

Wright

How do we remain positive in such a negative environment, especially with plummeting stock prices, the devastating housing market, record-high gas prices, and astronomical unemployment rates?

Johnson

That's a great question, which I am asked frequently! As I mentioned, I travel all over the country, so I see the devastation, anxiety, and discouragement all over—it's everywhere!

I remember a time when my husband, son, and I went on vacation. I ended up lying wide awake at 2 AM in our hotel. Hoping it would help me fall asleep, I turned on the television and the only thing on was the news. Within ninety seconds, my stomach was in knots and my heart literally ached after learning about a ninety-year-old woman being beaten at an ATM, people dying at sea because their boat capsized, a female jogger being raped during her morning jog, and a child dying in a house fire. I turned off the television and laid there next to my husband and son in fear, sadness, anger, disgust, and pure anxiety—solely as a result of ninety seconds of the news. Needless to say, one of the best and immediate ways you can remain positive, especially in an economic crisis, is limiting the time you spend watching, listening to, and reading the news.

Another great tactic to employ during challenging times is to ask yourself powerful questions such as: Are you going to let other people, the economy, CEO decisions, gas prices, or housing markets affect *your* life? Are you going to let what's happening to other people crush *your* dreams? What courageous actions do *you* need to take to thrive, especially during difficult times? Asking yourself these questions allows you to focus on taking action toward what is best for you instead of becoming paralyzed with fear, anxiety, or discouragement.

My high school teachers and college professors often referred to me as "Pollyanna" because I chose (and continue to choose) to see the positive in almost every situation. Of course, I am human and I have my dippy days as well, however, for the most part, I *am* Pollyanna because I choose to put on rose-colored glasses and see things from that great, rosy perspective. David, it's all about choices. Living your life to its full potential is all about choices. The questions are: will you choose positive or negative? Scarcity or abundance? Fear or faith? Merely survive or absolutely thrive? The choice is yours!

Wright

What a fantastic conversation, Johnna. I know our readers are going to learn a lot about attitude and be inspired to make some changes in their lives! I really do appreciate all this time you've taken with me to answer these questions.

Johnson

It has been an absolute pleasure. Thank you so much for the invitation to join you, along with all of the other fabulous authors on this project.

Wright

Today we've been talking with international speaker and trainer, author, and success coach, Johnna Johnson. This high-energy, excellence-driven Idaho native exudes genuine passion, not only in what she delivers but also in those she teaches. With over sixteen years in the speaking and training industries, she has worked extensively in both private and government sectors, along with numerous professional associations, corporations, and individuals. Johnna has served as the first female non-commissioned training officer for the largest law enforcement agency in the state of Idaho. She has earned her way to the top 2 percent of over a million representatives of an international direct sales company and was one of four hundred international instructors for the largest financial institution in the world.

Johnna, thank you so much for being part of this great project, *Discover Your Inner Strength.*

About the Author

Johnna Johnson & Co. inspires organizations, teams and individuals to Just Jump: From Mediocrity to Excellence. Throughout her keynotes, workshops and coaching, you will experience not only her energetic and interactive methods but most importantly, her essential elements of excellence: Ambition, Attitude & Action!

With over 15 years in the Training & Development industry, Johnna has worked extensively in both the private and government sectors along with numerous professional associations and individuals. Johnna has served as a Training Officer for the largest law enforcement agency in the state of Idaho, earned her way into the top 2% of an International Direct-Sales Company as a Sales Director and was an Instructor for the largest financial institution in the world!

Whether she was receiving a college scholarship for her distinction of excellence, breaking numerous sales & performance records or starting her own companies, Johnna certainly has first-hand experience and know-how when it comes to taking courageous action and jumping! With an impressive success rate and being an expert in her field, thousands have sought out Johnna's expertise to assist them with personal, professional and organizational excellence including colleagues, executives, military leaders and Fortune 500 companies.

In addition, Johnna received her Bachelor's Degree in General Communication with an emphasis in Training & Development from Boise State University, where she also teaches as Adjunct Faculty. She possesses a variety of additional certifications that are a result of her commitment to continuing education and on-going professional development. Her articles have been featured in journals, forums and columns around the world, her message has been broadcast on radio waves from California to New York and she has authored two books, "Just Jump!" (Trieste Publishing House, 2008) and "Discover Your Inner Strength" (Insight Publishing, 2009)

Johnna Schuck Johnson

P.O. Box 191008
Boise, ID 83719
Toll free 888.694.4487 | 208.376.3734
ContactUs@JohnnaJohnson.com
www.JohnnaJohnson.com

Chapter Two

Attitude is Everything

An Interview With...

Dr. Kenneth Blanchard

David Wright (Wright)

Few people have created a positive impact on the day-to-day management of people and companies more than Dr. Kenneth Blanchard. He is known around the world simply as Ken, a prominent, gregarious, sought-after author, speaker, and business consultant. Ken is universally characterized by friends, colleagues, and clients as one of the most insightful, powerful, and compassionate men in business today.

Ken's impact as a writer is far-reaching. His phenomenal best-selling book, *The One Minute Manager®*, coauthored with Spencer Johnson, has sold more than thirteen million copies worldwide and has been translated into more than twenty-five languages. Ken is Chairman and "Chief Spiritual Officer" of the Ken Blanchard Companies. The organization's focus is to energize organizations around the world with customized training in bottom-line business strategies based on the simple, yet powerful principles inspired by Ken's best-selling books.

Dr. Blanchard, welcome to *Discover Your Inner Strength*.

Dr. Ken Blanchard (Blanchard)

Well, it's nice to talk with you, David. It's good to be here.

David Wright (Wright)

I must tell you that preparing for your interview took quite a bit more time than usual. The scope of your life's work and your business, the Ken Blanchard Companies, would make for a dozen fascinating interviews.

Before we dive into the specifics of some of your projects and strategies, will you give our readers a brief synopsis of your life—how you came to be the Ken Blanchard we all know and respect?

Blanchard

Well, I'll tell you, David, I think life is what you do when you are planning on doing something else. I think that was John Lennon's line. I never intended to do what I have been doing. In fact, all my professors in college told me that I couldn't write. I wanted to do college work, which I did, and they said, "You had better be an administrator." So I decided I was going to be a Dean of Students. I got provisionally accepted into my master's degree program and then provisionally accepted at Cornell because I never could take any of those standardized tests.

I took the college boards four times and finally got 502 in English. I don't have a test-taking mind. I ended up in a university in Athens, Ohio, in 1966 as an Administrative Assistant to the Dean of the Business School. When I got there he said, "Ken, I want you to teach a course. I want all my deans to teach." I had never thought about teaching because they said I couldn't write, and teachers had to publish. He put me in the manager's department.

I've taken enough bad courses in my day and I wasn't going to teach one. I really prepared and had a wonderful time with the students. I was chosen as one of the top ten teachers on the campus coming out of the chute!

I just had a marvelous time. A colleague by the name of Paul Hersey was chairman of the Management Department. He wasn't very friendly to me initially because the Dean had led me to his department, but I heard he was a great teacher. He taught Organizational Behavior and Leadership. So I said, "Can I sit in on your course next semester?"

"Nobody audits my courses," he said. "If you want to take it for credit, you're welcome."

I couldn't believe it. I had a doctoral degree and he wanted me to take his course for credit—so I signed up.

The registrar didn't know what to do with me because I already had a doctorate, but I wrote the papers and took the course, and it was great.

In June 1967, Hersey came into my office and said, "Ken, I've been teaching in this field for ten years. I think I'm better than anybody, but I can't write. I'm a nervous wreck, and I'd love to write a textbook with somebody. Would you write one with me?"

I said, "We ought to be a great team. You can't write and I'm not supposed to be able to, so let's do it!"

Thus began this great career of writing and teaching. We wrote a textbook called *Management of Organizational Behavior: Utilizing Human Resources.* It came out in its eighth edition October 3, 2000, and the ninth edition was published September 3, 2007. It has sold more than any other textbook in that area over the years. It's been over forty years since that book first came out.

I quit my administrative job, became a professor, and ended up working my way up the ranks. I got a sabbatical leave and went to California for one year twenty-five years ago. I ended up meeting Spencer Johnson at a cocktail party. He wrote children's books—a wonderful series called *Value Tales*® *for Kids.* He also wrote *The Value of Courage: The Story of Jackie Robinson* and *The Value of Believing In Yourself: The Story of Louis Pasteur.*

My wife, Margie, met him first and said, "You guys ought to write a children's book for managers because they won't read anything else." That was my introduction to Spencer. So, *The One Minute Manager* was really a kid's book for big people. That is a long way from saying that my career was well planned.

Wright

Ken, what and/or who were your early influences in the areas of business, leadership, and success? In other words, who shaped you in your early years?

Blanchard

My father had a great impact on me. He was retired as an admiral in the Navy and had a wonderful philosophy. I remember when I was elected as president of the seventh grade, and I came home all pumped up. My father said, "Son, it's great that you're the president of the seventh grade, but now that you have that leadership position, don't ever use it." He said, "Great leaders are followed because people respect them and like them, not because they have power." That was a wonderful lesson for me early on. He was just a great model for me. I got a lot from him.

Then I had this wonderful opportunity in the mid-1980s to write a book with Norman Vincent Peale. He wrote *The Power of Positive Thinking*. I met him when he was eighty-six years old; we were asked to write a book on ethics together, *The Power of Ethical Management: Integrity Pays, You Don't Have to Cheat to Win*. It didn't matter what we were writing together; I learned so much from him. He just built from the positive things I learned from my mother.

My mother said that when I was born I laughed before I cried, I danced before I walked, and I smiled before I frowned. So that, as well as Norman Vincent Peale, really impacted me as I focused on what I could do to train leaders. How do you make them positive? How do you make them realize that it's not about them, it's about who they are serving? It's not about their position—it's about what they can do to help other people win.

So, I'd say my mother and father, then Norman Vincent Peale. All had a tremendous impact on me.

Wright

I can imagine. I read a summary of your undergraduate and graduate degrees. I assumed you studied Business Administration, marketing management, and related courses. Instead, at Cornell you studied Government and Philosophy. You received your master's from Colgate in Sociology and Counseling and your PhD from Cornell in Educational Administration and Leadership. Why did you choose this course of study? How has it affected your writing and consulting?

Blanchard

Well, again, it wasn't really well planned out. I originally went to Colgate to get a master's degree in Education because I was going to be a Dean of Students over men. I had been a Government major, and I was a Government major because it was the best department at Cornell in the Liberal Arts School. It was exciting. We would study what the people were doing at the league of governments. And then, the Philosophy Department was great. I just loved the philosophical arguments. I wasn't a great student in terms of getting grades, but I'm a total learner. I would sit there and listen, and I would really soak it in.

When I went over to Colgate and got into the education courses, they were awful. They were boring. The second week, I was sitting at the bar at the Colgate Inn saying, "I can't believe I've been here two years for this." This is just the way the Lord works: Sitting next to me in the bar was a young sociology professor who had just gotten his PhD at Illinois. He was staying at the Inn. I was moaning and groaning about what I was doing, and he said, "Why don't you come and major with me in sociology? It's really exciting."

"I can do that?" I asked.

He said, "Yes."

I knew they would probably let me do whatever I wanted the first week. Suddenly, I switched out of Education and went with Warren Ramshaw. He had a tremendous impact on me. He retired some years ago as the leading professor at Colgate in the Arts and Sciences, and got me interested in leadership and organizations. That's why I got a master's in Sociology.

The reason I went into educational administration and leadership? It was a doctoral program I could get into because I knew the guy heading up the program. He said, "The greatest thing about Cornell is that you will be in the School of Education. It's not very big, so you don't have to take many education courses, and you can take stuff all over the place."

There was a marvelous man by the name of Don McCarty who eventually became the Dean of the School of Education, Wisconsin. He had an impact on my life; but I was always just searching around.

My mission statement is: to be a loving teacher and example of simple truths that help myself and others to awaken the presence of God in our lives. The reason I mention "God" is that I believe the biggest addiction in the world is the human ego; but I'm really into simple truth. I used to tell people I was trying to get the B.S. out of the behavioral sciences.

Wright

I can't help but think, when you mentioned your father, that he just bottom-lined it for you about leadership.

Blanchard

Yes.

Wright

A man named Paul Myers, in Texas, years and years ago when I went to a conference down there, said, "David, if you think you're a leader and you look around, and no one is following you, you're just out for a walk."

Blanchard

Well, you'd get a kick out of this—I'm just reaching over to pick up a picture of Paul Myers on my desk. He's a good friend, and he's a part of our Center for FaithWalk Leadership where we're trying to challenge and equip people to lead like Jesus. It's non-profit. I tell people I'm not an evangelist because we've got enough trouble with the Christians we have. We don't need any more new ones. But, this is a picture of Paul on top of a mountain. Then there's another picture below that of him under the sea with stingrays. It says, "Attitude is everything. Whether you're on the top of the mountain or the bottom of the sea, true happiness is achieved by accepting God's promises, and by having a biblically positive frame of mind. Your attitude is everything." Isn't that something?

Wright

He's a fine, fine man. He helped me tremendously. In keeping with the theme of our book, *Discover Your Inner Strength,* I wanted to get a sense from you about your own success journey. Many people know you best from *The One Minute Manager* books you coauthored with Spencer Johnson. Would you consider these books as a high water mark for you or have you defined success for yourself in different terms?

Blanchard

Well, you know, *The One Minute Manager* was an absurdly successful book so quickly that I found I couldn't take credit for it. That was when I really got on my own spiritual journey and started to try to find out what the real meaning of life and success was.

That's been a wonderful journey for me because I think, David, the problem with most people is they think their self-worth is a function of their performance plus the opinion of others. The minute you think that is what your self-worth is, every day your self-worth is up for grabs because your performance is going to fluctuate on a day-to-day basis. People are fickle. Their opinions are going to go up and down. You need to ground your self-worth in the unconditional love that God has ready for us, and that really grew out of the unbelievable success of *The One Minute Manager.*

When I started to realize where all that came from, that's how I got involved in this ministry that I mentioned. Paul Myers is a part of it. As I started to read the Bible, I realized that everything I've ever written about, or taught, Jesus did. You know, He did it with the twelve incompetent guys He "hired." The only guy with much education was Judas, and he was His only turnover problem.

Wright

Right.

Blanchard

This is a really interesting thing. What I see in people is not only do they think their self-worth is a function of their performance plus the opinion of others, but they measure their success on the amount of accumulation of wealth, on recognition, power, and status. I think those are nice success items. There's nothing wrong with those, as long as you don't define your life by that.

What I think you need to focus on rather than success is what Bob Buford, in his book *Halftime,* calls "significance"—moving from success to significance. I think the opposite of accumulation of wealth is generosity.

I wrote a book called *The Generosity Factor* with Truett Cathy, who is the founder of Chick-fil-A. He is one of the most generous men I've ever met in my life. I thought we needed to have a model of generosity. It's not only your *treasure,* but it's your *time* and *talent.* Truett and I added *touch* as a fourth one.

The opposite of recognition is service. I think you become an adult when you realize you're here to serve rather than to be served.

Finally, the opposite of power and status is loving relationships. Take Mother Teresa as an example—she couldn't have cared less about recognition, power, and status because she was focused on generosity, service, and loving relationships; but she got all of that earthly stuff. If you focus on the earthly, such as money, recognition, and power, you're never going to get to significance. But if you focus on significance, you'll be amazed at how much success can come your way.

Wright

I spoke with Truett Cathy recently and was impressed by what a down-to-earth, good man he seems to be. When you start talking about him closing his restaurants on Sunday, all of my friends—when they found out I had talked to him—said, "Boy, he must be a great Christian man, but he's rich." I told them, "Well, to put his faith into perspective, by closing on Sunday it costs him $500 million a year."

He lives his faith, doesn't he?

Blanchard

Absolutely, but he still outsells everybody else.

Wright

That's right.

Blanchard

According to their January 25, 2007, press release, Chick-fil-A was the nation's second-largest quick-service chicken restaurant chain in sales at that time. Its business performance marks the thirty-ninth consecutive year the chain has enjoyed a system-wide sales gain—a streak the company has sustained since opening its first chain restaurant in 1967.

Wright

The simplest market scheme, I told him, tripped me up. I walked by his first Chick-fil-A I had ever seen, and some girl came out with chicken stuck on toothpicks and handed me one; I just grabbed it and ate it; it's history from there on.

Blanchard

Yes, I think so. It's really special. It is so important that people understand generosity, service, and loving relationships because too many people are running around like a bunch of peacocks. You even see pastors who measure their success by how many are in their congregation; authors by how many books they have sold; businesspeople by what their profit margin is—how good sales are. The reality is, that's all well and good, but I think what you need to focus on is the other. I think if business did that more and we got Wall Street off our backs with all the short-term evaluation, we'd be a lot better off.

Wright

Absolutely. There seems to be a clear theme that winds through many of your books that has to do with success in business and organizations—how people are treated by management and how they feel about their value to a company. Is this an accurate observation? If so, can you elaborate on it?

Blanchard

Yes, it's a very accurate observation. See, I think the profit is the applause you get for taking care of your customers and creating a motivating environment for your people. Very often people think that business is only about the bottom line. But no, that happens to be the result of creating raving fan customers, which I've described with Sheldon Bowles in our book, *Raving Fans*. Customers want to brag about you, if you create an environment where people can be gung-ho and committed. You've got to take care of your customers and your people, and then your cash register is going to go ka-ching, and you can make some big bucks.

Wright

I noticed that your professional title with the Ken Blanchard Companies is somewhat unique—"Chairman and Chief Spiritual Officer." What does your title mean to you personally and to your company? How does it affect the books you choose to write?

Blanchard

I remember having lunch with Max DuPree one time. The legendary Chairman of Herman Miller, Max wrote a wonderful book called *Leadership Is an Art.*

"What's your job?" I asked him.

He said, "I basically work in the vision area."

"Well, what do you do?" I asked.

"I'm like a third-grade teacher," he replied. "I say our vision and values over, and over, and over again until people get it right, right, right."

I decided from that, I was going to become the Chief Spiritual Officer, which means I would be working in the vision, values, and energy part of our business. I ended up leaving a morning message every day for everybody in our company. We have twenty-eight international offices around the world.

I leave a voice mail every morning, and I do three things on that as Chief Spiritual Officer: One, people tell me who we need to pray for. Two, people tell me who we need to praise—our unsung heroes and people like that. And then three, I leave an inspirational morning message. I really am the cheerleader—the Energizer Bunny—in our company. I'm the reminder of why we're here and what we're trying to do.

We think that our business in the Ken Blanchard Companies is to help people lead at a higher level, and to help individuals and organizations. Our mission statement is to unleash the power and potential of people and organizations for the common good. So if we are going to do that, we've really got to believe in that.

I'm working on getting more Chief Spiritual Officers around the country. I think it's a great title and we should get more of them.

Wright

So those people for whom you pray, where do you get the names?

Blanchard

The people in the company tell me who needs help, whether it's a spouse who is sick or kids who are sick or if they are worried about something. We've got over five years of data about the power of prayer, which is pretty important.

One morning, my inspirational message was about my wife and five members of our company who walked sixty miles one weekend—twenty miles a day for three days—to raise money for breast cancer research.

It was amazing. I went down and waved them all in as they came. They had a ceremony; they had raised $7.6 million. There were over three thousand people walking. A lot of the walkers were dressed in pink—they were cancer victors— people who had overcome it. There were even men walking with pictures of their wives who had died from breast cancer. I thought it was incredible.

There wasn't one mention about it in the major San Diego papers. I said, "Isn't that just something." We have to be an island of positive influence because all you see in the paper today is about celebrities and their bad behavior. Here you have all these thousands of people out there walking and trying to make a difference, and nobody thinks it's news.

So every morning I pump people up about what life's about, about what's going on. That's what my Chief Spiritual Officer job is about.

Wright

I had the pleasure of reading one of your releases, *The Leadership Pill*.

Blanchard

Yes.

Wright

I must admit that my first thought was how short the book was. I wondered if I was going to get my money's worth, which by the way, I most certainly did. Many of your books are brief and based on a fictitious story. Most business books in the market today are hundreds of pages in length and are read almost like a textbook.

Will you talk a little bit about why you write these short books, and about the premise of *The Leadership Pill?*

Blanchard

I really developed my relationship with Spencer Johnson when we wrote *The One Minute Manager*. As you know, he wrote, *Who Moved My Cheese*, which was a phenomenal success. He wrote children's books and is quite a storyteller.

Jesus taught by parables, which were short stories.

My favorite books are *Jonathan Livingston Seagull* and *The Little Prince*. Og Mandino, author of seventeen books, was the greatest of them all.

I started writing parables because people can get into the story and learn the contents of the story, and they don't bring their judgmental hats into reading. You write a regular book and they'll say, "Well, where did you get the research?" They get into that judgmental side. Our books get them emotionally involved and they learn.

The Leadership Pill is a fun story about a pharmaceutical company that thinks they have discovered the secret to leadership, and they can put the ingredients in a pill. When they announce it, the country goes crazy because everybody knows we need more effective leaders. When they release it, it outsells Viagra.

The founders of the company start selling off stock and they call them Pillionaires. But along comes this guy who calls himself "the effective manager," and he challenges them to a no-pill challenge. If they identify two non-performing groups, he'll take on one and let somebody on the pill take another one, and he guarantees he will outperform that person by the end of the year. They agree, but of course they give him a drug test every week to make sure he's not sneaking pills on the side.

I wrote the book with Marc Muchnick, who is a young guy in his early thirties. We did a major study of what this interesting "Y" generation—the young people of today—want from leaders, and this is a secret blend that this effective manager uses. When you think about it, David, it is really powerful in terms of what people want from a leader.

Number one, they want integrity. A lot of people have talked about that in the past, but these young people will walk if they see people say one thing and do another. A lot of us walk to the bathroom and out into the halls to talk about it. But these people will quit. They don't want somebody to say something and not do it.

The second thing they want is a partnership relationship. They hate superior/subordinate. I mean, what awful terms those are. You know, the "head" of the department and the hired "hands"—you don't even give them a head. "What do I do? I'm in supervision. I see things a lot clearer than these stupid idiots." They want to be treated as partners; if they can get a financial partnership, great. If they can't, they really want a minimum of a psychological partnership where they can bring their brains to work and make decisions.

Then finally, they want affirmation. They not only want to be caught doing things right, but they want to be affirmed for who they are. They want to be known as individual people, not as numbers.

So those are the three ingredients that this effective manager uses. They are wonderful values when you think about them.

Rank-order values for any organization is number one, integrity. In our company we call it ethics. It is our number one value. The number two value is partnership. In our company we call it relationships. Number three is affirmation—being affirmed as a human being. I think that ties into relationships, too. They are wonderful values that can drive behavior in a great way.

Wright

I believe most people in today's business culture would agree that success in business has everything to do with successful leadership. In *The Leadership Pill*, you present a simple but profound premise; that leadership is not something you do to people; it's something you do *with* them. At face value, that seems incredibly obvious. But you must have found in your research and observations that leaders in today's culture do not get this. Would you speak to that issue?

Blanchard

Yes. I think what often happens in this is the human ego. There are too many leaders out there who are self-serving. They're not leaders who have service in mind. They think the sheep are there for the benefit of the shepherd. All the power, money, fame, and recognition move up the hierarchy. They forget that the real action in business is not up the hierarchy—it's in the one-to-one, moment-to-moment interactions that your frontline people have with your customers. It's how the phone is answered. It's how problems are dealt with and those kinds of things. If you don't think that you're doing leadership *with* them—rather, you're doing it *to* them—after a while they won't take care of your customers.

I was at a store once (not Nordstrom's, where I normally would go) and I thought of something I had to share with my wife, Margie. I asked the guy behind the counter in Men's Wear, "May I use your phone?"

He said, "No!"

"You're kidding me," I said. "I can always use the phone at Nordstrom's."

"Look, buddy," he said, "they won't let *me* use the phone here. Why should I let you use the phone?"

That is an example of leadership that's done *to* employees, not *with* them. People want a partnership. People want to be involved in a way that really makes a difference.

Wright

Dr. Blanchard, the time has flown by and there are so many more questions I'd like to ask you. In closing, would you mind sharing with our readers some thoughts on success? If you were mentoring a small group of men and women, and one of their central goals was to become successful, what kind of advice would you give them?

Blanchard

Well, I would first of all say, "What are you focused on?" If you are focused on success as being, as I said earlier, accumulation of money, recognition, power, or status, I think you've got the wrong target. What you need to really be focused on is how you can be generous in the use of your time and your talent and your treasure and touch. How can you serve people rather than be served? How can you develop caring, loving relationships with people? My sense is if you will focus on those things, success in the traditional sense will come to you. But if you go out and say, "Man, I'm going to make a fortune, and I'm going to do this," and have that kind of attitude, you might get some of those numbers. I think you become an adult, however, when you realize you are here to give rather than to get. You're here to serve, not to be served. I would just say to people, "Life is such a very special occasion. Don't miss it by aiming at a target that bypasses other people, because we're really here to serve each other."

Wright

Well, what an enlightening conversation, Dr. Blanchard. I really want you to know how much I appreciate all the time you've taken with me for this interview. I know that our readers will learn from this, and I really appreciate your being with us today.

Blanchard

Well, thank you so much, David. I really enjoyed my time with you. You've asked some great questions that made me think, and I hope my answers are helpful to other people because as I say, life is a special occasion.

Wright

Today we have been talking with Dr. Ken Blanchard. He is coauthor of the phenomenal best-selling book, *The One Minute Manager.* The fact that he's the Chief Spiritual Officer of his company should make us all think about how we are leading our companies and leading our families and leading anything, whether it is in church or civic organizations. I know I will.

Thank you so much, Dr. Blanchard, for being with us today.

Blanchard

Good to be with you, David.

About the Author

Few people have created more of a positive impact on the day-to-day management of people and companies than Dr. Kenneth Blanchard, who is known around the world simply as "Ken."

When Ken speaks, he speaks from the heart with warmth and humor. His unique gift is to speak to an audience and communicate with each individual as if they were alone and talking one-on-one. He is a polished storyteller with a knack for making the seemingly complex easy to understand.

Ken has been a guest on a number of national television programs, including *Good Morning America* and *The Today Show*. He has been featured in *Time, People, U.S. News & World Report,* and a host of other popular publications.

He earned his bachelor's degree in Government and Philosophy from Cornell University, his master's degree in Sociology and Counseling from Colgate University, and his PhD in Educational Administration and Leadership from Cornell University.

Dr. Ken Blanchard

The Ken Blanchard Companies
125 State Place
Escondido, California 92029
800.728.6000
Fax: 760.489.8407
www.kenblanchard.com

Chapter Three

Living a Strategic Life: The Seven C's of Success

An Interview With...

Dr. Howard M. Knoff

David Wright (Wright)

Today we're talking with Dr. Howard M. Knoff, President of Project ACHIEVE Incorporated. Howie (as everyone knows him) is a nationally known consultant, author, and lecturer, a licensed psychologist, a twenty-year university professor, and a past-president of the National Association of School Psychologists. Howie works extensively across the country in the areas of organizational development and strategic planning, and school effectiveness, continuous improvement, and school safety. He also works to turn around failing schools and other human service agencies, to improve the academic progress and social-emotional health of children and adolescents, and to help parents succeed with their children at home especially relative to discipline and behavior management. Known for his incredibly popular *Stop & Think Social Skills Program,* with separate books and materials for both schools and parents, Howie helped to write the *Early Warning, Safe Schools* guide commissioned by President Clinton after the first wave of school shootings. He also was invited to participate in the White House Conference on "Character and Community" by then-First Lady Laura Bush, and he has been seen on *NBC News, 20/20,* and other national news programs. Howie is an expert in strategic planning— whether applied to education, home, or life. He is an engaging, charismatic, and "audience-friendly" presenter.

Dr. Knoff, welcome to *Discover Your Inner Strength.*

Dr. Howard Knoff (Knoff)

Thank you, David. It's nice to be here.

Wright

Where do we begin? You have accomplished so many things in your professional life—at a national leadership level, for community agencies and organizations, with failing and ineffective schools, helping challenging students, and supporting parents who are struggling with parenting. What guides what you do?

Knoff

In many areas of my life, I am guided by a number of "blueprints" or "road maps" that help me to organize what I am doing, to problem-solve effectively, and to respond successfully to the many challenges that sometimes occur on a daily basis. I often cite a quote from *Alice in Wonderland:* "If you don't know where you're going, any road will get you there." For me, this means that without these road maps, I may get lost and become unproductive or unsuccessful!

Thus, when I find myself in extreme, emotional, chaotic, or crisis-oriented situations, I use these blueprints to systematically identify the problem, analyze why it is happening, select and implement the best strategies or solutions, and evaluate my success. In a sense, I just described Blueprint number one: the problem-solving process. This process, again, involves four critical steps:

1. Identifying and describing, at an operational level, the Problem (i.e., what is happening?). This is not always so easy, as sometimes, what we think is a problem is really a symptom and not the real problem.

2. Analyzing the problem to systematically determine *why* the problem is occurring (i.e., why is this happening?). This is a most essential step because if we do not know why a situation is occurring, we may not choose the right intervention to effectively eliminate the problem now while preventing it in the future.

3. Choosing and implementing Strategies, Solutions, and/or Interventions (i.e., how are we going to solve the problem?). Here, we need to link our strategies or interventions directly to the confirmed reasons that explain why the problem is occurring in the first place.

4. Evaluating our success (i.e., did the interventions work?). This, again, is not as easy as it sounds. To be successful here, we need to recognize that our "criteria for success" at the beginning of the intervention may be different at the end of the intervention. Thus, we need to identify short-term and long-term goals so that we can recognize different phases or levels of success.

Now, I'm not saying that difficult problems or challenges don't get me emotional (e.g., confused or tense or even angry). What I *am* saying is that "inner strength" means that, at some point, you need to put the emotionality aside, and you have to problem-solve your way to success.

Wright

How do you tell the difference between a problem and a symptom?

Knoff

Well, let's use an example wrapped around a metaphor, and then, another example. The first example is a school-aged child who is throwing chairs in his classroom. Naturally, this is *a* problem. But, I would suggest, the chair-throwing is not *the* problem.

Let's "cut away" to the metaphor. You wake up in the morning and you are running a 104-degree temperature. That's pretty serious! So, you call your doctor who immediately admits you into the hospital. Once there, your doctor and his or her team begin a diagnostic process. Part of the diagnostic process is a clinical interview with you. Part of the process, depending on your answers during the interview, may include running blood tests, taking throat cultures, completing different physiological scans. In all of this, the ultimate goal is to figure out *why* you are running such a high fever.

Point 1: While the doctors see your fever as *"a"* problem, they are not focusing on it as *"the"* problem. Your fever is *a symptom*. The doctors need to figure out which of three, five, or eight possibilities is the *source* of your fever. Once they identify this, then they have identified *"the"* problem. Then, with further analyses, they can determine why the problem is occurring and then how to medically treat you.

Point 2: In order to determine the most appropriate medical treatment, your doctor conducts *a problem analysis* and confirms the reasons for your medical condition. Only then does your doctor begin the medical treatment (or intervention). Thus, doctors are continually using a data-based, diagnostic, problem-solving process. Doctors do not do *random intervention*. They do *strategic interventions* that focus on resolving identified problems (not just symptoms) that are linked to systematic problem analysis.

And now, let's return to our chair-throwing child. Once again, I would suggest that the chair-throwing is a symptom. In order for us to solve this problem, we need to identify the *reason* for the chair-throwing. To do this, we need to generate some hypotheses. Some examples are: Is the student throwing chairs because he or she is academically frustrated, wants peer attention, wants to be sent to the principal's office to miss the bus and avoid the bully who was on the bus in the morning, or because the student's parents are getting a divorce?

All of these are great hypotheses. But we need to test and confirm these hypotheses to determine which one (or ones) is correct. This is because the interventions for an academically frustrated student differ from those for a student motivated by peer attention, and these differ from those for a student who has been dealing with a bully on the bus. Once again, I want to reinforce the following points: 1) we need to determine "the" problem, instead of focusing on the chair-throwing symptom and 2) our strategic interventions must be based on hypotheses that have been tested and confirmed during the data-based problem analysis step.

Now, I am not saying that we do not take the chair away from the student. What I am saying is that if we want to eliminate future chair-throwing, we need to eliminate the reasons for it.

Wright

So, what does this have to do with "discovering our inner strength?"

Knoff

I believe that important parts of our "inner strength" are used when solving problems or accomplishing personal and professional goals. In order to have the highest probability of success when setting goals for ourselves, we must create strategic plans that identify the skills and resources needed to solve "the" problem(s) or accomplish "the" goal(s). We need to set and implement realistic timelines and the activities required. And, we need to specify the short- and long-term outcomes expected and how they will be evaluated. Clearly, this involves the problem-solving process we are now discussing.

When a situation, dilemma, or crisis arises, the problem-solving process is even more essential—even though a) it often needs to be done faster, b) it initially focuses on stabilizing the crisis situation, and c) its long-term solutions need to be implemented under intensive conditions. In an emergency room, the medical staff first triage the patient, then stabilize the patient, and then move to long-term medical and "quality of life" solutions.

But, challenging situations or crises must be addressed head-on. The chair-throwing must solved. Taking the chair away or suspending the student is not likely to change the conditions underlying this dangerous behavior. Indeed, James Baldwin said, "Not everything that is faced can be changed . . . but nothing can be changed unless it is faced." And so, in order to face our problems, we need to discover and develop our "inner strength" characteristics, attributes, and skills.

Now, let's explore our second example. As a supervisor at work, you have a small number of staff members who are resistant to change. These are frustrating colleagues! They detract from the morale, momentum, and productivity of your organization. And yet, it would take months to gather the documentation needed to potentially fire them, you would lose all of the training and supervision already invested in them, and you would still need to go through a time-consuming re-hiring and re-training process.

Using the problem-solving process, once you get past your feelings of aggravation, resentment, or resignation, you must recognize that your staff members' resistance is a symptom of *"the"* underlying problem(s). For some of these individuals, the resistance might be "covering" their lack of skill and expertise (regardless of how much training you have done with them). For others, it might be covering their fear of failure or fear of success—if they surpass their goals now, they worry that that will always be expected. For others, they may figure that, if they can "wait" you out, you will decrease your expectations or leave them alone entirely. For still others, the resistance may represent a lack of motivation, or anger or revenge (e.g., over past evaluations or perceived unfairness). And finally, for some, perhaps there is a medical or substance abuse issue underlying the behavior.

Once again, these are all hypotheses that need to be assessed so that the actual problem and the reason(s) for the problem can be addressed through strategic intervention. As a brief sidebar, let's understand that the data needed to confirm or reject your hypotheses can be collected using one of six approaches. These approaches are summarized in the acronym, RIOTSS. The approaches are:

- **R**eview records, personnel files, other collected documentation.
- **I**nterview clients of the staff member of concern, colleagues, others.
- **O**bserve the staff member in different settings or situations.
- **T**est. Complete personality or other assessments of the staff member through your HR office or private clinicians.
- **S**urvey clients of the staff member, colleagues, others.
- **S**elf-Report. Interview the staff member.

To summarize, when you have difficult staff members or colleagues, you need to use your inner strength to determine why they are having difficulties or exhibiting "challenging" behavior. As part of the problem analysis, it is important to determine your staff members' strengths, inner resources, and previous successes (an "Asset Analysis"), as well as explain their current weaknesses. In the end, by connecting your inner strength and your problem analysis, your strategic interventions, and your staff members' inner strengths, you will ultimately have the highest probability of success—both for your staff members and for you.

Wright

Wow! I can see where your training as a psychologist pays off in applying the problem-solving process to difficult situations and circumstances. So, what else helps you to problem-solve? Are there other problem-solving blueprints that you use in different areas of your life?

Knoff

Yes. The next blueprint that I'd like to discuss involves the "Seven C's of Strategic Living." Strategic Living[1] is important to every part of our life—to our personal, interpersonal, relationship-oriented, professional, and spiritual interactions. Indeed, when done systematically and effectively, Strategic Living helps individuals of all ages to develop the knowledge, skill, and confidence that results in continuous and positive growth. Strategic Living also helps to prevent some of the situations, dilemmas, or crises that we discussed earlier. And, finally, Strategic Living helps to build resilience and self-competence, self-control and self-management, and self-reliance and independence over time.

As noted, children, adolescents, young adults, families, older adults, businesses, complex organizations, communities, and states can all engage in Strategic Living through "Strategic Life Planning." Blueprint number two helps to guide this process—a process that is organized by the "Seven C's of Strategic Living." These Seven C's involve:

- **C**harting the Course
- **C**ollecting the Supplies
- **C**ruising with Purpose
- **C**hecking Coordinates
- **C**orrecting for Drift

---

[1] A Google search of the terms "Strategic Living" and "Strategic Life Plan or Planning" resulted in the realization that a number of individuals, businesses, and even religious organizations are using these terms. The term is used here as a concept and not as the title of a specific approach that is being used to advance a particular idea or methodology.

- **C**ontaining Crises
- **C**elebrating the Voyage

Let's briefly describe each of these components.

Step number one: Charting the Course. Joel Barker said, "Almost all successful individuals and organizations have one thing in common—the power and depth of their vision of the future." This is the essence of strategic life planning and, especially, its first step. Charting the Course focuses on specifying the goals, objectives, and outcomes of your current or desired journey or "voyage"—whether in the personal, interpersonal, relationship-oriented, professional, spiritual, or combined areas.

Critically, and as much as possible, your desired outcomes should be described in specific, behavioral terms so that they are observable and measurable. For example, rather than setting a goal stating: "I want to improve my public speaking skills this year," you might specify, instead, that "I want to make at least twelve presentations during the next twelve months to audiences with at least twenty-five participants in my field, receiving feedback ratings averaging at least 4.0 on a 5.0 scale in the areas of a) is knowledgeable in the topic presented, b) was clear and organized, c) was interesting and kept my attention, and d) added to my professional knowledge and skills."

Relative to Barker's quote, your goals are your "vision of the future." Without your goals and vision, there truly is no strategic plan.

Step two: Collecting the Supplies focuses on identifying and gathering the needed resources so that the journey has the highest probability of success. Significantly, many people think only about money as their primary resource. And yet, there are other resources that sometimes are more powerful. For example, other people— colleagues, friends, mentors, consultants, teachers, other professionals—can be resources. Written, audio-visual, or multi-media information sources—books, DVDs, web-based trainings or references—can be resources. Time—to do research, to engage in training, to devote to self-improvement, to focus tenaciously on a strategic goal—is an essential resource. Places and facilities—libraries or other research sites, model or exemplary practice sites, simulation or job-related training sites—are possible resources. And, finally, technology—with all of its wondrous innovations and advances—is a resource.

The point here is that goal-setting is not enough. If we are under-resourced, we may never build the momentum needed to reach our goals or we may need to abandon the journey because we run out of provisions. And so, part of strategic life planning is to "plan for the journey before embarking on the journey." However, relative to this planning, we sometimes need to over-plan and over-resource for the journey. That is, we need to plan not just for "best-case scenario" conditions, but also for "worst-case scenario" conditions. Functionally, this means that sometimes we need to have more resources available to help us meet our goals than needed. Goals are not successfully attained when challenges are underestimated or when resources are not available to address emergency situations.

The strategic over-resourcing of an initiative sometimes is called the "Powell Principle," after General Colin Powell. In preparing for the 1991 Gulf War, General Powell made a strategic decision to transport more soldiers, more armament, more equipment, more reserves, and more support systems to our forces in Kuwait and Iraq than needed. He did this because he wanted to ensure a quick, efficient, and resounding victory in the Gulf with a minimum of casualties and loss. As a psychological consultant with the Department of Defense (DoD) during the January 1991 airstrikes that preceded the ground war in the Gulf, I saw firsthand—while working with the DoD's American schools in Germany—the wisdom of this strategy. The result was an American victory in less than three days with fewer than 150 battle-related deaths from among the over 600,000 American soldiers deployed.

Wright

Yes. I understand that you led a four-member national association team of psychological experts to help the Department of Defense prepare to address the mental health needs of American military families living in Germany in case the high number of war-related casualties predicted actually occurred.

Knoff

Yes. We were in Germany, helping the American schools and mental health community there to strategically plan for a worst-case scenario. When we were there, the advanced air strikes into Iraq were already occurring and the start of the ground war was imminent. The tension across Germany and the European theater was sky-high, but we had an important job to do—plan services to provide the social-emotional support needed by the military and civilian families living there. Thank God that the war was won so quickly under General Powell's command and his strategic planning.

Step number three: Cruising with Purpose occurs when you have developed your strategic plan, identified and gathered the resources needed, prepared for potential difficulties, chosen the optimal time to begin, and determined how and when you are going to evaluate your progress. With all of this accomplished, you can embark on your journey with direction, determination, confidence, and purpose.

While all of this sounds natural and easy, many people complete all of the planning and preparation, but never embark on the journey. Sometimes this occurs because of a fear of failure, a fear of the unknown, or a fear of taking or being in the lead. Sometimes, it is due to competing priorities, a resistance to change, or the belief that a secure present is better than a challenging future. And sometimes, it is because of a lack of confidence, determination, or motivation.

Here, again, is where inner strength is essential. Critically, while there are no certainties in life, are we truly living life when we are determined to keep everything certain? Inner strength allows us to conquer our fears, it motivates us to make the future our priority, and it inspires us to take the first steps along the path to accomplishment and success. Trammell Crow said, "There's as much risk in doing nothing as in doing something." And so, in order to make planning and preparation meaningful, we must take action. Said another way, once ready, we need to hoist the anchor, engage the rudder, and let out the mainsails—confident in our ability to take advantage of the good and to adjust to the bad.

Step number four: Checking Coordinates is all about "formative evaluation." Formative evaluation involves planned, periodic evaluations that occur at different points in time *during the journey* to ensure that we are on course and not in need of mid-course corrections. Formative evaluation is important because most goals are not accomplished in a direct, straight-line fashion. Typically, progress involves different pathways, requires different levels of energy, and occurs at different speeds. Progress also, at times, requires detours, rest periods, and moments to consolidate the advances made.

Without formative evaluation, the "checking of coordinates," people sometimes get lost, miss the progress made, or prematurely believe that they have reached their destination. This is true for adults as well as for children. For example, psychological research has long shown that when students chart and graph their progress toward long-term goals, not only does the documentation of the short-term gains (for example, on a chart) increase their motivation, it also increases their actual success in reaching their goals.

Formative evaluation, then, is the feedback process that all of us need when long-term goals involve a series of short-term steps. If you think about it, most mountains are not climbed by ascending a single steep path to the summit. Mountains are conquered by patiently negotiating a gradual series of switchbacks that increase the potential for success. Similarly, most large bodies of water are navigated by tacking the sailboat back and forth, maximizing the power of the wind to successfully arrive at the desired destination. Without formative evaluation, we may not tack at the right time, we may tack too many times, or we may not tack at all. William Drayton said, "Change starts when someone sees the next step." Mr. Drayton understood formative evaluation and the Seven C's of Strategic Life Planning.

Step number five: Correcting for Drift is the action needed when formative evaluations tell us that we are off-course.

Let's face it—life is complex. There's a retirement commercial on television right now that begins with an older gentleman chiding us, "What did you think—life was an expressway?" Clearly not. With all the complexities in life, and everything that seems to be bombarding us at the same time, it is easy to get lost in the irrelevant details, the inevitable detours, or the "crisis of the day." At times, all of this causes us to lose our focus and drift from our path.

And so, using our formative evaluation results, we need to periodically make mid-course corrections to stay on track. Think about it this way: Many of you would be surprised to learn that when a plane travels across the country, it is off-course 90 percent of the time. This is because airplanes travel from one air traffic control center to the next—at least, until they are within fifty or so miles of their final destination. Thus, because the control centers are not aligned with your departure and destination cities, during the flight, the captain, the computers, and the air traffic control centers are constantly programming the plane to make mid-course corrections based on their current formative evaluation data.

Formative evaluations must be built into and executed as part of the personal or professional goals in our strategic life plans. This helps us to make the necessary mid-course corrections so that we stay on track to reach our goals. Without these corrections, we could get so off course or so lost that our only option would be to give up the journey and start over again. The time we spend in periodically evaluating and correcting our progress over time often saves us ten times the time required to restart the process from the very beginning.

Wright

It seems like the first two steps of the strategic planning process focuses on identifying our personal or professional goals, designing the action plan, and collecting the resources needed to begin executing the plan.

Steps three through five appear to involve the actual implementation of the plan, along with the periodic evaluations needed to ensure that we are progressing toward our goals—making needed mid-course corrections if we are drifting or getting off-track.

Step six seems to involve both planning and execution. It looks like it is about planning ahead of time so that most crises are prevented, but taking the right steps when crises do occur so that they are quickly addressed.

Finally, Step seven seems to emphasize enjoying the entire journey—not just the end of the journey when success occurs. Is that correct?

Knoff

You've got it! As you've just outlined, Step number six, Containing Crises, focuses on the planning that prevents crises (while you are trying to attain your personal or professional goals), and the responses that resolve them.

While we have talked some about prevention, I want to introduce what I call the "NASA Approach to Crisis Prevention." This involves thinking, during the development of a strategic life plan, about everything that could possibly go wrong while actually executing the plan, developing an "early warning system" as an alert for potential crises, and then preparing response systems or contingency plans to address any crises that might actually occur.

The reason why I call this the "NASA Approach" is because this is exactly what NASA did when designing the space shuttle, and what it does before every space mission. More specifically, NASA spends an incredible amount of time in development and training in the areas of crisis prevention, intervention, and response.

For example, when they designed the shuttles, they built them with what are called "redundant" or "back-up" systems. That is, during the design process, NASA engineers tried to envision every possible hardware or software system failure or misfortunate that might confront the shuttle from lift-off to touch-down. Guided by these "worst-case scenarios," they built back-up systems into the shuttles—extra fuel cells, additional computer capacity, by-pass systems and strategies, and emergency procedures for unlikely, but possible, events.

Now, clearly, given the tragic loss of the Columbia and its courageous crew when re-entering the Earth's atmosphere on February 1, 2003, NASA did not have redundant systems for everything—most notably the thermal protection tiles. And so, they had to re-visit the strategic planning process, redesign critical parts of the shuttle (including the external fuel tanks which lost the foam that damaged the thermal tiles), and add important safeguards and repair procedures to prevent future catastrophic losses. At this point, while another shuttle disaster could occur, at least the potential has been minimized to the greatest extent possible.

Crisis prevention is also integrated into every astronaut's training prior to leaving on a mission. Indeed, beyond preparing for the scientific parts of their mission, astronauts spend a large amount of time on "crisis response" procedures. Once again, after imagining every possible crisis that might occur on the shuttle, NASA conditions the astronauts so that they can respond to any crisis situation at virtually an automatic level. This training and response is essential—especially when the difference between survival and catastrophe, at times, is counted in seconds, not minutes.

The point here is that people should think, as part of their strategic life planning, about the potential crises that may affect or completely ruin their potential to accomplish their personal or professional goals and objectives. While good planning may actually prevent most crises from happening, planning also results in interventions that are available to contain and minimize crises if they do occur, and responses to repair the damage once they are over.

While most individuals are born with inner strength, this strength is not automatically available during a crisis. When active and visible, it often is the result of high levels of planning, training, and experience. Indeed, as stated by Captain "Sully" Sullenberger, one of the heroes of U.S. Air Flight 1549 whose passengers all survived a crash landing in the Hudson River in January of 2009, "I needed to touch down with the wings exactly level. I needed to touch down with the nose slightly up. I needed to touch down at a descent rate that was survivable. And I needed to touch down just above our minimum flying speed but not below it. And I needed to make all these things happen simultaneously. [And he had to keep his cool.] The physiological reaction I had to this was strong, and I had to force myself to use my training and force calm on the situation," he explained. "It just took some concentration. . . . I think, in many ways, as it turned out, my entire life up to that moment had been a preparation to handle that particular moment." (From an interview on *60 Minutes*, CBS News, February 8, 2009.)

Step number seven: Celebrating the Voyage focuses on celebrating the fact that a) we can plan and try to improve ourselves on personal, interpersonal, relationship-oriented, professional, and spiritual levels, b) we can make incremental progress toward our goals by succeeding at different stages in the process, and c) we can commemorate our major successes that result in significant achievement, growth, recognition, or contribution. This step, then, celebrates the journey itself, the short-term accomplishments, and the major results.

Of these three areas of celebration, I would suggest that the first one is the most important. Too many times, we focus on "the win," "the award," or "the recognition." And yet, the reality is that we will not always reach our goals. Given this, we need to refocus our "perceptions of success"—demonstrating sincere motivation and appreciation for the accomplishment of creating the strategic life plan itself, for the care in preparing for the journey, for the thrill of taking the first steps, and for the excitement of experiencing new challenges and opportunities.

We also need to teach our children this lesson. Indeed, when working with parents and teachers, I often remind them that "it may take a whole village to raise a child, but it also takes a whole child to raise a village." By this, I mean that we need to help our children, at levels appropriate to their development and maturity, to create strategic life plans for themselves (at different age levels and across the stages of their lives). Moreover, we need to help them understand that life plan "success" is represented—as above—by the journey itself, the short-term accomplishments, *and* the major results.

As a final step in "Celebrating the Voyage," I would like to define "failure" so that we can contrast it with "success." I firmly believe that "the only failure . . . is not being able to explain why you have been successful or unsuccessful." To me, then, failure does not occur when we do not win or meet a goal or accomplish a task. Failure occurs when we do not fully understand *why* these situations have happened, and when we do not learn from and improve upon them in the future. Conversely, when we are successful, it is important to know *how* that has occurred. Indeed, only when we understand the *"how"* can we duplicate the effort or conditions so that we can continue to succeed in the future.

And so, now included in *Celebrating the Voyage* is not just the fact that we *can* celebrate, but exactly *why* we are able to celebrate.

Wright

To summarize, you believe that everyone needs to live a "Strategic Life," and that the most effective way to do that is to create and implement a "Strategic Life Plan." In order to do this, we can follow the *Seven C's of Strategic Living*. And, finally, successful Strategic Living helps to build resilience and self-competence, self-control, self-management, self-reliance, and independence over time—some of the most important "inner strengths."

Knoff

That is a fantastic summary!

Wright

You've now discussed two blueprints: the Problem-solving process, and the Seven C's of Strategic Living. Is there a third blueprint?

Knoff

Yes. I'd like to finish our discussion by introducing Blueprint number three, the *Seven C's of Success*. Many people have said that "Choice, not chance, determines one's destiny." If that is true, and I believe that it is, then we need to understand what "inner strength" skills and choices best help us to lead a strategic life and fulfill our strategic life plans.

Complementing the Seven C's of Strategic Living, the Seven C's of Success involve the following inner strengths:

- **C**ommunication
- **C**aring
- **C**ommitment

- **C**ollaboration
- **C**onsultation
- **C**elebration
- **C**onsistency

One of the keys here is that we need to develop these inner strengths ourselves while we also "pay them forward"—helping others to develop these inner strengths in themselves. Briefly, let's describe these Seven C's.

Communication involves the formal and informal, oral and written, explicit and implicit, person-to-person interactions that involve, teach, reinforce, and validate individuals who are working toward common goals.

Caring involves the interest, recognition, understanding, validation, support, and reinforcement that we give to others in the personal, interpersonal, relationship-oriented, professional, and/or spiritual areas of their lives.

Commitment involves the steadfast dedication that we actively demonstrate to ideas, beliefs, initiatives, programs, plans, people, families, organizations, systems, communities, and societies. Commitment is long-standing in nature, and it endures through good times and bad.

Collaboration involves people, working together as teammates or in well-functioning teams, who a) plan and implement projects together; b) build consensus and partnerships; c) discuss, analyze, and compromise to resolve disagreements; and d) "agree to disagree" when compromise does not work, keeping disagreements on a professional, not personal, level.

Collaboration, significantly, differs from "cooperation." Where collaboration includes a willingness to directly address differences and disagreements, cooperation typically occurs only when people support each other's goals or are willing to work together. That is, cooperative groups tend to ignore or avoid conflict.

Consultation involves the recognition that when we do not have the understanding, knowledge, skill, confidence, objectivity, or interpersonal capacity to address a need, meet a goal, or solve a problem, we must have the willingness to find, listen to, and accept assistance from a friend, colleague, or expert who can help us. For example, when doctors are not sure about a patient's symptoms, or simply need some reassurance on a challenging case, they get a "consult" or a "second opinion." We need to do exactly the same thing across the different facets of our lives. In a sentence, "If you don't know, get a consult."

Celebration, as we have already discussed, involves the formal or informal, intrinsic or extrinsic, individual or collective, and random or planned observances that acknowledge the strategic life goals and plans we set, the short-term achievements we complete, and the major accomplishments we realize.

Consistency involves an active, ongoing focus on the six areas above—communication, caring, commitment, collaboration, consultation, and celebration—that reflects a dedication to growth and development across time, people, settings, situations, and circumstances. Consistency helps us build the momentum that we need for many life goals. It is the "glue" that makes the Seven C's work.

Clearly, these inner strengths look different from childhood through adolescence to adulthood and into our elder years. They also look different across gender, race, culture, and generations. But despite these differences, the "common denominator" involves a focus on people, how they develop and grow in the Seven C areas, and how they use the positive potential of the Seven C's in their interactions with others.

Wright

Well, our time is almost up. Do you have any final thoughts?

Knoff

Somehow, I don't think I'll surprise you by saying, "Yes." Actually, I would like to conclude with a quote: "Do not follow where the path may lead . . . Go instead where there is no path and leave a trail."

You know, there are many paths that we travel during our lives. Some of our paths touch others' paths for brief moments. And other paths are shared for long periods of time with people who significantly influence our lives. But in the end, each of us needs to blaze our own path through life. We must set goals. We must make decisions. We must make plans. And we must take our first steps.

Every one of us is different. And so, every one of us goes "where there is no path," and every one of us "leaves a trail."

In order to live a strategic life, we need to live a meaningful life. In order to live a meaningful life, we need to nurture our inner strengths, share these strengths, and not be afraid of the path ahead.

Wright

Thank you, Howie.

Knoff

Thank you. It was my pleasure!

About the Author

After 22 years as a university professor, Howard M. Knoff is a national consultant, author, and lecturer known for his work in strategic planning and organizational change; effective consultation processes; and helping parents to succeed with their children at home, so that they can be more productive at work.

The President of Project ACHIEVE Incorporated, a federally-designated National Model Prevention Program focused on implementing comprehensive school improvement practices to maximize students' academic and behavioral success, "Howie" has authored twelve books and over 75 articles or book chapters. A licensed psychologist, his *Stop & Think Parent Book: A Guide to Children's Good Behavior* is regarded by parents as essential to their parenting success, and educators as essential to their school and classroom success.

Constantly "in-demand" as a speaker and consultant, Howie is engaging, innovative, practical, and insightful. With a Ph.D. from Syracuse University and numerous national awards and honors, he was the 21st President of the National Association of School Psychologists.

Howard M. Knoff, Ph.D., President

Project ACHIEVE Incorporated/Project ACHIEVE Press
49 Woodberry Road
Little Rock, Arkansas 72212
Phone: 501-312-1484
Fax: 501-312-1493
knoffprojectachieve@earthlink.net
www.projectachieve.info

Chapter Four

Happiness and Ultimate Wealth: The Power of Inner Strength

An Interview With...

Dr. Neera Puri

David Wright (Wright)

Today we're talking with Dr. Neera Puri, she holds a PhD in Psychology from the University of Southern California and an MSW from the University of Houston. A senior international business coach and trainer, Dr. Neera is the principal of Bay Area Coach, LLC, providing executive and leadership coaching. Her coaching practice includes international clientele from Australia, Canada, India, Israel, Mexico, Nigeria, and the United States. She is committed to multicultural training, being a founding member of the South Asian Psychological Networking Association and a member of the Asian American Psychological Association. She has been interviewed as a pioneer for her work with South Asian mental health in the American Psychological Association and is a credentialed member of the International Coach Federation. With over fifteen years of experience, Dr. Puri has worked with Fortune 50 companies, health care systems, diversity programs for corporations and universities, and women's organizations. Her investment with women and children led her to work at the USC Career Center, UCLA Student Psychological Service, UC Davis Counseling and Psychological Services, Catholic Charities, and Mary Kay cosmetics.

She was a faculty instructor and supervisor for the nationally renowned Multicultural Immersion Program at the University of California Davis and was a senior international trainer for the MentorCoach program. Dr. Puri was also involved with the University Women's Centers and non-profit boards to address sexual discrimination, sexual assault, trauma, and crisis response strategies. Dr. Puri has taken on leadership positions with the San Francisco East Bay Coaches and International Coach Federation. She was on the Marketing Committee of the 2005 International Coach Federation Annual Conference, the largest worldwide gathering of coaches to date. She consults with corporations, universities, and non-profits on marketing with print, television, and online technology.

Dr. Puri is an invited speaker for seminars on motivation, spirituality, positive psychology, and work-life balance, strong women leaders, and team-building using the Myers-Briggs type inventory.

She lives in the San Francisco Bay area where she enjoys going on hikes with her two boys, and her two puppies, Smokey and Twixie. An avid animal lover, she has actively trained and rehabilitated shelter dogs, and hopes one day to open "Smokey Ranch" to connect shelter dogs with loving, invested people.

Dr. Puri welcome to *Discover Your Inner Strength*.

Neera Puri (Puri)

Thank you, David, for the lovely introduction.

Wright

So describe for us a pivotal moment when you discovered your inner strength?

Puri

One of the most pivotal moments when I discovered my inner strength is when I hit rock bottom and I was making the decision to get divorced from an abusive husband. He was very cruel and froze my access to all cash. I had no money and two baby boys and two puppies to support and feed. I went from being an established business coach and therapist with a decent income, to being poorer than a person on welfare because I didn't qualify to get any assistance. I joke now that I went from a doctor in Psychology to a doctor in Poverty overnight. Though I have worked in homeless shelters and in places like South Central Los Angeles with young people in gangs, I still had lived a financially privileged life until I was left with no money and my baby boys depending upon me.

When I was at rock bottom, that's when I tapped into my faith and I prayed to Jesus Christ for a way out. At that point, I realized I had a choice to either fall flat on my face and continue to feel depressed or I could trust that the Holy Spirit would provide for me.

The Holy Spirit did provide for me because spiritual people would randomly show up to help me and my boys keep a roof over our heads, have food in our bellies, and laughter in our hearts. I learned that with *faith* and *focus* you can accomplish many successes when things feel insurmountable.

Sometimes when things were really bad and I was feeling hopeless, I would think, "Well, if I had a million dollars, things would be better."

Then, I had the good fortune to read a research study by Michael Freeman, Ph.D. on inheritors who by the age of 21 had wealth substantial enough to render working a choice rather than a necessity. This showed me that lots of money did not guarantee happiness either, and money was just a spiritual tool. According to Dr. Michael Freeman's research, true wealth was really about being able to work hard and experience the joy of accomplishment through struggle. And so I reframed my sudden poverty as an opportunity to grow spiritually and experience the joy of rebuilding everything in my life from scratch.

Wright

So how did you know you had hit rock bottom?

Puri

There was nothing in my bank account but bouncing checks and overdraft fees. I was contemplating escaping to a shelter or temporary housing with my two little boys and two puppies. Many people I thought were good friends of mine and close family members were not there for me when things were horrible—*that* was rock bottom.

But I never lost my inner strength. I never lost the hope and the love that I felt from God and the Holy Spirit. From praying to the Holy Spirit I felt that I had to be prepared to lose every material possession to follow Jesus Christ faithfully out of the darkness we were in. Later, very spiritual people entered my life that taught me what life was really about and what really mattered.

Wright

So where did you find the strength?

Puri

I had the sense to pray and to connect with my inner voice and the Holy Spirit, rather than take in all the negative chatter around me. I came from a very conservative bicultural Asian Indian family where all my ancestors had arranged marriages and never divorced. Divorce, especially for women with children, had a bad stigma and shame attached to it. I actually had a relative want to make me swear that I would not disclose that I was divorced to any person in our community, which was quite ridiculously unsupportive.

My response to this was you really ought to be proud that I had the courage to leave an abusive marriage with two young children under age three, and that is something to hold my head high for, not hide in shame. I found that this kind of negative chatter was wrong for me. I knew clearly from professionals that I was in the wrong situation, and I couldn't professionally grow because the person I was with was threatened by my spiritual growth and success as a person.

I was ready to launch one of the biggest projects of my lifetime, and my partner was progressively getting angrier, more controlling, and more abusive toward me in front of my children. So, to counter the negative chatter, I sought out positive, success-oriented people who had been through divorce and came out on the other side as better people.

I also tapped into the strength of creativity, so when other people might be falling apart during a process like this, I was able to think about creative ways that I could make more money for basic survival, and eventually start my life all over.

I learned invaluable lessons from my situation about spirituality and maintaining wealth. It is amazing that many people come out of their rock bottom place as a better soul, better at business or their career, and better with their relationships. Many of the top and best-selling authors were at rock bottom right before their biggest breaks such as J. K. Rowling (author of the Harry Potter books) who was a divorced single mother on welfare prior to her bestselling book series.

San Francisco Bay-area psychologist and minister, Darcy Ing follows the Japanese spiritual tradition of Johrei. She describes a process of "purification" that is necessary for spiritual growth. Purification is a really difficult, intensely painful struggle that can take many forms, but is necessary for immense spiritual growth. You can find this idea of purification in every faith tradition from Christianity talking about the soul being polished by hardship, to Hinduism discussing the importance of learning from your past.

In my darkest moments, when I started to lose faith from exposure to wicked behavior, I remembered the value of going through a spiritual purification. I sought out spiritual lessons from spiritual people who seemed to show up just at the right time.

Wright

How did your faith create abundance in your life?

Puri

My faith has been there for me in every aspect of my life, and every good decision. First of all, I had a mom who hated what she did for her career and work was just a way to get a paycheck. So I made it my goal in life to do something I love while I earn money. From my faith, prayers, and tapping into my inner source, I was guided toward a career where I helped others find their purpose in life and live their dreams fully.

Over time, I found people needed to slow down for themselves. We can be caught in the rat race of trying to work and climb the ladder of success, and then suddenly realize we are climbing the wrong ladder. I found from coaching many successful people that it is essential for everyone to make time to slow down to listen to their purpose in this world. The joy you will feel when you connect with something meaningful and purposeful is unimaginable. When you are authentic with yourself and your purpose, then you can do nothing but smile in the hardest of circumstances. I think it is important for people to know the saying, *"The hardest path is sometimes the best path."*

Many times successful people had unpopular, unsupported ideas, and they had to take the road less travelled to really make a difference. Galileo, for example, was considered a sinner for his views by people who misused the Christian Bible as a way to condemn people. In modern times, the Christian Bible is misused against people who identify as gay, lesbian, bisexual, or transgendered, people who have divorces or affairs, people in the sex industry, and people of different faiths. And yet we forget that Jesus Christ, in the book of John, took the harder path when asked what to do about a woman accused of adultery, given the laws at that time required stoning for adultery. Jesus Christ said, "Let He who is without sin among you, let him throw a stone at her first."

Jesus Christ was eventually killed for taking the harder path of questioning the laws of the religious people in power in His time. However, His hard sacrifice lead to His rebirth and the salvation of the entire world. So I learned you must be willing to climb the higher mountain, and struggle toward the harder path, because eventually you will reach salvation in your circumstances.

There are times when we may feel like quitting or giving up because it seems that there is no end to that mountain, and our feet are bleeding from the jagged stones. However, this is when you reach out to God or a spiritual soul to remind you of the power of faith and that *you only need to take one step at a time, and you are much closer to your goal than you can ever imagine.* Many people stop when they were actually really close to meeting their goals.

And taking the harder, yet best path requires learning to overcome and eventually master your fears. You learn to replace these fears with joy and celebration. My faith in the Holy Spirit helped me overcome fear from being in that deep, dark, bottomless pit while I was on the harder path and eventually step into a better life far different from my past life.

So my faith helped guide me toward helping others find their purpose and live their dreams. From coaching many successful people, I think people need to slow down to tap into our own inner strength. Many times we're socialized to speed through this rat race to compete with everybody for the best paid job or look like the ideal family, when what *we really need is to slow down and check in with who we are, what we dream of, what we want to be, have, or do in this world.*

I believe every one of us has a mission in this world that is going to make this world a better place and leave us feeling so very happy. When you are connected with your purpose and authentic with yourself, then you can smile in the hardest of circumstances.

Wright

How do you practice the faith that gave you so much strength?

Puri

For me, because I'm a very busy person, I had to adapt rituals in my life where faith became my top priority. I learned from my Mary Kay mentor, Thea Elvin, how important faith was in creating a wealthy life. Thea Elvin is a woman guided by the Holy Spirit who earned the elite position as a national sales director who literally accrued two million in commission from enriching women's lives through the top selling cosmetics company, Mary Kay.

Mary Kay was a brilliant woman, recognized as globally one of the top businesspeople. She created a company where you put *faith first, then family, and then career.* Mary Kay has created more U.S. women millionaires than any other company. *And Mary Kay herself taught by example that it is important to make faith a regular part of your daily routine. Mary Kay believed in setting six top priorities daily and said, "If you fail to plan, then you plan to fail."*

So I schedule my inner work time for my faith routine daily. I do things such as pray to the Holy Spirit, study all faith scriptures for wisdom such as Shamanism, Hinduism, Islam, Judaism, Johrei, Christianity, etc. I envision my life as I want it to be, and write in my gratitude journal daily to make certain I am focusing on the joy in my life. *I learned that where there is joy and love, there is no room for fear.*

So every day, the first thing I do when I get up in the morning, is I pray. Very simply, I pray and ask for wisdom for the greatest challenges I have in my life that day and to give me focus, and every evening I have that same ritual. I do this every single day. It's nothing fancy, but *when you look across all the different world religions, in the end it's not fancy—it's just showing up and doing it.*

Wright

Hmmm, that's a great line—showing up and doing it.

So how can people become self-aware of their own inner strengths?

Puri

You can identify your strengths by talking with an optimistic person or mentor, and share your "best moment" story with them. The best moment story is any time in your life you really felt great. When you share this best moment story, also ask the person listening to your story to identify your strengths in the story.

One of the best moments in my life was when I was in college and I worked with the international students from India and the domestic students from America in order to learn more about different cultures because I was raised in Wisconsin. When I was at the University of Wisconsin-Madison, I put together a cultural festival called Holi, where you throw colored water at people and colored powder. It's just a fun festival based in Hinduism, where you can get red color all over your face and clothes.

What I did is I came up with a creative way of getting people from completely different cultures to play together. So suddenly, here are two opposing groups, one thinking, "Oh you foreigners, you're fresh off the boat, you're so backward," and another group thinking, "Oh you Americans are so spoiled and we just don't get you." Suddenly they're playing together for the first time in their lives, laughing, giggling, and bridges are crossed.

I realized from my best moment story my strength was creativity and my high moments were creative. Then you look at how your strength has been used throughout your life. In my case, I used creativity to diffuse high conflict tension between Palestinian and Jewish university students by having them interact with music and dance, which created a joyful connection between two very opposing groups of people.

Another thing you can do to identify your strengths is take the online Values In Action (VIA) Signature Strengths Survey from Chris Peterson and Martin Seligman. The VIA Signature Strengths Survey has taken research from religion, philosophy, business, etc. to categorize twenty-four character strengths and virtues that are cross-cultural. If you take the VIA Signature Strengths Survey online, you will be given a list of the top five character strengths and virtues you have. If you take this or any test, it is a good idea to discuss the results with someone familiar with interpreting it.

Wright

So what about people who say they have a lot of money and status and don't need to know about their inner strengths? In other words, what makes it important to discover your inner strengths?

Puri

There are people who think that if they have money and status, why do they need to discover their inner strengths? The reality is that when you look at the happiness and success literature coming out of positive psychology, you are happy with money only up to a certain point. The average middle-income wage earner has met that point already. So if someone says, "I'm happy because of money and status," you can't really believe that person; it does not agree with the research on happiness. It somewhat goes back to the Beatles' song, "Money Can't Buy You Love." In the end, happiness is based on other things that are more important such as using your strengths in your career to make a difference in this world or using your strengths in your relationships.

Wright

I understand you have been working on a book about women and happiness. What have you found about successful women?

Puri

I asked women across the globe to write about what made them happy. We're talking about perspectives of women from Israel around the war-torn areas in Jerusalem, Argentina, India, Japan, the United States, and Canada. Women from all parts of the world wrote their stories about what made them happy. What's amazing is, from the orthodox Jewish woman to the lesbian identified third age couple who did not believe in religion, they all first referred to their inner faith, whether they referred to God or whether they talked about their inner voice, it was their inner faith that tied them to happiness.

The second thing that happy women do is help others. I still remember the story from Jerusalem from author and coach Yehudit Yosef about the sadness from mothers who see their children who are soldiers dying. I couldn't imagine such a sad situation as a mother.

How can one feel happiness in this situation? What the women did is they got together and they decided they were going to put on a huge fundraiser with a play. So they turned their energy toward doing something productive and happy for their children. They created happiness in the middle of despair. That was very moving to hear about.

Helping others, no matter what your circumstance, can really bring you *happiness*.

A homeless man named Rob who lived in Philadelphia had to get food and shelter in the biting cold rain. He taught me a spiritual lesson. He said being Christian to him means always being kind to others.

One day a young lady was dropped off on the street by police because she had been discharged from the psychiatric hospital and did not have any relatives or home. Rob tried to approach her, and realized with his hunched back and crippled hands that he probably looked scary to her. He said, "You don't have to be scared of me, I can help you if you need it. I know the best places to sleep out of the rain." She kept her distance initially, then over time she started getting closer and closer to Rob. Eventually, Rob was tucking her in to sleep in safe, sheltered areas away from the wind and rain. Later, he went to the train station and gathered a crowd of people to raise money to send this young lady to her relatives. Rob, the homeless man from Philadelphia, taught me a valuable spiritual lesson—*no matter who you are, no matter what your circumstances, you will benefit from helping others.*

The third important area for happy women is social relationships. For example, author therapist, Diane Sue, wrote about how many times we're isolated in our neighborhoods, and we don't bother to connect with each other. Diane Sue shared how she befriended an older woman in her neighborhood. Diane eventually found out that this elderly grandmother was a holocaust survivor with such amazing insights for Diane that they became lifelong friends who were like family.

Happier women extend themselves in social relationships. My mother, a very social woman, always extended herself when people were ill or there was a death in the family. She would go above and beyond to provide homemade dinners and social support. My mother is also someone who has maintained the same social circle for twenty years. Happier women are socially connected women.

Wright

As a psychologist and successful business coach, what have you found out about your search with successful multimillionaires and CEOs?

Puri

This to me has been the most mind-blowing thing—the people who continue to be wealthy, well-rounded millionaires point to having a strong inner faith. They make time to pray, and they make time to meditate and focus on their vision for the future.

Every major religion talks about setting time aside to be quiet and connect with spirit. This quiet time or meditation is a key factor for wealthy people. Wealthy people constantly have a vision of where they're heading.

In Mary Kay cosmetics, the national sales directors who earn a million plus in commission, without counting product sales, were often steadfast believers in having pictures of their goals such as the Pink Cadillac all around their home, or affirmative statements from the Bible on their mirrors. They also focused on their message and what they were going to do to enrich women's lives, rather than making their business about a cosmetics product. Many of them have a message that they want to give out to the world; it's just amazing to see it. I think they're so in tune with how they're going to make a difference for people, that they're just driven every day. It's really exciting to see that in action.

A fine example of this is Annette Sym, the number one Australian low fat, cookbook author who sold two and a half million books, at last count. She turned her life around from a two-hundred-pound unhealthy lifestyle into a healthier way of eating and living. Annette Sym's vision was to get her message out in her cookbook, *Symply too Good to be True,* that there was a healthier, happier, and more fit lifestyle available to everyone.

In the end, successful people combine faith and consistent focus on an inner vision to achieve a wealthy lifestyle.

Wright

So what are the steps that people can take to identify their top strengths and become successful?

Puri

I really do believe in mentorship. Whatever avenue of life you want to enter, succeed, and lead in, go find a person who is doing it, and ask that person to mentor you. I invite people to contact me so I can use my spiritual intuition to help them identify their strengths and purpose. I sit down, talk, and then really look at what is it that they are good at. I then look at what's blocking them from being more successful.

Another thing I recommend people do is take some of those online tests. They're easy enough to take, and they're free right now. I do highly recommend talking with a trained, successful person who is familiar with whatever tests you do take.

Wright

So what resources do you have available for people?

Puri

I always keep up on my Web site free tools that will help you identify your strengths, because I just think it's doing so much good for our children, for our relationships, career, businesses, etc. So you can go to www.bayareacoach.com and get free resources that will show you how to take these surveys and exercises in identifying your strengths. You can contact me if you need someone to speak to about strengths and spiritual purpose or if you need an authentic and reliable referral for people who are trained at identifying your strengths. I also have a very strong network of spiritual women in Mary Kay cosmetics with local, support meetings for any woman who wants a better life for her children.

Wright

Well, very interesting. You have come from rock bottom, so how are you doing now?

Puri

I have faith in myself that I am at the top, and that's what it takes. If you look at the most successful people—not just material success, but personal success—they always have faith in their vision of how they're going to live their lives. I think you have to start from the inside first; you have to start with courage to live out your strengths to their fullest.

Wright

A wise man once told me, if I were walking down a road and saw a turtle sitting on top of a fencepost, that he didn't get up there by himself. Are there people in your life who are mentors and others who are helping you along the way?

Puri

Absolutely, and this is the amazing thing again because I've always been so focused on prayer and my mission. I have always had mentors enter my life for everything that I wanted to learn and do. I think that you have to have the openness, willingness, and humility to learn from others who have done what you want to do. I've told my students to "never reinvent the wheel—there is someone out there doing what you dream of doing."

For example, my personal mission was to create a global company that sold products to generate substantial revenue for empowering abused women and children in shelters. I found out that Mary Kay cosmetics is already doing this. In the first quarter of 2009 selling one product—apple berry lipstick—produced over 1.4 million dollars for shelter funding! Now that is powerful—to purchase one product line and help that many women and children in shelters!

When I saw this, I humbly retrained as an independent beauty consultant in Mary Kay to follow my purpose. This was not a "popular" decision, yet successful people have good instincts that outshine popularity. And now I have a sisterhood of elite Mary Kay women guided by the Holy Spirit to create wealth for women even during financial recessions!

Take the time to dream and decide what you want to have, be, or do. Then find someone who is already doing it. There are many people who would love to share their wisdom and have someone quietly absorb their life lessons—the lessons they learned that got them to where they are.

I have been very, very blessed to have been guided toward some of the best mentors for pretty much every phase of my life. I believe, though, that if you work on your inner faith and your inner strength, the right mentors will appear from the universe.

Wright

Well, what a great conversation. I really appreciate all this time you've spent with me today answering these questions. I have learned a lot and I'm sure our readers will.

Puri

And thank you, David, because it's been a very pleasant conversation with you also.

Wright

Today we've been talking with Dr. Neera Puri. Dr. Puri is a senior international business coach and trainer and a principal of Bay Area Coach, LLC providing executive and leadership coaching. She is committed to multicultural training, as a founding member of the South Asian Psychological Networking Association and a member of the Asian American Psychological Association, American Psychological Association, and the International Coach Federation. She is also actively involved in Mary Kay cosmetics to enrich women and children's lives toward more peace.

Dr. Puri, thank you so much for being with us today on *Discover Your Inner Strength*.

Puri

And thank you, David, for putting together such a wonderful book.

About the Author

Neera Puri, she holds a PhD in Psychology from the University of Southern California and an MSW from the University of Houston. A senior international business coach and trainer, Dr. Neera is the principal of Bay Area Coach, providing executive and leadership coaching. Her coaching practice includes international clientele from Australia, Canada, India, Israel, Mexico, Nigeria, and the United States. She is committed to multicultural training, being a founding member of the South Asian Psychological Networking Association and a member of the Asian American Psychological Association. She has been interviewed as a pioneer for her work with South Asian mental health in the American Psychological Association and is a credentialed member of the International Coach Federation. With over fifteen years of experience, Dr. Puri has worked with Fortune 50 companies, health care systems, diversity programs for corporations and universities, and women's organizations. Her investment with women and children led her to work at the USC Career Center, UCLA Student Psychological Service, UC Davis Counseling and Psychological Services, Catholic Charities, and Mary Kay cosmetics.

Dr. Puri is an invited speaker for seminars on motivation, spirituality, positive psychology, and work-life balance, strong women leaders, and team-building using the Myers-Briggs type inventory.

She lives in the San Francisco Bay area where she enjoys going on hikes with her two boys, and her two puppies, Smokey and Twixie. An avid animal lover, she has actively trained and rehabilitated shelter dogs, and hopes one day to open "Smokey Ranch" to connect shelter dogs with loving, invested people.

Dr. Neera Puri

PO Box 5730

Hercules, CA 94547-5730

(866) 528-0553

info@bayareacoach.com

www.bayareacoach.com

Chapter Five

Character Strengths

An Interview With…

Tana Sherwood

David Wright (Wright)

Today we are talking with Tana Sherwood, founder of Crystal Cove Coaching, who partners with others to create healthier, happier more abundant lives. She leads monthly Master Mind groups, coaches small business owners and individuals in transition, delivers corporate workshops and is frequently invited to serve as a guest speaker. Speaking venues include the Ford Motor Company, WISE (Women Investing in Security and Education), Woman Sage, and the Orange County Christian Outreach. Ms. Sherwood earned a MBA from Pepperdine University, a Certified Financial Planning Certificate, a California Secondary Teacher Life Credential, and is a Certified Coach through the International Coaching Federation.

Tana, welcome to *Discover Your Inner Strength.*

What is the standard, universally understood definition of the term "character strengths?"

Tana Sherwood (Sherwood)

I am not certain we have a universally accepted definition of anything. Character strengths can range from the very broad to the very specific and might depend on whom you ask or the context in which it is being used. Think for a moment of what character strengths come to mind if referring to a job applicant, a parent, or the desired qualities in a significant other, or a world leader. We would most likely choose different strengths for each of these roles.

However, most philosophical discussions of character are indebted to the analysis of Aristotle who wrote, "Character is that which reveals moral purpose, exposing the class of things a man chooses or avoids." Many philosophers since have approached character not as an esoteric study, but as a necessary guide for life. They often use strength of character as a gauge for maturity.

Wright

The topic of character strengths is of great interest to you. What fascinates you with regard to character strengths and the human condition?

Sherwood

Strength of character is not just a good attribute to have but is also something to be—the most important thing to be. When looking at the human condition around much of the world, we see so much unhappiness and personal distress. Much of this unhappiness comes from the inability or unwillingness to control tempers, impulses, passions, and appetites. Being able to exercise one of the virtues, the virtue of temperance—the strength that protects us from excess—would greatly improve the present condition.

One of my favorite college classes in literature was Greek mythology. The ongoing message from each myth was that excess—excess in anything—will destroy, excess vengeance or love are just two examples. We are easily reminded of excesses every time we watch television or read the newspaper. Several recent studies report that two thirds of the people in our country are obese, which has devastating consequences, not only for each obese person but also for our culture and economy. Another example is excess greed by people at all levels, which has contributed to the economic challenges we face.

I want to be a contribution, and creating awareness about character is one way to contribute. I encourage people to take character development seriously to enhance the quality of their existence. When we face the inevitable challenges in life, our character strengths help us make important decisions and sustain new, necessary behaviors and attitudes.

When a person lives a life grounded in character strengths, and commits to ongoing reflection on and improvement of those strengths, that individual will live a life of possibilities, and possibilities afford us freedom.

Wright

What is the connection between character strengths, possibilities, and freedom?

Sherwood

Being aware of our character strengths and committing to growing them creates a life of possibilities—the more possibilities, the more freedom we will experience.

The word "possibility" is an amazing word. I am inspired by the book, *The Art of Possibility*. I had the wonderful opportunity to meet one of the authors, Benjamin Zander, who is the conductor for the Boston Philharmonic, at a Young President's Organization (YPO) Conference in Russia. Mr. Zander cowrote the *The Art of Possibility* with his wife, Rosamund Stone Zander, who is a therapist and runs accomplishment groups. Their book reminds us that we must focus our gaze on the person we want to be and momentarily silence the voice in our head that tells us we will fail. What a great example of freeing oneself from imagined negative self-talk that keeps us from being free to be our best selves and to accomplish our life's work.

We can all feel freedom—freedom to be healthy, freedom to treat ourselves and others kindly, and freedom to create our own realities. As Mr. Zander says, "It is all invented anyway, so we might as well invent a story or framework of meaning that enhances our quality of life and the life of those around us." Without freedom, there are no choices. The higher we develop our character strengths, the more freedom we will experience. The Zanders remind us in their book of rule number six, which is *don't take yourself so seriously.* This attitude of not taking ourselves so seriously greatly contributes to our feeling free and creating new possibilities

Wright

What role do you believe your faith in Christianity plays in character strengths?

Sherwood

I love the foundation, support, and encouragement my faith has given to me. Through faith in God, I get my moral code and compass. I love the statement by Pastor Rick Warren, "God is more interested in why we do something than in what we do." He suggests we ask ourselves the following questions: Do we approach our lives as servants or only focus on ourselves? Do we strive to be good stewards of the many blessings God has loaned us while we are here? Do we compare ourselves to others and compete with them, or do we stay focused on our own purpose? Do we treat those we love as an opportunity to serve or an obligation?

Recently I moved my ninety-three-year-old, legally blind mom from another state to be closer to her. The move was not without challenges, both logistically and emotionally. My adult son had recently graduated college and moved away. I was experiencing a new freedom from certain responsibilities. After relocating my mother, I found myself in the caretaker role again. My faith enables me to embrace this opportunity and to draw on my character strengths in order to be a good servant. This is truly a "get to" and not a "have to." She questions why she is still on this earth, but I believe this is the opportunity for me to serve and for us to complete that circle of love that started with her doing for others, which she did all of her life.

Wright

What is the relationship between character strengths, or good character, and virtues?

Sherwood

Aristotle says that a "virtue is a state of character that makes its possessors behave in ethically appropriate ways." We build character by practicing virtues and using our inherent strengths toward our divine purpose on earth.

Virtues are powerful, and several formulations of virtues have been proposed through the years. The classical Greek philosophers considered the foremost virtues to be *The Cardinal Virtues,* which are prudence, temperance, courage, and justice. *The Theological Virtues* are love, hope, and faith.

The Seven Contrary Virtues were derived from the poem "Psychomachia," which meant "Battle for the Soul," written by Prudentius in approximately 410 ACE. When a person practiced these virtues, it was alleged to protect him or her against temptation toward the Seven Deadly Sins: *humility* against pride, *kindness* against envy, *abstinence* against gluttony, *chastity* against lust, *patience* against anger, *liberality* (giving freely) against greed, *diligence* against sloth.

The study of character and virtues has continued throughout history and has had a renewed interest the last few years. I took a class with Marty Seligman who wrote *Authentic Happiness* and *Learned Optimism.* He spearheaded the research connecting happiness with character strengths and virtues. Seligman's group classified and measured widely valued, positive traits. Their research classified twenty-four specific strengths under six broad virtues that have consistently emerged across culture and history. Those six virtues are: wisdom, courage, humanity, justice, temperance, and transcendence.

Wright

What "model" of character strengths do you use when working with clients in your personal coaching business?

Sherwood

Almost all of my clients complete the Values in Action (VIA) assessment available on Seligman's Web site—www.authentichappiness.com. This assessment ranks in order a person's twenty-four character strengths. The VIA is one of my favorite assessments, as it provides great value in creating awareness about the strengths in which an individual ranks highly and those in which improvement may be desired.

Seligman's research further shows how possessing five of these strengths greatly contributes to happiness. After working with many clients, I modified the list of five and added two character strengths that I find are essential for creating a best life. The two I added are spirituality or purpose in life and self-regulation. I call my list "the Sacred Seven." The words identifying the strengths have a recognizable meaning and can be immediately practiced in one's life. They are: curiosity, love, optimism, gratitude, spirituality or life's purpose, courage, and self-regulation,

Wright

How do you make the Sacred Seven practical and accessible for the average client? Will you walk us through them?

Sherwood

Nothing makes an impression like a good story! I always employ examples of individuals who personify each one of the Sacred Seven. I also help clients focus and commit to practicing all seven in order to successfully confront the unexpected that often comes our way.

Wright

How does being curious contribute to high character?

Sherwood

Curiosity falls within the virtue of wisdom. A cognitive strength, it represents one's intrinsic desire for knowledge and experience. A person who loves to learn gains a new perspective through wisdom. My mantra is that it is better to be interested than interesting. When people are truly interested and open to new information and experiences, the world becomes their playground. I find I am happier when I am curious and not overly focused on myself—how I feel, what I own, or what is or is not working in my own life.

All of our famous inventors had an insatiable curiosity in creating something new and making it better. Henry Ford's curiosity propelled his obsessive attention to detail. He wanted people to be curious about how to think better and not just remember facts. This strength allowed him to imagine something the world would really need—the Model T automobile—and then sell it to them for an affordable price. His curiosity, coupled with vision, made him a major figure in the twentieth century.

As a personal coach, I am privileged to share in the journey of an individual pursuing knowledge and wisdom through curiosity.

Wright

How can people embrace the character strength of love when there is so much suffering in the world?

Sherwood

Love is the basis of our humanity. This character strength includes the capacity to love and be loved, to be kind, show patience, have emotional intelligence, and be generous. Through love, we tend to and befriend others. We demonstrate appreciation of others when we care as much about other people's needs as much as our own, and when we acknowledge and value what is important to them.

Viewing circumstances as part of a larger, loving plan allows us to endure and to persevere. This was the philosophy of the life of Jesus. He saw God as His only Source and accepted that God's love was in control of His life's plan. When Jesus was thrown in prison unjustly and later crucified, He saw injustice as part of this same loving plan.

I believe that one of our greatest challenges is to continue to love when bad things do happen. Knowing when to offer compassion and when to challenge an individual's resistance to change requires insight and patience for a personal coach. Either approach, if offered in the spirit of love, can constructively serve.

Wright

Can optimism be learned?

Sherwood

Optimists have hope. Their mindset is future thinking and the future looks better. Dr. Martin Seligman, who wrote *Learned Optimism,* determined that optimists have less depression, live healthier and longer lives, are more active socially, and perform better at school and work. Most importantly, he offers instruction on how optimism can be learned. On the flip side, he shows the causal link between pessimism, or learned helplessness and depression. Our habitual patterns of thought lead us to being pessimists or optimists.

One of the best examples of an optimistic thinker was Thomas Edison. He tried ten thousand times to develop an electric lamp. With each unsuccessful attempt, Mr. Edison quipped, "I have not failed. I've just found another way that won't work." We can extrapolate three useful tips from Mr. Edison's perspective and end result:

1. There is no such thing as failure—only unexpected outcomes, which will provide guidance for future work.
2. Decide with full commitment to accomplish something.
3. Look on the bright side of everything (no pun intended here).

Wright

What character strength do you personally value the most?

Sherwood

I am most grateful for having the attitude of gratitude. Gratitude is a strength that forges a connection to the larger universe and provides meaning to our individual lives. Gratitude is a cornerstone in my life and in my coaching practice. Eight years ago, after being diagnosed with Stage III non-Hodgkin lymphoma, I lay in a hospital bed for nearly two weeks. After a few days of intense tests, morphine, and many visitors, I found myself alone. The hospital room suddenly became very white and appeared to be enveloped in a cloud. I felt the warm presence of God. I quietly said, "Father in heaven, I am in so much pain." His only response was, "I know my child, just be grateful."

I knew I was already grateful for so many things—grateful after several months to be finally out of unbearable intense pain, grateful for the love of my family and friends, and grateful for the doctors' and nurses' dutiful care. My gratitude became increasingly powerful, as I soon realized that this challenge was to help me formulate my real purpose in being on this earth—a purpose I wasn't completely clear about prior to cancer.

After many months of treatment, I met with a personal coach who directed me into coaching. All of my life's experiences and knowledge gleaned by earning several degrees (MBA, teaching credential, and financial planning certificate) could be channeled toward helping others. My life's purpose is to partner with others to create healthier, happier, more abundant lives. This purpose nourishes me and glorifies God. God's purpose for me was revealed through cancer, and for that, I am most grateful

Wright

When are people at their absolute best?

Sherwood

People are at their best when they realize they are spiritual beings having human experiences, and they are clear about their divine purpose while here on earth. I believe spirituality and purpose are our greatest character strengths. I do not believe we can really begin to understand purpose without having a spiritual perspective. Life has an inner purpose, which is "being" and an outer purpose, which is "doing."

The goal of inner purpose is to be still and let go of ego. I read once that ego stands for easing God out. An overly active ego can be a source of negativity and unhappiness. Part of the outer purpose is to practice acceptance and enjoyment in the present and have enthusiasm for what you do.

One of the most profound and popular selling books is *The Purpose Driven Life* by Rick Warren. Pastor Warren defines "purpose" as being and doing what God intended for you. In religious circles, it is having clarity about your calling in life, whereas in business and education circles, "purpose" is described as clarity of your personal mission statement—that to which you aspire to be or wish to accomplish. When an organization or people have clarity and passion about purpose, they provide an irresistible attraction. Your purpose is the way you use your character strengths and gifts in service to others that make a difference in the things that are important to you.

Our weaknesses also can have a great role in living our purpose. Rick Warren writes, "God has never been impressed with strength or self-sufficiency. In fact, He is drawn to people who are weak and admit it."

Prior to getting cancer, I had great pride in my independence, my endless energy, and my thick, beautiful hair. Suddenly those perceived strengths were gone. I was then left relying on the help and support of others to meet my daily needs. Health challenges provide the opportunity to be real—real with compassion to others' pain, real about knowing who is really in charge, and real about how community is truly created.

When others perceive only your strengths, they can be discouraged by you or want to compete with you. My self-sufficiency was a weakness until I learned humility and being honest about my own vulnerabilities and fears. I feel so blessed that I acquired the gifts of that health challenge—that God loves me and is in charge, there are no guarantees for anyone that life will go a certain way, and through my surrender to Him, His grace will see me through anything. Although my hair and energy are back better than ever, I still struggle with the tendency toward self-sufficiency.

Wright

How does knowing our purpose help us?

Sherwood

Knowing your purpose gives your life focus, simplifies the struggle of when to say yes or no, increases motivation, and prepares us for the life hereafter. Knowing and living my purpose gives me profound gratitude.

On the flip side, there are consequences to not knowing and living your purpose. Life can seem tiresome, unfulfilling, and uncontrollable. Without a spiritual perspective of God's hand in our lives, it is, again, almost impossible to manage and control our lives. Ask anyone who has tried to rely on willpower alone to make changes. We are meant to surrender to God and put Him first. Then real change can happen.

Wright

Who else really talks about good character and the influence of courage?

Sherwood

Aristotle wrote, "You will never do anything in this world without courage. It is the greatest quality of the mind next to honor."

Eleanor Roosevelt has been called the "First Lady of Courage." She wrote in her book, *You Learn by Living,* "Courage is more exhilarating than fear, and in the long run it is easier. We do not have to become heroes overnight. Just a step at a time, meeting each challenge that presents itself, seeing it is not as dreadful as it appeared, and discovering we have the strength to stare it down." Eleanor Roosevelt did learn by living one challenge after another beginning with a painful childhood. Before the age of ten, she lost both parents and a brother. Her courage was tested many times in her marriage to Franklin Roosevelt. She experienced loss, pain, and suffering, and as a result, she had great empathy for the oppressed and worked tirelessly on their behalf. She championed women's rights and civil rights until her death.

Wright

Why is it so difficult for people to have discipline and to self-regulate?

Sherwood

I believe that people do not want to acknowledge that they are flawed and that it is human nature to fall short or to sin. As Dr. Phil says, "You can't change what you don't acknowledge." During the twentieth century, Americans shifted from self-denial to immediate gratification. Our "me culture" is stimulated by advertising to the consumer that promotes obsession with ourselves. We end up taking ourselves far too seriously and compromising our freedom. How can a person feel free when obsessed with constant gratification?

The wonderful payoff of freedom comes at a price—the choice of exercising self-regulation. Ask any poor soul who struggles with addiction, whether it is with substances or choosing unhealthy relationships. These people are not free. They live in bondage. God does give us free will to create abundance or to mess up our lives. The choice is ours, and the degree to which we own that choice also molds our character.

To live balanced lives, we need to acknowledge that much of life is guided by habits and routines. We tend to stop questioning what we are doing and how we are doing it. Living on automatic pilot, we may be living a life of less than constructive habits. Stephen Covey says, "Our character, basically is a composite of our habits . . . and that the first step on the road to success is good character." Covey's influence has shaped the thinking of so many people, as he encourages them to be proactive in wisely renewing their physical, spiritual, mental, and social domains. His book, *The 7 Habits of Highly Effective People,* has set the foundation for people to take charge of their destiny by getting clarity of their goals and using discipline to keep their commitments in all dimensions of their lives.

Cheryl Richardson writes in *Take Time for Your Life,* that it takes self-care to create a balanced life. It is much too easy to live on adrenalin and not put good self-care as a priority. It is always appropriate to ask what price are you paying and is the payoff worth that price? If your choices leave wreckage behind such as neglected family members and an unhealthy body and spirit, the price does become too great. Self-management or discipline becomes necessary.

I like to ask my clients, "What do you need to let go of that keeps you off balance? If you do let go, what might you gain in the journey going forward?"

Wright

What are the benefits of character strengths?

Sherwood

We certainly experience the downside when they are lacking. There are benefits to the individual and then, by extension, the benefits to others who live or work with a person who lives a life grounded in character strengths.

The easiest internal measure is to ask yourself how you feel. You are most likely living a life of character when *you:*

feel love—not fear
feel connected—not separate
feel hopeful—not hopeless
feel peaceful—not chaos
feel abundance—not scarcity
feel gratitude—not entitlement
feel joy—not depression
feel known—not invisible
feel abundance—not scarcity
feel inspired—not stuck
feel safe—not vulnerable
feel light—not dark or heavy
feel free—not chained
feel open—not closed

If more of your feelings are positive, you are probably committed to living good character. Which of these feelings are serving you rather than limiting you? Where and with whom do you feel these positive feelings?

Wright

How can we know if we are living a life of good character?

Sherwood

If you are seeking something very simple, take this self-audit of seven statements:

1. *Curiosity*—I am more interested in others and in the world around me than being interesting.
2. *Love*—I have people in my life whose happiness matters as much to me as my own.
3. *Optimism*—I am highly optimistic from the time I wake up until I go to bed.
4. *Gratitude*—I am grateful and appreciate what I have been given, and do not resent what I lack.
5. *Spirituality/Purpose*—I know why God created me and am committed to living His purpose for me. I look to a Higher Power for support, guidance, and strength.
6. *Courage*—I am bold in my approaches to moral dilemmas.
7. *Self-regulation*—I exert control over my responses to reach goals and live up to standards.

Wright

What do others use as a basis for judging one's character strengths?

Sherwood

It always helps to fast-forward from today and ask yourself this question, "What would I like said about me at my ninetieth birthday or at my funeral?" If you took inventory of your habits, behavior, and relationships, would they result in a life story that you would be happy to have told to your grandchildren? If there are some contradictions, you have a great opportunity to address them.

Some people assess a life of good character through external measures such as church attendance, tithing, volunteer work, respecting others, donating to charity, being an involved parent, and commitment to worthy causes such as education, peace, elderly, animals, environment, country, democracy, church, and God. These external measures are important but not complete.

Many religious people measure character as defined by God. Christians look to Jesus as the one person who has perfect character. He is the perfect model, along with the Word. God created us to be His children, to be saved and to live in eternity with Him. God is the ultimate judge of our character. He gave us His love letter—the Bible—which is his manual to those who seek. Christians also believe that living a virtuous life is the greatest reward—although not a perfect life—as it is man's nature to sin and be flawed.

Often the "judgment" day on Earth takes place when an individual, or individuals representing an organization, perform in a contradictory manner. We have some very recent and painful examples of this contradiction.

Wright

Recent disgraces indicate a lack of character strengths in at least some of corporate America. Will you address this?

Sherwood

For example, since the credit crash we now ask ourselves how we view organizations that gave big money to charity and yet ruined their companies with unscrupulous practices. How do we view the mortgage industry that may have been well intentioned to offer loans to the poor, but, in reality, greatly harmed those people and millions of others? The industry neglected a basic financial moral principle—all people must commit to living within their means. Individuals borrowing did not exercise prudence or self-control, neither did many of the participants in the mortgage and lending industries nor in our governing bodies.

The virtue of temperance protects against excess by requiring people to exercise caution, prudence, and self-control. In a world where anything goes, the virtue of temperance and the strength of self-regulation were absent.

Wright

How can character strengths better impact the workplace?

Sherwood

Our world has been shaken due, in large part, to the inability of corporate and government leaders to demonstrate good character. Many of the scandals and the economic fallout are due to the inability of leaders to be Omega leaders. The Omega leader motivates others by building up, nurturing, and enhancing employees', family members', and colleagues' inherent strengths of character and gifts. Laurie Beth Jones writes in *Jesus, CEO* that Jesus was the original Omega leader.

Traditionally, leaders have had the masculine or alpha style, while beta is the more feminine style. Today, women are the fastest growing segment of business owners and 80 percent of all businesses employ twenty or less. We need more Omega leaders—those who have mastery of self, good relationship skills, and can take action. When a leader is aware of his or her character strengths, commits to using and improving them, his or her company will most likely prosper. The qualities of the Omega leader are ones to which men and women leaders should aspire.

In our hectic work life today, personal resources are getting to be more important. Executives have to cope with very demanding, complex issues in this global marketplace, and they need the highly developed strengths to make good decisions under pressure.

In a study done in 2004 for the International Positive Psychology Summit, a correlation was proven between high work life satisfaction for executives and their scoring high on leadership, open-mindedness or curiosity, and bravery or courage. When executives are highly satisfied in their work life, everyone around them benefits, including their employees or families. It would behoove any leader to especially improve on these particular strengths.

As a business and life coach, I help my clients develop all three skills of self-mastery, relationship-building, and taking action to the highest levels by also getting clarity on other issues. I partner with them in:

- Developing a more accurate belief system about capabilities, resources and opportunities,

- Discovering character strengths and how to use them to best advantage and not overuse them,
- Recognizing what motivates them and what puts them "on hold,"
- Unleashing the passion that energizes,
- Learning how to confidently adapt to change, and
- Creating a vision founded on clarity.

Wright

How can we develop character strengths in order to live our very best life?

Sherwood

There are so many resources on the Internet that provide practical, free advice on setting and achieving new goals and developing other skills. If it is in your budget, one of the best ways is to have a personal coach who serves as your accountability or results partner. A coach keeps you focused on the journey out the windshield and not so much as the rear view mirror. We all have to be aware of our thoughts and self-talk. I remind my clients that we have about fifty thousand to sixty thousand thoughts each day and that about 95 percent of them are the same day after day. If you are thinking the same thing every day, how likely is it that you will have a new experience or new result? Not likely.

I have a free tool on my Web site, www.CrystalCoveCoaching, that aids people in being aware of their thoughts. It is called "15 minutes for thoughts" and can be downloaded free from the Discovery page. Individuals can create quiet time to write down each thought for fifteen minutes on this form. Then they could make a check in the column provided to see if each thought limited or served them.

One of my clients realized that every thought about herself was negative and critical. Incidentally, critical thinking was one of her top character strengths on the Values In Action assessment. This was an example of a character strength being overused and then becoming a weakness. We then strategized how she could develop more positive self-talk to aid her in her goals to lose weight as well as grow her small business.

All of our character strengths can be overused, becoming weaknesses. One of my strengths is love of learning. I became obsessed with taking every certification program and attending every conference before I started my business. I finally had to say to myself, "Look, you already have an MBA, a certified financial planning certificate, and are now a certified coach. Just start your business knowing that nothing will be perfect and there will be things you learn along the way." Again, a strength being overused.

Another question that is often asked is, "How much should you focus on those strengths in which you scored lower on the assessment?" For example, one client scored very low on optimism (twenty-three out of twenty-four) and her husband often complained about her negativity. I asked her if this pessimism was a real barrier in happiness in her marriage. If it was, she could choose to work on that strength or really focus more on her strengths of kindness and love. Some practical tips on improving her optimism were:

1. Read about someone who succeeded despite setbacks such as the people we have talked about.
2. Forgive yourself or someone else for bad decisions and choose to do better.
3. Visualize where you will be in one year and all of the benefits of reaching that goal by being more positive.

Wright

How can we teach our children character strengths?

Sherwood

Parents can be role models by practicing how character strengths begin on the inside. We can share with them our own strengths and how we commit to developing them further in our personal and professional lives. This is a great way to introduce the concept of setting goals and modifying one's thoughts and behaviors to get new results.

Have your children take the VIA assessment for their age bracket so they have their own awareness of their strengths. Discuss as a family how you will acknowledge, appreciate, and celebrate each other's strengths. For example, if creativity is one of your child's strengths, plan an outing to see an art museum or take a new class together as a family.

It is also important that parents allow their children to have natural consequences. How often do you rescue your child from the consequences of his or her own choices out of your own inability to keep a healthy boundary? The role of parents is important in instilling self-control in their children. When parents are indulgent and have an excessive concern for self-esteem, children may develop weak, narcissistic, self-indulgent personalities. We must remember that we ourselves have learned the most when we have been in that wilderness of pain and confusion. It is through confronting fears and challenges that we build the character muscle we need all through life. Balancing good boundaries with love and affection and a healthy dose of forgiveness is the tightrope all parents walk. The benefits are endless when we commit to those behaviors and attitudes.

Wright

What is your closing message?

Sherwood

This quote by Frank Outlaw says so much:

Watch your thoughts, for they become words.
Watch your words, for they become actions.
Watch your actions, for they become habits.
Watch your habits, for they become character.
Watch your character, for it becomes your destiny.

Wright

Thank you for being with us today.

About the Author

Tana Sherwood, founder of Crystal Cove Coaching, partners with others to create healthier, happier more abundant lives. She leads monthly Master Mind groups, coaches small business owners and individuals in transition, delivers corporate workshops and is frequently invited to serve as a guest speaker. Speaking venues include the Ford Motor Company, WISE (Women Investing in Security and Education), Woman Sage, and the Orange County Christian Outreach. Ms. Sherwood earned a MBA from Pepperdine University, a Certified Financial Planning Certificate, a California Secondary Teacher Life Credential, and is a Certified Coach through the International Coaching Federation.

Tana Sherwood

Crystal Cove Coaching
Newport Coast, CA
tana@CrystalCoveCoaching.com
www.CrystalCoveCoaching.com

Chapter Six

Discovering The Secret to Your Sales Power

An Interview With…

Lee Knapp

David Wright (Wright)

Today we are talking with Lee Knapp, president of Knapp Consultants based in Fort Myers, Florida. She is a motivational speaker and sales training specialist. For over three decades, Lee's contagious passion for the selling profession has inspired people to believe in themselves, raise their personal expectations, and achieve outstanding sales success. As one of the first female executives to benefit two Fortune 500 companies, Lee is the unstoppable trailblazer. She has trained and developed a national/international sales team of over twenty thousand people. She has also trained, recruited, and developed a one-thousand-person sales team in Melbourne, Australia. Her "in-the-trenches" selling techniques and experiences provide her with the ability to lead and inspire people to achieve their wildest dreams.

Lee, welcome to *Discover Your Inner Strength*.

Lee Knapp (Knapp)

Thanks, David.

Wright

What is your secret to your sales power?

Knapp

I love sales. Let me tell you how I started my selling career.

When I was three years old, my father had a grocery store in Detroit, Michigan. Sitting on the shelves of the store, within my short reach, were Maxwell House coffee cans. On the bottom of those cans, there was a small metal key that was used to open the lid of the coffee can. Without this key, you could not open the coffee can. I must have realized the importance of this small key, even at three years old. I would pick the key off the bottom of the can and sell it for a penny. That's how I actually started my selling career.

Obviously, my career didn't last very long because as soon as my father realized where those coffee can keys were going, my career came to a screeching halt. My parents told me that this early taste of success started my belief in sales. I was one of those kids who just sold anything and everything I could get my hands on. I learned the excitement of gaining the sale at three years old.

My secret lies in my belief that there are no limits in sales. Having no limits in what I can accomplish in life has provided me with my motivation to always believe in the opportunity of sales and continue to get out there and make things happen.

When I want to sell more, I raise my expectations, feed my mind with new information, get creative, remain flexible with my thinking, and become proactive. I stay aware of what's going on around me and tuned in to what I am doing that works and what doesn't work. The answers are usually right under my nose; all I have to do is take off my blinders and look for them.

When I think about my sales power secrets, I also think about the ability to connect with people. When I connect with people, I feel the difference in the relationship. Truly connecting with people is a valuable sales skill. Yes, it can be learned, too. Since making a sale is all about defining the need of the customer and filling that need, I want to make a solid connection with my customers.

Wright

You are such a believer in the sales profession and the opportunities that it offers people, what has created this positive belief for you?

Knapp

I stay focused on having a clear goal, a game plan to achieve that goal, and a burning desire to succeed. I believe in myself, my product, and my company. Actually, David, I learned this lesson when I was about seven years old, growing up in Detroit, Michigan.

As an easily-impressed seven-year-old with no television at home, my favorite thing to do was go to the Saturday movie matinee. Twelve o'clock sharp at the RKO Theatre was where it all happened for me. Just thinking about it brings back the excitement. This was a full day event because there were two feature films, lots of cartoons, newsreels, and other surprises.

It cost twenty-five cents to get into the movies. My weekly allowance of twenty-five cents covered the cost of the movies. However, what is a movie without snacks? My snacking goal consisted of JuJu Bees, popcorn, and soda pop.

These snacks were going to cost me an additional twenty cents. I knew that I was expected to earn that extra twenty cents on my own. No problem—I had a goal, a game plan, and a burning desire to succeed. I could taste the JuJu Bees and the warm salty popcorn.

I went into my backyard, under the porch, where I kept my red flyer wagon, as my enthusiasm for meeting my goal was building. Down the street I would go, pulling my empty red wagon. The sounds of my red wagon clanging behind generated more enthusiasm.

The corner grocery store always smelled rather strange and actually had sawdust on the floor. The grocer, Sam, would always welcome me with a friendly smile. He told me I was good for business. I'm not sure about that, but it made me feel great about being there. I would position my wagon right next to the cash register and sit at the end of the wagon with my legs hanging over the edge. Every lady, without exception, who came through the grocery line was my potential customer. I would look each one directly in the eye, put a big smile on my face, and bravely ask, "How would you like me to carry those heavy groceries home for you in my wagon for only five cents a trip?"

I never lost sight of my goal. I stayed focused on four trips and twenty cents. I also had a time frame on my goal. I had to earn my twenty cents no later than 11:30 AM so I could get to the RKO Theatre before noon. Nothing stopped me from asking every lady coming past the cash register. I never thought about all the "what ifs."—I was too busy thinking about my four trips. I never stopped to think what if they say no, what if they don't like me, what if they don't like my wagon, what if they think I'm being pushy, what if I make them mad? I didn't worry about rejection because I didn't know about rejection at seven years old. I knew that I had a goal, a game plan, and a burning desire to spend the rest of my Saturday at the RKO Theatre enjoying my movies and snacks. Yes, I could taste those JuJu Bees

Now, many years later, I keep a small red flyer wagon in my office as a visual reminder of this time in my life when nothing stopped me because I was able to stay focused on my goal, my game plan, and my burning desire to succeed.

Not succeeding was never an option for me at seven years old and it isn't an option for me today. Quitting was never a part of my game plan then and isn't a part of my game plan today.

Wright

How did you begin your professional sales and sales management career?

Knapp

I have Avon Products to thank for the start of my professional sales management career. I was hired as a district manager in Cleveland, Ohio, responsible for a field sales team of about one hundred and seventy-five Avon representatives.

I was soon promoted to become a division manager responsible for a team of thirty-five hundred Avon representatives throughout the Ohio River Valley. During that time, Avon continued to provide me with exceptional management and leadership training that would further develop my professional skills and help me be the best I could be. I never lost sight of always having my goal, my plan, and my burning desire to succeed.

Years later, I remain forever grateful to this wonderful corporation for the many future opportunities it provided. It allowed me to accomplish my most exciting career goal in Melbourne, Australia.

Wright

What has been your greatest achievement in your career?

Knapp

I was hired by Stanley Home Products and sent to Melbourne, Australia, to build a door-to-door field selling organization. I made a commitment to the board of directors that I would recruit, train, and develop a sales team of a thousand sales people who would go door-to-door, selling home cleaning products in Melbourne. My time frame for this goal was eighteen months. I moved to Melbourne full of determination, fears, and uncertainty but I stayed focused on my goal, my game plan, and my burning desire to succeed.

I didn't know anyone in Melbourne so I started from the ground up. This meant that I recruited almost everyone I met. I recruited my next-door neighbor, the local grocer, and anybody and everybody who would talk to me. Recruiting really took off. It was working. The news media was fascinated by this "female Yank" who was building a field sales team throughout the city. We received lots of free media attention and the sales team grew rapidly.

Within the eighteen-month time frame, we recruited, trained, and retained over one thousand sales people and developed a company there called Happy Home Proprietary Limited. The Australian people made every day a sheer delight for me. They treated me with tremendous respect and welcomed my children and me into their homes and into their hearts. How could I have ever asked for more? It was actually a sad day when I left Australia and I do hope to return someday. Most definitely, I remain thankful to Avon products and Stanley Home products for giving me the opportunity to achieve goals and create memories that I will hold in my heart forever.

Wright

When the going gets tough what keeps you going?

Knapp

Well, of course I have to do my daily check-ups from the neck up. My favorite motivational speaker, Zig Ziglar, introduced me to the importance of that message many years ago. In other words, I have to remind myself every day that my attitude is my choice. No one is responsible for my attitude but me.

I look for the humor in every day because I love to laugh—especially at myself. I remind myself to lighten up and enjoy the day to the fullest. A healthy fun-loving sense of humor is critical during difficult times. I am personally very fortunate and am richly blessed with an incredible supportive, loving family. Of course, my grandchildren continue to remind me what is most important in life. They are all a part of what I call my "attitude of gratitude." This is my morning ritual. It helps keep me grounded and helps keep everything in perspective. I take ten minutes and start my day with my wonderful mug of coffee. I sit in peace and focus on everything I have to be grateful for. I feed my mind with positive messages from one of my many self-help books and pray for the strength to do and say the right things to everyone I meet that day.

I fine-tune my selling skills by analyzing my results and revising my game plan. I reflect on my networking results. Is my net working for me? I take a good critical look at where I am spending my time because my time is my most valuable resource. I ask myself some good basic questions, such as:

- How much actual face-to-face time am I spending with prospects?
- Am I associating with positive, successful, upbeat people?
- Am I reaching outside the box and searching for new opportunities?
- Am I assuming total responsibility for my sales results?
- Am I whining or am I celebrating?
- How will I redesign my sales process?

- How much income-producing time am I actually spending with qualified prospects?
- Am I focused on my strengths and my sales successes?
- Am I working on the numbers game of contacting people?
- Am I focused on recapturing any lost customer opportunities?
- Am I rewarding myself for positive results and having fun?
- When did I last tell myself "doggone, you're great?"

I reward myself for exceptional efforts. It keeps me motivated, excited, and upbeat about what I am doing. I always want to make sure I am sharing the successes of everyone around me. Good news brings results that are more positive. I maintain high expectations and substantial goals for myself. I make sure that I review customer challenges or objections so that I feel confident and competent when I am in front of my customer. When I get objections, I know I'm ready to handle them.

Finally, I remain conscious of the need to stay energized. The best way to re-energize myself is to gain more successes. I ask for referrals and gain them. I look for fun, laugh a lot, and maintain my healthy sense of humor. It all seems to work for me.

Wright

In your years of teaching and coaching people how to sell, what are the most critical traits that salespeople should have?

Knapp

I have seven critical traits I practice on a consistent basis. They might be somewhat different than the norm. Of course, there are more, but I find all of these seven traits critical to success.

1. *Understanding:* To make sure that I understand the needs of my customer and to also make sure that my customers understand that I know what their needs are. We can then communicate that understanding together. Too often, we don't take the extra time to make sure we are all on the same wavelength and understand how we can benefit each other. Sometimes, it's just a matter of asking a few extra open-ended questions to gain some

additional information. It also sends the message to the customer that "we care" about clarifying their needs.

2. *Anticipation:* For me, I want to be ready. I don't want to be surprised or blind-sided with things that I didn't anticipate. It just says to me that I am anticipating the needs of my prospects and my customers and that I am ready for anything they might throw my way.

3. *Expectations:* The expectations that I have for myself, the expectations that I have for my customers, for the goals, for the successes, and their expectations of me—to make sure that I am meeting all of those expectations at all times.

4. *Confidence:* Actually, if I am doing the above three, then my confidence level will be soaring. My self-confidence will be obvious to my prospects and customers. I believe people can read our self-confidence level just by the way we walk into the room. I know I want to buy from confident people, how about you, David?

5. *Patience:* Having the patience to know that not everybody buys the same way. Some people need more time, need to think more, need to ask more questions, and need to ask more people. I need to be patient enough to know that I am going to follow up one more time. I am going to be there to answer questions and I am going to have the tone and patience in my voice that says to customers that I really do care about them and their needs.

6. *Humility:* A lot of times, when I am coaching or working with younger sales people, they don't get it. They will say to me, "What do you mean by 'humility'?" To me, humility is just the practice of making the other person feel important. It is always critical to me that my customer or prospect feels so much more important than I feel. I think that people can pick that up in your voice, in your tone, in your willingness to help them, and they like to associate with and buy from people who have some humility.

7. *Belief:* Believing in myself, my product, my service, and believing that my product and service is going to be the best that there is out there for that customer.

I think that the attitude and the emotions that come from these fundamentals are very contagious. Of course, that just helps motivate my customers to buy.

Wright

Many people leave sales because they cannot handle rejection. How can you teach people to handle rejection and never give up?

Knapp

After spending a lot of time and effort to gain an appointment with the customer, I want to make sure I am not letting the fear of rejection keep me from moving forward and making the sale.

Rejection can be a major fear that stops people from ever asking for the order and closing the sale. Some people fear hearing "no," so they never ask. Since I already have a good deal of time invested in meeting with my customer, I want to make sure that I'm totally on top of my game and ready to ask for the order. Unfortunately, fear of rejection can stop us from achieving that goal. The more confident *I feel* in overcoming any fear of rejection, the more successful I will be in closing the sale. Sales and rejection go hand-in-hand. I know it is all part of the process. Many years ago, I learned that selling is not for sissies. Well, that sure was a true statement.

I need to remind myself that if I experience customer rejection, the customer isn't necessarily rejecting me. The customer is rejecting my message. My goal is to find out why my message is being rejected. I cannot afford to take it personally. I have to assess whether my product meets my customers' needs and how effective I was in helping prospects see the value of my product. I need to consistently fine-tune my skills and make sure I close all my sales. I remind myself of the following message: "SW SW SW SW Next." This stands for "Some will. Some won't. So what? Someone's waiting. Next!"

Wright

Are there any specific sales tools you have used that have helped you with your sales success?

Knapp

The most effective sales tool I have ever used is a behavioral profile called DiSC. Many people have utilized the DiSC behavioral tool over the years. The most recent update called Everything DiSC Sales Profile has been an incredible tool for my customers. This twenty-plus-page profile clearly describes everything I need to know to effectively communicate with my customers. We have been using the DiSC tools in our business for the past twenty years and our customers value these tools. In fact, customers continue to express their delight for DiSC and claim this is the most effective sales tool they have used for their sales team.

The Sales Profile helps me in three different ways: 1) it allows me to better understand myself and the way I tend to communicate, 2) it allows me to identify the communication styles of other people, and 3) it tells me how I should be flexible with my communication style in order to meet the sales needs of my customers. When you think about that, it's just like an open book on how to sell to every customer just the way he or she would like to buy. Yes, this tool has definitely helped me both professionally and personally.

Wright

What do you mean when you say that "closing begins with hello"?

Knapp

That expression started when customers would say to me, "Lee, we want you to come in and help us with our sales skills. All we really need is closing techniques. We know how to do the rest." So that's when I came up with "closing really does begin with hello." If I don't start off on the right foot, I may never have a chance to get to the closing. I may be turning people off before I have a chance to turn them on.

If closing begins with hello, how about the importance of making a positive first impression? Within the first nine seconds we meet someone, first impressions are being created. People are starting to form opinions on whether they would like to do business with us.

POINTS TO FOCUS ON:
- Maintain a comfortable confident look on my face
- Make eye contact and smile.
- Offer a professional handshake.
- Clearly exchange names.
- Maintain a friendly confident tone of voice.
- Feel great about my appearance.
- Feel great about the appearance of my marketing materials.

- Be enthusiastic and show high energy.
- Search for common ground.
- Ask meaningful questions.
- Listen like I care.
- Build trust.
- Determine mutual follow-up.
- Show appreciation for their time.

Wright

How can beginning salespeople jump-start their success?

Knapp

That question sounds like another book opportunity. Smart new salespeople are continually evaluating everything they do on a day-to-day basis. They are looking to learn and grow from their successes as well as their failures.

Most importantly, what goes on between our ears is directly related to our sales results. Having a positive attitude is critical to the overall success of every salesperson. Successful salespeople realize the need to consistently believe in their potential opportunities. They cannot afford to allow negative self-talk get in their way. Staying focused on "I can" instead of "I can't" needs to be a constant mindset.

When we surround ourselves with smart, supportive people who help feed our dreams and goals, great things happen. Spend time with people who encourage our growth and success—people who will listen, offer reinforcing feedback, laugh with us, and be there when we need them the most. Search out those special friends. Remember, if you want to have a friend, you must be a friend, first.

If I am going to feel good about myself and my presentation, I need to feel good about my overall appearance. My appearance sends a message of confidence, professionalism, attention to detail, and caring for people to prospects and customers. People like to buy from successful people who look well put together. Look in the mirror—is this you?

Maybe it's time to take an honest look at your closet. Is it time to "dump the frump"? If you have clothes hanging in your closet that you haven't worn for years, donate them to someone who can use them. If you haven't worn them, there must be a reason. Don't wear anything that doesn't make you feel like a success. Clothes make a difference in people's perception of you and your business.

Smart salespeople build long-term relationships with customers, which means, don't burn any bridges. Your reputation should always be priceless. Long-term relationships generate repeat business, customer referrals, and satisfied customers.

In building those relationships, focus on building customer trust. I remind myself of the three ways to build customer trust: 1) show the customer that I *want* to help, 2) show the customer that I *can* help, 3) show the customer that I *will* help. When I accomplish these three points, I generate customer trust and build relationships.

Jump-starting my success also says that I have to learn the difference between selling value versus price. Leading salespeople sell the value of their product. Marginal salespeople sell price, discounts, concessions, and slim margins. I look for the added value of every product and the added value that I bring to the product. I use the expression or the term "added value." I use it my proposals. I use it in my conversations. If I am adding something for someone I will say, "That represents added value to you because you are a special customer to me." Companies set prices but customers establish value.

The best salespeople are the best listeners. If you are listening to your customers, you are learning as well as helping the customer feel important. If I hear myself talking, I need to mentally tell myself to stop. I am supposed to be listening instead of talking. The other part of this is that I need to be asking good, meaningful questions. If I ask good questions, then I will be listening because the customer is going to be providing me with good information.

As I look to develop those meaningful questions, I ask myself, what do I need to learn from this customer that will help me present my product and make the sale? After listing what I want to know, I simply wrap a good open-ended question around my point. It's really effective and easy.

Wright

What a great conversation. I really appreciate the time you have given me here today to answer all these questions. I have learned a lot about selling and I have you to thank for that.

Today we have been talking to Lee Knapp. She is president of Knapp Consultants. Lee is a motivational speaker and sales training specialist. She has successfully trained a national and international sales team of over twenty thousand people. She also recruited, trained, and developed a one-thousand-person sales team in Melbourne, Australia.

Lee, thank you so much for being with us today on *Discovering Your Inner Strength*.

Knapp

Thank you, David, very much. It has been my pleasure.

About the Author

Lee Knapp, President and founder of Knapp Consultants, is a business development consultant, motivational speaker and training specialist. For over three decades, Lee has been using her successfully proven techniques as a basis for helping individuals and companies achieve personal and professional success.

One of the first female executives to benefit two Fortune 500 companies, Lee is known as an unstoppable trailblazer. As a corporate executive vice president, she was responsible for sales development and training of a 21,000 person national/international sales organization.

Lee was recruited to build a sales force in Melbourne, Austraila. During her 17 month tenure, she was responsible for successfully recruiting, training and developing over 1,000 salespeople.

Lee designs and presents motivational programs based on the specific needs of her clients, including an upbeat, fun-loving approach that consistently drives her message home. Her goal is to bring out the best in people and help then exceed their greatest expectations.

Lee Knapp
Knapp Consultants, Inc.
5260 Harborage Drive
Fort Myers, FL 33908
239-481-8557
lknappconsulting@aol.com
www.LeeKnapp.com

Chapter Seven
A Values-Based Approach

An Interview With…

Dr. Stephen Covey

David Wright (Wright)

We're talking today with Dr. Stephen R. Covey, cofounder and vice-chairman of Franklin Covey Company, the largest management company and leadership development organization in the world. Dr. Covey is perhaps best known as author of *The 7 Habits of Highly Effective People,* which is ranked as a number one best-seller by the *New York Times*, having sold more than fourteen million copies in thirty-eight languages throughout the world. Dr. Covey is an internationally respected leadership authority, family expert, teacher, and organizational consultant. He has made teaching principle-centered living and principle-centered leadership his life's work. Dr. Covey is the recipient of the Thomas More College Medallion for Continuing Service to Humanity and has been awarded four honorary doctorate degrees. Other awards given Dr. Covey include the Sikh's 1989 International Man of Peace award, the 1994 International Entrepreneur of the Year award, *Inc.* magazine's Services Entrepreneur of the Year award, and in 1996 the National Entrepreneur of the Year Lifetime Achievement award for Entrepreneurial leadership. He has also been recognized as one of *Time* magazine's twenty-five most influential Americans and one of *Sales and Marketing Management's* top twenty-five power brokers. As the father of nine and grandfather of forty-four, Dr. Covey received the 2003 National Fatherhood Award, which he says is the most meaningful award he has ever received. Dr. Covey earned his undergraduate degree from the University of Utah, his MBA from Harvard, and completed his doctorate at Brigham Young University. While at Brigham Young he served as assistant to the President and was also a professor of Business Management and Organizational Behavior.

Dr. Covey, welcome to *Discover Your Inner Strength*.

Dr. Stephen Covey (Covey)

Thank you.

Wright

Dr. Covey, most companies make decisions and filter them down through their organization. You, however, state that no company can succeed until individuals within it succeed. Are the goals of the company the result of the combined goals of the individuals?

Covey

Absolutely—if people aren't on the same page, they're going to be pulling in different directions. To teach this concept, I frequently ask large audiences to close their eyes and point north, and then to keep pointing and open their eyes. They find themselves pointing all over the place. I say to them, "Tomorrow morning if you want a similar experience, ask the first ten people you meet in your organization what the purpose of your organization is and you'll find it's a very similar experience. They'll point all over the place." When people have a different sense of purpose and values, every decision that is made from then on is governed by those. There's no question that this is one of the fundamental causes of misalignment, low trust, interpersonal conflict, interdepartmental rivalry, people operating on personal agendas, and so forth.

Wright

Is that primarily a result of an inability to communicate from the top?

Covey

That's one aspect, but I think it's more fundamental. There's an inability to involve people—an unwillingness. Leaders may communicate what their mission and their strategy is, but that doesn't mean there's any emotional connection to it. Mission statements that are rushed and then announced are soon forgotten. They become nothing more than just a bunch of platitudes on the wall that mean essentially nothing and even create a source of cynicism and a sense of hypocrisy inside the culture of an organization.

Wright

How do companies ensure survival and prosperity in these tumultuous times of technological advances, mergers, downsizing, and change?

Covey

I think that it takes a lot of high trust in a culture that has something that doesn't change—principles—at its core. There are principles that people agree upon that are valued. It gives a sense of stability. Then you have the power to adapt and be flexible when you experience these kinds of disruptive new economic models or technologies that come in and sideswipe you. You don't know how to handle them unless you have something you can depend upon.

If people have not agreed to a common set of principles that guide them and a common purpose, then they get their security from the outside and they tend to freeze the structure, systems, and processes inside and they cease becoming adaptable. They don't change with the changing realities of the new marketplace out there and gradually they become obsolete.

Wright

I was interested in one portion of your book, *The 7 Habits of Highly Effective People,* where you talk about behaviors. How does an individual go about the process of replacing ineffective behaviors with effective ones?

Covey

I think that for most people it usually requires a crisis that humbles them to become aware of their ineffective behaviors. If there's not a crisis the tendency is to perpetuate those behaviors and not change.

You don't have to wait until the marketplace creates the crisis for you. Have everyone accountable on a 360-degree basis to everyone else they interact with—with feedback either formal or informal—where they are getting data as to what's happening. They will then start to realize that the consequences of their ineffective behavior require them to be humble enough to look at that behavior and to adopt new, more effective ways of doing things.

Sometimes people can be stirred up to this if you just appeal to their conscience—to their inward sense of what is right and wrong. A lot of people sometimes know inwardly they're doing wrong, but the culture doesn't necessarily discourage them from continuing that. They either need feedback from people or they need feedback from the marketplace or they need feedback from their conscience. Then they can begin to develop a step-by-step process of replacing old habits with new, better habits.

Wright

It's almost like saying, "Let's make all the mistakes in the laboratory before we put this thing in the air."

Covey

Right; and I also think what is necessary is a paradigm shift, which is analogous to having a correct map, say of a city or of a country. If people have an inaccurate paradigm of life, of other people, and of themselves it really doesn't make much difference what their behavior or habits or attitudes are. What they need is a correct paradigm—a correct map—that describes what's going on.

For instance, in the Middle Ages they used to heal people through bloodletting. It wasn't until Samuel Weiss and Pasteur and other empirical scientists discovered the germ theory that they realized for the first time they weren't dealing with the real issue. They realized why women preferred to use midwives who washed rather than doctors who didn't wash. They gradually got a new paradigm. Once you've got a new paradigm then your behavior and your attitude flow directly from it. If you have a bad paradigm or a bad map, let's say of a city, there's no way, no matter what your behavior or your habits or your attitudes are—how positive they are—you'll never be able to find the location you're looking for. This is why I believe that to change paradigms is far more fundamental than to work on attitude and behavior.

Wright

One of your seven habits of highly effective people is to "begin with the end in mind." If circumstances change and hardships or miscalculations occur, how does one view the end with clarity?

Covey

Many people think to begin with the end in mind means that you have some fixed definition of a goal that's accomplished and if changes come about you're not going to adapt to them. Instead, the "end in mind" you begin with is that you are going to create a flexible culture of high trust so that no matter what comes along you are going to do whatever it takes to accommodate that new change or that new reality and maintain a culture of high performance and high trust. You're talking more in terms of values and overall purposes that don't change, rather than specific strategies or programs that will have to change to accommodate the changing realities in the marketplace.

Wright

In this time of mistrust among people, corporations, and nations, for that matter, how do we create high levels of trust?

Covey

That's a great question and it's complicated because there are so many elements that go into the creating of a culture of trust. Obviously the most fundamental one is just to have trustworthy people. But that is not sufficient because what if the organization itself is misaligned?

For instance, what if you say you value cooperation but you really reward people for internal competition? Then you have a systemic or a structure problem that creates low trust inside the culture even though the people themselves are trustworthy. This is one of the insights of Edward Demming and the work he did. That's why he said that most problems are not personal—they're systemic. They're common caused. That's why you have to work on structure, systems, and processes to make sure that they institutionalize principle-centered values. Otherwise you could have good people with bad systems and you'll get bad results.

When it comes to developing interpersonal trust between people, it is made up of many, many elements such as taking the time to listen to other people, to understand them, and to see what is important to them. What we think is important to another may only be important to us, not to another. It takes empathy. You have to make and keep promises to them. You have to treat people with kindness and courtesy. You have to be completely honest and open. You have to live up to your commitments. You can't betray people behind their back. You can't badmouth them behind their back and sweet-talk them to their face. That will send out vibes of hypocrisy and it will be detected.

You have to learn to apologize when you make mistakes, to admit mistakes, and to also get feedback going in every direction as much as possible. It doesn't necessarily require formal forums—it requires trust between people who will be open with each other and give each other feedback.

Wright

My mother told me to do a lot of what you're saying now, but it seems that when I got in business I simply forgot.

Covey

Sometimes we forget, but sometimes culture doesn't nurture it. That's why I say unless you work with the institutionalizing—that means formalizing into structure, systems, and processing the values—you will not have a nurturing culture. You have to constantly work on that.

This is one of the big mistakes organizations make. They think trust is simply a function of being honest. That's only one small aspect. It's an important aspect, obviously, but there are so many other elements that go into the creation of a high-trust culture.

Wright

"Seek first to understand then to be understood" is another of your seven habits. Do you find that people try to communicate without really understanding what other people want?

Covey

Absolutely. The tendency is to project out of our own autobiography—our own life, our own value system—onto other people, thinking we know what they want. So we don't really listen to them. We pretend to listen, but we really don't listen from within their frame of reference. We listen from within our own frame of reference and we're really preparing our reply rather than seeking to understand. This is a very common thing. In fact, very few people have had any training in seriously listening. They're trained in how to read, write, and speak, but not to listen.

Reading, writing, speaking, and listening are the four modes of communication and they represent about two-thirds to three-fourths of our waking hours. About half of that time is spent listening, but it's the one skill people have not been trained in. People have had all this training in the other forms of communication. In a large audience of 1,000 people you wouldn't have more than twenty people who have had more than two weeks of training in listening. Listening is more than a skill or technique; you must listen within another's frame of reference. It takes tremendous courage to listen because you're at risk when you listen. You don't know what's going to happen; you're vulnerable.

Wright

Sales gurus always tell me that the number one skill in selling is listening.

Covey

Yes—listening from within the customer's frame of reference. That is so true. You can see that it takes some security to do that because you don't know what's going to happen.

Wright

With this book we're trying to encourage people to be better, to live better, and be more fulfilled by listening to the examples of our guest authors. Is there anything or anyone in your life that has made a difference for you and helped you to become a better person?

Covey

I think the most influential people in my life have been my parents. I think that what they modeled was not to make comparisons and harbor jealousy or to seek recognition. They were humble people.

I remember one time when my mother and I were going up in an elevator and the most prominent person in the state was also in the elevator. She knew him, but she spent her time talking to the elevator operator. I was just a little kid and I was so awed by the famous person. I said to her, "Why didn't you talk to the important person?" She said, "I was. I had never met him."

My parents were really humble, modest people who were focused on service and other people rather than on themselves. I think they were very inspiring models to me.

Wright

In almost every research paper I've ever read, those who write about people who have influenced their lives include three teachers in their top-five picks. My seventh-grade English teacher was the greatest teacher I ever had and she influenced me to no end.

Covey

Would it be correct to say that she saw in you probably some qualities of greatness you didn't even see in yourself?

Wright

Absolutely.

Covey

That's been my general experience—the key aspect of a mentor or a teacher is someone who sees in you potential that you don't even see in yourself. Those teachers/mentors treat you accordingly and eventually you come to see it in yourself. That's my definition of leadership or influence—communicating people's worth and potential so clearly that they are inspired to see it in themselves.

Wright

Most of my teachers treated me as a student, but she treated me with much more respect than that. As a matter of fact, she called me Mr. Wright, and I was in the seventh grade at the time. I'd never been addressed by anything but a nickname. I stood a little taller; she just made a tremendous difference.

Do you think there are other characteristics that mentors seem to have in common?

Covey

I think they are first of all good examples in their own personal lives. Their personal lives and their family lives are not all messed up—they come from a base of good character. They also are usually very confident and they take the time to do what your teacher did to you—to treat you with uncommon respect and courtesy.

They also, I think, explicitly teach principles rather than practices so that rules don't take the place of human judgment. You gradually come to have faith in your own judgment in making decisions because of the affirmation of such a mentor. Good mentors care about you—you can feel the sincerity of their caring. It's like the expression, "I don't care how much you know until I know how much you care."

Wright

Most people are fascinated with the new television shows about being a survivor. What has been the greatest comeback that you've made from adversity in your career or your life?

Covey

When I was in grade school I experienced a disease in my legs. It caused me to use crutches for a while. I tried to get off them fast and get back. The disease wasn't corrected yet so I went back on crutches for another year. The disease went to the other leg and I went on for another year. It essentially took me out of my favorite thing—athletics—and it took me more into being a student. So that was a life-defining experience, which at the time seemed very negative, but has proven to be the basis on which I've focused my life—being more of a learner.

Wright

Principle-centered learning is basically what you do that's different from anybody I've read or listened to.

Covey

The concept is embodied in the Far Eastern expression, "Give a man a fish, you feed him for the day; teach him how to fish, you feed him for a lifetime." When you teach principles that are universal and timeless, they don't belong to just any one person's religion or to a particular culture or geography. They seem to be timeless and universal like the ones we've been talking about here: trustworthiness, honesty, caring, service, growth, and development. These are universal principles. If you focus on these things, then little by little people become independent of you and then they start to believe in themselves and their own judgment becomes better. You don't need as many rules. You don't need as much bureaucracy and as many controls and you can empower people.

The problem in most business operations today—and not just business but non-business—is that they're using the industrial model in an information age. Arnold Toynbee, the great historian, said, "You can pretty well summarize all of history in four words: nothing fails like success." The industrial model was based on the asset of the machine. The information model is based on the asset of the person—the knowledge worker. It's an altogether different model. But the machine model was the main asset of the twentieth century. It enabled productivity to increase fifty times. The new asset is intellectual and social capital—the qualities of people and the quality of the relationship they have with each other. Like Toynbee said, "Nothing fails like success." The industrial model does not work in an information age. It requires a focus on the new wealth, not capital and material things.

A good illustration that demonstrates how much we were into the industrial model, and still are, is to notice where people are on the balance sheet. They're not found there. Machines are found there. Machines become investments. People are on the profit-and-loss statement and people are expenses. Think of that—if that isn't bloodletting.

Wright

It sure is.

When you consider the choices you've made down through the years, has faith played an important role in your life?

Covey

It has played an extremely important role. I believe deeply that we should put principles at the center of our lives, but I believe that God is the source of those principles. I did not invent them. I get credit sometimes for some of the Seven Habits material and some of the other things I've done, but it's really all based on principles that have been given by God to all of His children from the beginning of time. You'll find that you can teach these same principles from the sacred texts and the wisdom literature of almost any tradition. I think the ultimate source of that is God and that is one thing you can absolutely depend upon—"in God we trust."

Wright

If you could have a platform and tell our audience something you feel would help them or encourage them, what would you say?

Covey

I think I would say to put God at the center of your life and then prioritize your family. No one on their deathbed ever wished they had spent more time at the office.

Wright

That's right. We have come down to the end of our program and I know you're a busy person. I could talk with you all day, Dr. Covey.

Covey

It's good to talk with you as well and to be a part of this program. It looks like an excellent one that you've got going on here.

Wright

Thank you.

We have been talking today with Dr. Stephen R. Covey, cofounder and vice-chairman of Franklin Covey Company. He's also the author of *The 7 Habits of Highly Effective People,* which has been ranked as a number one bestseller by the *New York Times*, selling more than fourteen million copies in thirty-eight languages.

Dr. Covey, thank you so much for being with us today.

Covey

Thank you for the honor of participating.

About the Author

Stephen R. Covey was recognized in 1996 as one of *Time* magazine's twenty-five most influential Americans and one of *Sales and Marketing Management's* top twenty-five power brokers. Dr. Covey is the author of several acclaimed books, including the international bestseller, *The 7 Habits of Highly Effective People*, named the number one Most Influential Business Book of the Twentieth Century, and other best sellers that include *First Things First, Principle-Centered Leadership*, (with sales exceeding one million) and *The 7 Habits of Highly Effective Families*.

Dr. Covey earned his undergraduate degree from the University of Utah, his MBA from Harvard, and completed his doctorate at Brigham Young University. While at Brigham Young University, he served as assistant to the President and was also a professor of Business Management and Organizational Behavior. He received the National Fatherhood Award in 2003, which, as the father of nine and grandfather of forty-four, he says is the most meaningful award he has ever received.

Dr. Covey currently serves on the board of directors for the Points of Light Foundation. Based in Washington, D.C., the Foundation, through its partnership with the Volunteer Center National Network, engages and mobilizes millions of volunteers from all walks of life—businesses, nonprofits, faith-based organizations, low-income communities, families, youth, and older adults—to help solve serious social problems in thousands of communities.

Dr. Stephen R. Covey

www.stephencovey.com

Chapter Eight

The SENSE of Humor

An Interview With…

Juli Burney

David Wright (Wright)

Today we are talking with Juli Burney. Juli Burney, MA, is a multiple-award-winning teacher, communication specialist, humorist, and author. She is able to train or motivate her audiences as she entertains with the ability of a headlining comedian. Juli has received several honors because of her ability to help improve people's lives through humor and the effective use of communication tools. She has presented in every state in the continental United States as well as in Canada. She has been commissioned by a variety of associations from the National Endowment for the Arts to Fortune 500 companies to develop training programs that stick. Juli brings thirty years of experience and humor to each of her programs. She is the author of *Shifting Gears: A Communication Ownership Manual.*

Juli, welcome to *Discover Your Inner Strength.*

Juli Burney (Burney)

Thank you very much for having me!

Wright

You call yourself a motivational humorist. What exactly does that mean?

Burney

I'm glad you asked that question. Usually after I am done explaining to people what I do, they say, "Oh, you're a comedian." And yes, I am; however, there is always a message within the stories I tell.

I actually started my career doing stand-up comedy and making people laugh. That is a wonderful thing, yet I wanted to do something more. I wanted people not just to escape their lives for an evening with laughter, I also wanted to help people realize they could improve and change their lives by taking the humor home with them as well.

At the time I was entertaining, I was also a college assistant professor teaching all areas of communication, so I merged those two careers into one thus the self-given title of motivational humorist. I believe that what I'm doing leaves a smile on people's faces, though I also hope that it motivates them to continue that smile throughout their lives.

Wright

So through your presentations you attempt to teach lessons with humor.

Burney

Absolutely! I hope to help people realize that there are many benefits to having a humorous perspective. It helps us to detach from things we are emotional about or are having trouble getting a handle on. It helps us to see a more positive perspective of situations that might otherwise seem unbearable.

For example, I know you can't tell just from talking with me, but throughout my entire life a lot of people have thought I struggled with a weight problem. In changing my thought process with humor, I see myself differently. I have weight, it goes with me, and it's no problem. Yes, it's true that I'm above average in that department but, isn't above average something we all strive to be in one area or another?

And let's apply that changing perspective to you. Have you ever noticed that every time you're running late you are slowed down by stoplights? Because you're a mature adult, how do you respond to that situation? You yell at the stoplights, right? Yes, you yell at stoplights that are on a timer—like that will make it change! I find that humorous. We yell at the light as if there is a man sitting there watching us, giggling, saying, "It looks like they're late" and then switches the light to red just to mess with us. The truth is that we run into stoplights even when we are not in a hurry; however, when we are calm and relaxed we don't assign them any value in our lives. Our perspective changes because we have changed how we have decided what is important to us—what we value. That's where humor comes in; it can help us keep things in perspective.

Wright

You've been talking to my wife, right?

Burney

About life?

Wright

No, no—to my wife about my problem.

Burney

Oh! Talking to your wife about *your* problem. No, I haven't, but thank you for making my point for me. As you see, what I'm talking about is pretty universal. I have found that stoplight story applies to almost everyone who drives. We all react to situations depending on how we are feeling at the time.

Wright

You seem equally as passionate about communication. How is it that you've merged the two areas of expertise together?

Burney

My structured education has been in interpersonal communication and theater. When I was in college, I had a wonderful communication professor who helped me realize that many of the communication challenges we have are really technically difficulties that we can control by taking ownership of our communication.

Communication, as with humor, is about timing and delivery. Choosing the correct words, deciding what tone they should be delivered with, and when they should be delivered makes all the difference in the world on how the message is received. Also, listening and paying attention are key factors in the success of messages in both areas of communication and humor. It is important to know your audience. Making the choice to communicate responsibly, choosing language so that it is positive, and recognizing that when I deliver the information is as important as the information itself, has improved my life immensely. Being in better humor has a domino effect. The happier I feel, the better I interpret the world around me, and the clearer I communicate.

Wright

You know, many people believe that humor is all about making jokes. How is that helpful to discovering inner strengths?

Burney

Actually, jokes are just a symptom of humor. You have to experience situations in your life with a humorous perspective. Then, after you do, you turn that experience into a humorous story or joke.

If you think about your favorite comedians, the reason they make you laugh is because they have surprised you with their response to a certain situation. They found a totally new way to look at something you've looked at every day with just one perspective. It makes you laugh because you can relate to what they are describing, yet they show you a new way to look at it.

Humor has often helped me to gain perspective on a situation that enabled me to turn it into a positive experience. A few years ago, I spoke in Columbia, Missouri, which is the home of a big rival in football to the University of Nebraska here in Lincoln where I live. When I was introduced as being from Nebraska, I was booed on my way up to the stage, which is not the best way for a humorist to start. I asked them, "Are you booing me because I'm a Cornhusker?" (Cornhusker is the team name of course.)

They responded, "Yeah!"

"Well, you know," I said, "I never actually played for the team. But thanks for looking at me and thinking that I might have."

There was immediate laughter because you can tell by looking at me that I obviously never played for the team. I'm a five-foot, six-inch "well rounded" woman in my fifties. By finding the humor in the situation, I was able to diffuse a possible adversarial situation and bond with my audience.

Humor helps us to build rapport, cope with stress, diffuse uncomfortable situations, and establish relationships. There is strength in all of those abilities.

Wright

So, do you think humor is appropriate in serious situations?

Burney

I think our lives should be taken very seriously. However, taking them seriously does not mean they should be taken somberly. Of course, it's inappropriate to find humor in a tragedy or crisis, yet it's through that humor that healing can begin.

Recently my mother had a serious fall down some steps where she suffered a traumatic brain injury. In telling people what had happened and asking them to pray for her recovery, I said, "Could you please pray for her brain? As some of you know, it's not the first time we have prayed for a brain in this family." And of course, what I'd said brought laughter to people. We were able to face the healing process much stronger. She's doing great now and we just celebrated her eightieth birthday. She likes to point out that eighty is the new sixty, which of course makes me thirty. I like this positive way of thinking, however, my young nieces aren't very happy with the new classification because they would be embryos—another situation to find humor in!

Wright

So how does one discover one's own humor potential?

Burney

Here is what's interesting. Everyone was born with a sense of humor; the trick is to allow it to surface when needed. Do you remember when you were a child and you would get the giggles— uncontrollable giggles that would often come at the most inappropriate times like in church? Then the more upset the adults became with you, the funnier the situation got. Everyone has that humor inside of them; we hesitate to bring it with us into adulthood because so often we were discouraged by the adults in our lives. We needed to "grow up" and be more serious. But, you know, we don't need to suppress that humor. We just need to learn where it's appropriate.

As adults, we need to observe what it is that makes us smile in life, whether it's a cartoon or comic or a person. I often start smiling when I'm all by myself and I trip. No one is there to enjoy my human klutziness but me, yet I still enjoy it. Really, have you ever watched people trip? It's really quite funny. There are those who look around to see who tripped them, those who make a dramatic scene out of tripping, those who look around to see if anyone else saw it, and those who try to gracefully make it look as though it was their intention to trip. Everybody reacts differently to situations and it's truly humorous. People are funny creatures when you take the time to observe them.

Once we take the time to find humor in our own behavior, we find the humor in life as well. Once you start paying attention to what it is about you that makes you smile, then you can start looking for that in other areas of your life. It has to start with looking inward first.

Wright

Chevy Chase has made a great living out of it.

Burney

Out of tripping! Yes! That is such a simple thing and we all do it. Yes, yes! Absolutely!

Wright

So, once we are able to see the humor in our lives, how is that helpful in improving our lives?

Burney

Once we start seeing the joy that surrounds us, our attitude changes and we are able to see more. I knew my attitude toward myself and my life had changed when one day I went out to get my mail. As I was looking through my mail and coming back into the house, I thought, "Juli, how can you ever feel bad about yourself when every day you get a letter saying, 'Juli Burney you're a winner!' " You get those letters too, right? However, I bet you never looked at them with that perspective. I believe that each of us personalize so much of what happens to us when really life moves along and we either move with it or against it.

We are evolving and changing, yet so much of what is happening to us right now has happened to someone else as well. Let's take a look at fashion. What is the youth of America wearing right now? It is the same thing we wore back in the seventies. In fact, I was with my twenty-two-year-old niece a while back and I told her I had the exact same pair of bellbottoms when I was her age.

Indignantly she said, "These are *not* bell bottoms, they are flares!"

"Then they are in the witness protection program," I countered, "because I had the same pair."

You see, we may constantly rename things in our life, however, some of the challenges we face have been faced by others. They not only survived but the challenges caused them to thrive. That's where we need to look to improve our lives. I'll grant you that some things do change. For example, teens today wear flip-flops and in the seventies we called them thongs. Now, that thong strap is someplace else. The trick is adapting to the changes and challenges in our lives with humor, wherever the strap is. Humor sends positive endorphins to our brains and it causes us to see things more joyfully.

Wright

You say that humor is an effective communication tool. Will you explain how that works?

Burney

I think most people believe that humor is only about laughing out loud, but it's so much more than that. It's also about smiling inside. If you're in a bad mood, you tend to interpret everything around you accordingly. Most of the time, I see the world with a positive perspective, yet every once in a while even I have a bad day.

In fact, when I do have a bad day, I usually call it a bad hair day. I had one of those not too long ago. I told my friend I was having a bad hair day and because she's my friend she said, "Your hair looks the same as it did yesterday." Of course, what she said and what I heard were two different things. I thought she was telling me my hair was bad yesterday as well, but what she was really saying was that my hair looked fine. When I removed myself from what I heard and asked her to clarify what she meant, I realized that I had misinterpreted it because of my mood. It was my perspective that contaminated the message, not the actual communication. We laughed about it. Now I share that as a story when I speak.

Wright

What would you recommend for all of our readers, or for anyone who is struggling, to find the humor in their lives?

Burney

I was a crabby person when I was younger and when I first started college. I was fortunate enough to run into a communication professor—the one that I mentioned earlier. He saw that I had the ability to be more positive. He required me to keep a journal of all the positives in my life. I thought this would be easy since there were none. So that's what I wrote—nothing.

The first week that he saw I had written nothing, he told me that the journal was now worth half of my grade for the class. He gave the project value so I had to force myself to look for the positives.

On the very first page of that journal I wrote, "At least I didn't get hit by a truck today." That was the best I could do. However, the next day I noticed that the grass was turning green and that the convenient shop lady had been nice to me. So, now there were two things listed. The next day there were four and each day it continued to grow. The professor taught me to change my view of life and look for the positive. It had a huge affect on me.

That's what I would recommend as a process for anyone and for everyone. Look for the positive each day in your life.

I recently heard from an audience member at one of my speeches describing this. She was suffering from some very challenging setbacks. Her husband had been ill, they were having financial problems, jobs were in jeopardy, and they needed to take care of their children. She said that after hearing me speak, she went home, made supper, and had everyone at the table share the positives in their day. She couldn't believe what a difference that made in all of their lives. They now share those stories every evening at supper. They are excited to point out the great things that are happening in their lives and their approach to their challenges has changed. Their lives are turning around. Rather than focusing on their challenges, they are focusing on their blessings.

The truth is that life throws curve balls at all of us and we have the choice of standing in the way and getting hit or taking a step back so we can hit the ball out of the park. It's our choice.

Wright

Many people think they are funny and that other people are the ones who need help. So what would you tell them?

Burney

Well, I know those people. When trying to decide about appropriate humor, I would tell people that if your humor brings a smile to your face and a scowl from others then it's probably not funny. In order to understand others' humor, you need to listen to them. It goes back to effective communication. If your intentions are good, then your humor should follow that. Humor should help to enlighten a person's situation, not cause it more trouble.

Some people need a bit more time to discover their humor and they should be allowed to have that time. You can help them find their humor by asking questions about what makes them happy or encourage them to tell stories about things they are proud of or even their most embarrassing moment. You find out where the humor lives in their lives and then you share that humor with them. A good comedian or humorist will always be aware of the audience, whether it's in an auditorium or the office or home. It's all about being aware of the other people. Find out what makes others smile.

Wright

So, for all those who will be reading this, where do we start in applying humor to communication?

Burney

You start by detaching yourself from a situation—depersonalizing it. As I said, we have to recognize that life happens to all of us. Nobody is "out to get" us. I'm not out to get you—I'm busy tripping myself up so I don't have time to be out to get you. When we realize that not everything is about "us," we are able to be more effective communicators.

When I first started my career, I worked as a temporary to supplement my income. I was assigned to a mailroom at an insurance company for one week. The fourth day I was there, I was the only one in the mailroom when the phone rang. The man on the other end of the phone was yelling and calling me names. I was able to depersonalize that situation by being detached from it. I didn't have to take on his crabbiness because it wasn't mine to own—it was *his* crabbiness. Trust me, I realize that sometimes I do irritate people, however, not this time—not just from saying, "Hello, mail room" into the phone, which was the extent of my relationship with that gentleman. I knew the problem was his, not mine. I was able to stay calm in that situation. I was able to get the man what he needed, calm him down, and by the end of the conversation we were laughing. Since I didn't take on his crabbiness, I took ownership of what was mine and let him have ownership of what was his. That's how humor can help us with communication—it steers us in a positive direction.

Wright

So, how do we incorporate that into our work and personal lives?

Burney

Humor can be brought into our lives in many subtle ways. We can have little things that make us smile to help us de-stress during the day. We can have a cartoon or a funny picture of a family member at our desk or fun wallpaper on our computer. On my cell phone, I have the ring tone, "Always Look on the Bright Side of Life." Every time my phone rings, it makes me smile. This sends a positive message to my brain, which in turn helps me interpret life positively.

Once we are in a good place, we choose to listen and respond in a constructive manner. When I'm in a truly difficult situation, I try to find a metaphor to help me find perspective.

I travel a lot so I see a lot of crabbiness at airports when flights are delayed or canceled. I think of how that's a metaphor for why people get crabby in life. They are frustrated at having lost control of an aspect of their life. We need to recognize what we can control and what we can't control. Humor helps us do just that. So, instead of focusing on what I can't control, I focus on what I can control. I decide that the flight delay is something I can't control, however, I can control what I do with this gift of unexpected time. I use the time for my enjoyment or to finish work, giving me more free time when I get home. If we can find a metaphor to help us detach from a situation at work or in our personal lives, it can make all the difference in the world.

Last year, I had to go into the hospital for emergency surgery on an infected scratch. I was laying on the gurney dressed in a patterned gown. I had that balloon shower cap bag thing on my head. I was alone waiting to go into surgery so, needless to say, I was nervous. I thought to myself, "Juli, you're always telling people that they can change their thinking; you need to do that now. Find yourself a metaphor." So, as I lay there I decided I looked a bit like a float in a parade. When the nurse came back, I shared my metaphor and asked her if she could wheel me once around the ward so that I could princess wave to everyone before we went to the operating room. She complied and I waved to other patients, nurses, staff, and anyone who was around.

After surgery, when they were rolling me back to my room, the nurses lined up on each side of me, threw candy, and applauded. My parade was complete! It was wonderful! Good humor is contagious—everyone got involved in my metaphor. I laughed so much while I was there that I never needed pain medicine. That's how great laughing and humor is.

You don't have to teach people to be funny; we all have that inside of us. You just have to set up an environment to allow it to happen. Humor is contagious. It's healthy and it helps us to have better lives on so many levels.

Wright

Well, what a great conversation. I feel better all ready!

Burney

I am so glad!

Wright

I really appreciate all this time you've taken with me today to discuss this important topic. I learned a lot. You have given me a lot to think about and I think our readers will be pleased as well.

Burney

Great! That's wonderful!

Wright

Today we have been talking with Juli Burney, MA. She is the author of *Shifting Gears, A Communication Ownership Manual.* She is also a multiple award-winning teacher, communication specialist, and humorist. She has received several honors because of her ability to help people improve their lives through humor and the effective use of communication tools. After listening to her, I think she knows what she's talking about.

Juli, thank you so much for being with us today on *Discover Your Inner Strength.*

Burney

Thank you!

About the Author

Juli Burney, MA, is an adjunct assistant professor at Doane College in Lincoln, Nebraska, where she has been named "Teacher of the Year" five times. She works nationally as a communication specialist, humorist, and trainer. Juli has presented in all forty-eight continental United States and Canada. She has been commissioned by a variety of associations from the National Endowment for the Arts to Fortune 500 companies to develop training programs.

Recognized by her community as an outstanding leader, Juli is able to educate her audiences as she entertains them. She has received several honors, including the Toastmaster International Communication and Leadership Award. Juli brings thirty years of experience to each of her programs. She is the author of *Shifting Gears, A Communication Ownership Manual.*

Juli Burney
P.O. Box 22007
Lincoln, NE 68542
Green Light Speakers Group
877.974.8310
info@greenlightspeakers.com
www.greenlightspeakers.com

Chapter Nine

Little Courage – Big Rewards

An Interview With...

Sharon Jenks, CPBA

David Wright (Wright)

Today we're talking with Sharon Jenks, CPBA, and President of the Jenks Group. Sharon began her career in the banking business earning the title of Senior Vice President in a then male dominated banking industry at the age of twenty-seven. Having broken the glass ceiling herself she began to study the personal success strategy of executives who were able to achieve higher than normal levels of success. She is a professional behaviorist who has worked with thousands of individuals and companies in reaching their personal and professional goals. She does this through helping people discover their behavioral talents in order to increase their effectiveness in communication. Her foundational belief is that job performance is directly linked to how well a person knows himself or herself and how well he or she can adapt to other communication styles. Sharon, a survivor of cancer in 1980, is a sought-after keynote speaker and she has specialized in helping other cancer victims overcome their fear in reaching for the brass ring. Sharon is past chairperson of several non-profit boards. She and her husband have raised four children and now live in Truckee, California, with their four dogs.

Sharon, welcome to *Discover Your Inner Strength.*

Sharon Jenks (Jenks)

Thank you, David.

Wright

So courage has been defined by many to denote overcoming fear, acts of extraordinary feats, or acts of heroism. How do you define courage?

Jenks

I define courage as a person's ability to look straight in the eye all of those imaginary fears and claim a more powerful life than he or she could possibly ever imagine. Having courage does not mean having the absence of fear. That emotion is going to stay with you; but having courage, and more importantly, using it means that what you do or what you must do is more important because it has a bigger payoff than the fear that is holding you back. Courage is unleashed energy that people repress because fear has them stuck in their present reality.

Wright

So you believe that everyone possesses courage, but not everyone chooses to use it. What keeps that from happening?

Jenks

Well, do you remember the cowardly lion in *The Wizard of Oz?*

Wright

Absolutely.

Jenks

Aren't lions supposed to be the king of the jungle and fearless? The cowardly lion changed that belief by showing us that he learned his helplessness; it became a habit and he became a victim. He didn't like it; as a matter of fact, he complained about what wasn't working and he caved into his fears. He even showed his fear by constantly crying.

When you become a victim, you don't have to do anything else. Now you have a reason not to be courageous—being a victim is safe, it gives you an excuse for inaction. Being the victim really does bury the courage, where you don't even have to look at it anymore, because let's face it—you're helpless now. When you cry, people feel sorry for you and it reinforces your inner victim. The cowardly lion ended up seeking courage outside of himself when he joined the journey to Oz. He didn't realize that it lived inside of him, so he went looking for it like a "badge" of courage. Hey, whatever works! We all know he found it along the way, long before he got the badge.

Wright

So what are some of the characteristics of courageous people?

Jenks

They're risk-takers, they accept what it is, they're problem-solvers, they push their limits, and they're determined. They're willing to get rid of the old and embrace the new, to listen to their instincts, and live by their values no matter what fear is telling them.

Wright

Do fear and courage have anything in common?

Jenks

I don't think that one lives without the other. You must be afraid to have courage. Choosing courage over fear and suffering simply means that suffering isn't an option anymore.

I grew up living in fear, without a notion at first that I had any other options. It wasn't that I felt I could do something different but didn't possess the courage, but it has to be like an epiphany of sorts, that there's an option to do something different. As a small child, you aren't equipped knowing that you could take a courageous step to put an end to a life where you're being treated badly. Without something to compare it to, the knowledge that you can do something different is lost. You can live in fear without knowing that courage lies just ahead of you, and when you figure that out, you look back and you think, "Why didn't I push through that fear sooner?" Intellectualizing that your present state isn't serving you doesn't necessarily mean that you're not moving away from that state because you lack courage; but rather, once you realize that there are options to changing it you realize that courage is the antidote to the fear—the fear that has made you feel powerless for a long period of time. You then realize that you have another option that requires an act of courage. Believe me, it doesn't take long to act when you realize that act of courage can set you free.

Wright

Let me see if I get this clearly. If I feel as though I'm a victim, that can become a habit with me?

Jenks

It is a habit—it is a state of mind. You will often hear vigorous complaining from people who are victims. They really feel that there are no other options; they're just held in this strong belief that the world has "done them wrong" or they're a victim of circumstances and that there's no way out. It really is easier, I think, to be a victim. It's not easier for the people around you, but it's a heck of a lot easier because you don't have to do anything.

Wright

So what happens to an individual after a courageous moment?

Jenks

It's extremely liberating, it's a rush, it's an Ah-ha! moment. It can be accompanied by, I think, regret that you didn't do it sooner, but hindsight is 20/20 isn't it? You realize that you've given away your power for a very long time and once you reclaim it, you promise yourself to never do it again. I think that the first successful courageous moment paves the way for the next time. I believe that the next time is much easier and once you realize you lived through it, you're better off for it, and you know that you, alone, own your soul.

Wright

So what was the defining moment for you when you were courageous for the first time?

Jenks

Well, I was just fifteen years old. Unfortunately, I was raised in a very dysfunctional family. I was the product of child abuse. I truly didn't know from the age of four to twelve that this wasn't normal. We were not allowed to stay over at a friend's house, we were not able to go anywhere with friends, we were not allowed to talk on the phone with friends. We went to school and came directly home to do chores, and in my case, as the youngest girl, to do what I was told. In the 1950s and 1960s you didn't share your life with anyone outside of the family. We were taught never to discuss any personal details with anyone.

By the time I was twelve and in junior high school, I started to question my life. I think that there was always a small voice inside of me that questioned the unmentionable. I was raised a strict Catholic girl and we had confession available to us, so when confessing what I thought was wrong resulted in my receiving a bigger penance, that meant that I was wrong, not the situation, so I claimed the blame. That's what I mean when I say you can live in fear without the knowledge that you can create different conditions with courage. It wasn't the loss of courage that I had, but the knowledge, that there was actually another way.

So when I was fifteen I was confronted with a horrible dilemma. I knew that my life as I had been experiencing it had to end. With that decision to show courage in the face of my fear, for the first I time stood up to my father's demands. He threatened to kill me if I wouldn't do what he asked, but I had to stop this abuse. My first act of courage was to stand my ground and say, "Well, then kill me because I don't want to live like this anymore." With just that first act of courage, which didn't have the best plan to it I admit, the abuse came to an end. For me that first act of courage came when I knew I couldn't live in constant fear and shame, and it was the only way I knew, with the information that I had at the time, how to change my life.

Wright

Do you believe that courage is reactive or proactive emotion?

Jenks

I think it's both; however, I believe that you learn the first time that you're courageous is usually a reaction to suffering. You've allowed fear to take over, so when you use courage reactively for that first time and it's successful, you learn you don't have to live in fear or wait until something requires you to be reactive. Dr. Covey says that if you want a great future create it. That means using courage proactively to take a leap of faith trusting that your plans will be successful, stepping out of your comfort zone, and courageously going after your dreams.

Wright

So how many times in your life have you had to be courageous?

Jenks

I think at times more than I would like, yet they've been both proactive and reactive. Both take a lot of energy and conviction, no matter which they are. When I was twenty-nine I had to abort a five-month pregnancy because the fetus was combined with a tumor growing in my uterus. Six weeks after this I learned that it was malignant and that the cells had moved through the uterine wall and would attack my liver, my brain, or my lungs. I was immediately faced with the decision to have chemotherapy. I'd call that very reactive courage. My fear of needles is extremely high and the thought of a drug that had to be administered intravenously was really causing me to reconsider my options. Okay, well there weren't any really. This is the kind of courage you have when you face your fear and go forward.

I had two fears: the fear of needles and the fear of dying. In the first three months of chemo the doctors were not getting the results they had actually hoped for from the cancer drug. I had already lost my hair, was nauseous five days straight. I was losing weight rapidly, and I'd only weighed 106 pounds to begin with. A dietician at the hospital told me that I'd have to start drinking canned shakes that would actually keep my weight stable. I told her that they had too many calories in them and that I would get fat. So she put aside her dietician oration and told me that the truth is that chemotherapy wasn't going to save me if I didn't begin to use the power I had inside. The power she was talking about would give me the courage to do what it takes to survive. She told me that I could learn what she meant by reading two books: *Man's Search for Meaning* by Viktor Frankl and *Creative Visualization* by Shakti Gawain. Both of these books made me realize that courage does live in the very far reaches of our minds and it should be much closer than that; we can call upon it when we need to.

Seven months of chemotherapy was the physical cure, supported by exercising the extraordinary power of my mind, after reading these books. I believe that's where courage really lives. The courage that we use when we're faced with an immediate danger is the courage we need to change our life. It is a mental struggle because we start visualizing things that might happen when we listen to our fears. We have an emotional and a mental argument with ourselves and if we give in, we make that decision to suffer. That is also a courageous decision, it just isn't the courageous decision that is going to make our life better.

Wright

Have you ever witnessed anyone who grew tired of living courageously?

Jenks

Yes, my mom. She lived a totally courageous life in many, many ways. I think what she chose to do courageously made her life harder than it needed to be. Had she made a different courageous decision it wouldn't have taken such a toll on both her physical and mental health. She currently lives in a nursing home. She's ninety-two years old, she has severe dementia, and absolutely no quality of life. Yet she exists because I believe she has been on courageous autopilot for so long. This is a courageous way to suffer, but she doesn't know how to turn it off. Yet I know that she's tired of living courageously, and it's really hard to watch.

Wright

Do you know anyone whose courage shocked you?

Jenks

Yes, and I believe that even though I grew up in a dysfunctional family, there are some pretty admirable people in my family at the same time.

My sister, Vivian, is one of those whose courage shocks me. Thirty years ago, she was diagnosed with an illness called Machado-Joseph disease. It's similar to muscular sclerosis. She was a registered nurse and ran an intensively demanding wing of a big hospital, yet she selflessly stuck with this job just to care for others despite the toll that it was taking on her physically. Eventually she lost her ability to walk and had to quit her job. At first she could use a walker but shortly thereafter she went to a wheelchair. Her mental acuity never changed, and it hasn't changed to this day, but her speech slurs and people often think that she's drunk. Her emotions run from happy to sad at the drop of a hat. She's been in and out of hospitals more times than I can count with pneumonia. She's lost one of her legs to diabetes and continues each and every day to fight courageously to live. She does all this so that she can watch her grandchildren grow and be with her husband of over fifty years.

She's been a model of courage, in my opinion, throughout her entire life. She lost her first child to spinal bifida when that little girl was only three, and she's had five miscarriages and two stillborn full-term pregnancies. She's given birth to two sons and has never looked back. She dedicated her entire life as a nurse to helping others and has the character and determination that defines courage. She's still alive today at seventy-two despite many recent close calls. Does courage like that shock me? Yes it does!

Wright

So will you tell our readers how they can be courageous?

Jenks

I think that being courageous is different for everybody, but the best way I know to be courageous is to learn from others, and to know that you're never alone in taking that leap of faith. I've learned so much about life through reading great authors like Brian Tracy, Stephen Covey, and Ken Blanchard. As a consultant I tell people all the time that these authors' books are required reading for life.

I was a consultant in the Brian Tracy organization for five years, and I teach Covey and Blanchard's work through my consulting firm. Each of them provides practical models for taking control of personal challenges.

Courage takes great patience; we don't want to make a knee-jerk reaction to a situation; at the same time, we don't want to turn what we deem as patience into procrastination.

The word "encourage," sounds like "in courage" and is defined by Webster as to support and to inspire. To live in courage is to live an inspired and supported life. It's just too easy to live in discouragement and then become a victim. Being a victim does not allow you to live in gratitude and graciousness. My advice to everyone who look for that inspiration and support is to read, read, read.

When I was a little girl, I was called a bookworm. I loved the library and at an early age, I realized I could lose myself in reading books and stories of far away places. What I learned from books was how others conquered their fears and became courageous.

What I advise and encourage students in my workshops is to create a visual of what you want. Cut out pictures from magazines and create a collage or just draw it. Make it a picture that depicts a life that you could have with that one courageous step, and keep that picture where you can see it daily until it drives you to action.

If fear is holding you back, draw that picture of fear also, but instead of looking at that picture each day, get rid of it in a ritual that you design. Something like burning it or putting it in a bottle and throwing it into the ocean. Draw the picture on a balloon and let the balloon float away. Sometimes we just have to get rid of the old pictures that are holding us back in order to make room for the new pictures that will move us forward. Do it today and make the picture of the life that you want come true.

Wright

So how can you use courage to make your life the one that you really want?

Jenks

First you have to know what you really want! I know from talking with people in my workshops that many don't know and that is the first step. So many of them are frozen in the what if's or the I should haves. Look at your life and if it is not the life you want to live, then do something about it. If courage is what it takes, if fear is what is holding you back, then ask yourself if being a victim is providing you a payoff and if that payoff is greater than the change you could make if you took that leap of faith. Keep a journal and don't just write in it, read it! You might find that your journal pages haven't changed in a long time. That's when you know you're stuck! We will live the life we expect to live. Therefore, we will only stop being stuck when we stop expecting to be stuck. Courage versus victimhood—you decide.

Wright

Well, what an interesting conversation, I've never thought about courage in many of the ways you are thinking about it, and I appreciate all the information you've given here. I've taken copious notes and I think this is going to be a really great chapter; our readers are going to learn a lot.

Jenks

Thank you, David. I have a favorite quote, part of it is from Shakespeare I would like to leave you with it. The choices we make shall dictate the lives we lead—"to thine own self be true."

Wright

Today we've been talking with Sharon Jenks. Sharon is President of the Jenks Group. She's a professional behaviorist and has worked with thousands of individuals and companies in reaching their personal and professional goals through teaching people and helping them discover their behavioral talents in order to increase their effectiveness in communication.

Sharon, thank you so much for being with us today on *Discover Your Inner Strength*.

Jenks

You are very welcome. Thanks for having me.

About the Author

Sharon Jenks CPBA, President of The Jenks Group®, began her career in the banking business earning the title of Senior Vice President in the then male dominated banking industry at the age of 27. Having broken the glass ceiling herself, she began to study the personal success strategy of executives who were able to achieve higher than normal levels of success. Sharon is a professional behaviorist who has worked with thousands of individuals and companies in reaching their personal and professional goals. She does this through helping people discover their behavioral talents in order to increase their effectiveness in communication. Her foundational belief is that job performance is directly linked to how well a person knows themselves and how well they can adapt to other communication styles.

Sharon, a survivor of cancer in 1980, is a sought after keynote speaker where she specializes in helping other cancer victims overcome their fear in "Reaching for the Brass Ring" and is a past chairman of several non-profit boards. She and her husband have raised four children, and now live in Truckee, CA with their four dogs.

Sharon Jenks

10960 West River Street
Truckee, CA 96161
530 582-7265
sjenks@thejenksgroup.com
www.thejenksgroup.com

Chapter Ten

Has Your Vision Become an Illusion?

An Interview With...

Lyle R. Johnson

David Wright (Wright)

Today we're talking with Lyle R. Johnson, PhD, MBA, the CEO of LR Johnson, Inc. His company is known for providing a spectrum of advisory services, including management consulting, sales force stimulation, and coaching. The company also pioneered the Virtual Consulting service. Lyle is author of *Simply the Best,* a management training manual. He is one of those rare individuals who effectively combine academic discipline of a doctorate in motivational psychology and a master's degree in business administration with real-world experience in moving client companies from mediocrity to superior performance.

Dr. Johnson is considered an expert in cost containment as well as sales rejuvenation.

Lyle, welcome to *Discover Your Inner Strength*.

I understand you frequently speak on topics related to vision, goals, and inner strength. How did you become attracted to this area?

Lyle R. Johnson (Johnson)

Good question, thanks. How did I become attracted to this area? I believe my interest began in my late teen years when I was exposed to Earl Nightingale's book *The Strangest Secret.* There are many thought-provoking messages in that book, yet the one statement that really resonated with me was that you become what you think about most of the time. This concept was so profound and yet so simple. "Wow," I recall thinking, "is it really that easy?" I wanted to know more about this.

Once one becomes curious about a concept, there is a powerful inner strength that takes control in one's mind. This is your Reticular Activating System and everyone has it. Your Reticular Activating System is the phenomenon that causes you to notice red cars after someone tells you about their new red car. The red cars were always there, it is just that you are now more aware of them.

So my interest in this area began with my interest in the concept of becoming what one thinks about. After I became conscious of the process of thoughts creating reality, I found it easy to find information and to observe the situations people create for themselves.

My considered opinion, after years of study, is that the answer *is* that simple and easy. However, there are some qualifiers. For example, I have found that thinking, regardless of how positive the thought may be, is a necessary condition for success, but the "thought" alone is not sufficient; merely thinking about an accomplishment will not get you there, you must take action.

Furthermore, you must accept that you, alone, are responsible for where and what you are; no one or a single circumstance created your current condition. You must be accountable to yourself for your life as it is. The good news is that, since you are responsible for your life, you have the power to effect any change you desire.

Now, when I say you can effect any change, there are a couple of points to hold as trusts in this process. First, you must understand that your actions need to be congruent with your wants, goals, and visions. You also need to be sure your wants, goals, and visions are crystal clear and neither in conflict nor mutually exclusive. Next, one must avoid the overarching belief that has evolved in our collective consciousness—the thought that "easy/simple" accomplishments are not worthwhile. The prevalent thought that misleads many people is that one must work hard to accomplish anything meaningful and worthwhile.

I relish speaking and writing about how people can break out of the prison or mental confinement they have created for themselves to access their inner strength. When people free themselves from their self-imposed restrictions, they can break free of the shackles that hold them back and begin to achieve their goals, realize their visions, and enjoy the satisfying, fulfilling life that is within everyone's grasp. As George Eliot said,

"It is never too late to be what you might have been."

Wright

One of the questions I have heard you frequently ask your clients is, "Has your vision become an illusion?" What do you mean by this?

Johnson

I ask this question to separate a person from his or her currently perceived reality. In NLP (Neuro-Linguistic Programming) terminology, this a pattern interrupt. This means we stop the old worn pattern that no longer serves to generate passion or success and replace it with a new strategy that creates passion and results in the desired outcome.

I have found that the majority of people have allowed their vision to erode over the years. It has become vague and ethereal. Thus, I couple the focus on "vision" with the word "illusion" (something that is not quite real). My goal is to have them begin thinking, "I once believed my vision was attainable, so why haven't I achieved it?"

My belief is that people create a vision for their life, usually in their early years. Then, as the excuse goes, "life happens." The word "happens" in that excusing phrase, shifts responsibility from the person to circumstance. When you allow circumstances to rule you, you become a "victim." Successful people create their circumstances.

Sadly, I find that most people rarely revisit the vision they once created and held dear. This is unfortunate, but it is not an opportunity lost, rather, an opportunity in abeyance. Everyone can recapture the dreams and visions they once had. These visions are not illusions or fanciful thoughts from the past, they can be realized in the "Now."

All people have tremendous inner strength embedded in their very being that can be accessed to reprogram their thoughts and actions. In fact, you do not have to access it for it to work—your inner strength is always present and at work. Knowing how it works is critical to your success; it returns what it is given. Inner strength is neutral. When you feed it negative thoughts, it will work to create an aura of negativity around you. When you enrich your life with positive expectations, your inner strength will move you toward realizing those expectations. The issue, then, is how you use it.

The primary reason people don't consciously access their inner strength for a positive result is that they believe it is too simple and too easy. This idea of visualizing and taking action has been presented in literature for centuries. The message is everywhere and we have become desensitized to it. It can be found in the Bible in the "Sermon on the Mount" and in the writings of Confucius, Shakespeare, the Dalai Lama, Napoleon Hill, Tony Robbins, and Kevin Hogan, to name but a few. The message is clear, yet the very simplicity of it seems to be the major factor in why most people discount its value.

Ask, and it will be given to you; seek, and you will find; knock, and it will be opened to you. For everyone who asks receives, and he who seeks finds, and to him who knocks it will be opened.—Matthew 7:7–8.

Obstacles are those frightful things you see when you take your eyes off your goal.—Henry Ford.

Do, or not do; there is no try.—Yoda, Star Wars V

Whatever the mind of man can conceive and believe, it can achieve.—W. Clement Stone.

We can't solve problems by using the same kind of thinking we used when we created them.—Albert Einstein.

Your inner strength has always been with you, you simply need to tap into and seize it with a passion. You face no risk in doing so and you have your life's vision to gain or regain. There are no reasons or excuses when you accept total responsibility for everything that happens to you. Truly, you have created where you are. If you have used your inner strength to create a negative vision, change it now to a positive and passionately held vision.

Wright

What is the role of passion in this process?

Johnson

Let's examine the roles of accountability and passion in using your inner strength to realize your vision. Again, I prefer to think in terms of positively programming rather than discovering inner strength because it is there at all times. It does not have to be discovered—just know that it is always with you.

Accountability is critical in directing one's passion. Accountability is nothing more than accepting responsibility for the outcomes of one's actions or inactions. Now, just as your inner strength is ubiquitous so, too, are homilies justifying excuses.

You can't win them all.
Win some, lose some.
No one is perfect.

This bears repeating: only when you take away the excuses can you perform at a higher level.

Here is a real life example of a company that believed in perfection in an operational aspect. I have my daughter to thank for this example. She managed a location of a major national retail chain. The company's policy was that if an employee's cash drawer was out of balance twice it meant immediate termination. This policy applied to everyone, whether he or she had been with the company twenty days or twenty years. Many businesspeople with whom I have shared this example say that is a harsh policy. I do not think so; it focuses the employees' attention on what is important to the company. In addition, almost no one is ever terminated because of this policy; employees pay attention to the cash transactions.

Get rid of these excuses. If you accept them, they become a barrier to achieving your vision. Henry Ford's statement, "Whether you think you can, or think you can't, you are right," is applicable here. If you think you can, and personally accept responsibility for your actions, you cannot fail. Failure only occurs when you give up. If you do not immediately realize your vision, but keep moving forward, then you have not failed.

If you cannot bear the pain of accepting that you alone are responsible for where and what you are now, then you should read no farther. However, I encourage you to continue, as there is much to gain by being accountable. If you understand you are responsible for the life you created, then you will realize you have the power to change it to coincide with your vision. You can learn to be responsible for your success.

With that said, let's now talk about passion. Passion is another element that plays an important role in discovering your inner strength. First, however, I need to explain the difference that I believe exists between goals and visions to properly position my thoughts on passion. I consider a "vision" as substantially different from a goal. It is my opinion that the area of goal-setting has become so overworked and popularized, the effectiveness of the technique has eroded. Goal-setting is certainly a valid endeavor and the methodology is somewhat mechanical. Few people take the time to do goal-setting correctly even though they are aware of the value of having defined goals. Most people have wishes, not goals. A goal remains a wish, unless the following criteria are met:

First: It is a desired, specific accomplishment that is defined with the action steps required to achieve it.

Second: A metric is stated—how the progress toward the goal will be monitored (in terms of dollars, percentage, or other tangible measurement).

Third: A target date (or event occurrence) is established for the time at which the goal is to be realized.

Fourth: This criterion—the goal statement—must be committed to writing. A goal not documented is not really a goal at all, it is a wish.

I'll give you an example:

Our company will expand its overall market share by 15 percent within the next twelve months, in the Western sales region, through the launch of a secondary brand to directly compete with our flagship brand. The launch date for the brand will be January 1 and the target for achievement of the expansion goal is December 31. Gross profitable revenue will be the metric used to monitor progress toward goal achievement.

Again, very few people take the time to set goals properly. Yet, since it is such a popular "thing to do" consensus is that everyone must have a goal, so almost everyone says he or she has goals.

Consider the scene, somewhat factiously, of partners reviewing a final checklist for the start of their new business.

One partner says, "Okay, our line of credit should hold us for the first ninety days for emergencies, the staff is trained, signage is in place, the accounting software is loaded, the Web site is up, print ads are set. I think we have everything covered."

The other partner then asks, "What have you got written down as a goal?"

"Oh, I haven't anything yet," states the first partner, "I figured we would see how it goes for awhile and then decide what our goal should be."

That's about how casually goals are treated.

Visions, I believe, are substantially different because they contain a type of energy not present in goals. Visions lead one to outcome-based thinking. In positive envisioning, one projects oneself into a future ideal state and then looks back to determine with clarity how one got there. By contrast, goal-oriented behavior is pushing forward, going over, around, through, or under barriers to get from point A to point B. With a vision, you are where you want to be and you are able to see the detailed path you took to get there.

Perhaps the illustration below will clarify this. Illustrated are two mazes—a type familiar to most. The challenge is to get from point A to point B. The maze on the left has an A in the center representing a goal or "bottom-up-based" thinking. The concept of "outcome-based" thinking is highlighted in the maze on the right. In the maze to the right, you start at the desired result and work back to where you started. The purpose of this example is to illustrate that even though neither approach is difficult, it is easier to solve if you start at the outcome.

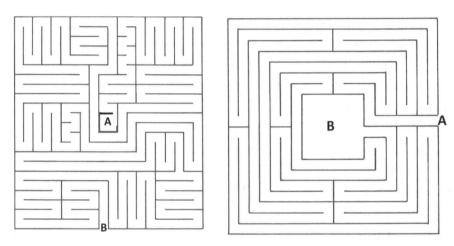

The illustration aside, the vision from where you want to be is more powerful and easier than pushing forward from where you are.

Some believe that vision evokes passion, while others believe that passion creates vision. Regardless of who is correct, when you transform what you really, really, want into to a vision, you almost automatically (whether consciously or subconsciously) develop a burning desire to achieve it. This is your inner strength surfacing.

You feel a driving passion and you are no longer "at effect," you are "at cause" of situations.

Your passion for realizing your vision is what creates the "I will do whatever it takes" attitude. Many people voice the "whatever it takes" mantra, but unless there is passion, it is meaningless. For example, the downsized employee may voice that he or she will do whatever it takes to continue employment, but it is too late. If, however, the employee had the passion to do whatever it takes to succeed in his or her position, the person would not be one of those selected for downsizing.

Think about that. How much emotional charge—passion—are you investing in the facets of your life right now? Are you "going through the motions" or causing them?

Wright

How does having a vision relate to discovering inner strength?

Johnson

Great question! Actually, I don't think having a vision assists the discovery of inner strength—I believe visions are your inner strength.

Your inner strength lies dormant until activated by a vision and the degree of strength you draw on is proportionate to your passion or desire to realize the vision.

The touchstone for your success then is to truly know what you really want. This is very important because many people only think they know, whereas they are operating based on what others—parents, siblings, co-workers, advisors, etc.—told them they wanted. Too many people have constructed their life story based on reasons and excuses they have accepted as fact because they were told that is what or how they should be.

The successful are the ones who knew what they themselves wanted, envisioned the outcome, and maintained their vision. They accessed their inner strength.

The wonderful, encouraging message is that your inner strength is available to you—to everyone—now, regardless of the current situation or condition. You merely need to know what you really want and pursue it with a passion.

There are great stories documenting the power of visions. One of my favorite business myths—I believe it to be true, but I can't cite a reference—concerns Walt Disney and Disneyland.

In the early fifties, before there was a Disneyland, there were ubiquitous recreational facilities and none of them charged an admission fee. His vision was a super entertainment facility to which admission would be charged. This concept was at odds with conventional wisdom and, therefore, certainly would not be accepted by the marketplace. Walt, however, had his passionately held vision and looked back from the perspective of being at his desired outcome—at the steps required to get where he was already. One of the steps was to obtain financing.

Now, the story is that he proposed his vision to four hundred and fifty-six banks. (This was in the days before all the consolidations, and there were, in fact, more than four hundred and fifty-six banks in the United States. His passion was so strong that he accepted "no" four hundred and fifty-six times. Ultimately, he received the financing. He did not listen to all the naysayers because Disneyland, his Vision, already existed for him. He merely needed to execute the steps he saw clearly to manifest it.

This is a great story, whether it is historically accurate or not. It cements my point about never giving up on your vision.

Other examples of vision abound. The sculptor sees the sculpture inside the block of marble and works to release it. The composer writes the notes required to represent the music he hears in his mind. The salesperson harvests the orders he or she has created.

These examples are to emphasize the power of a passionate vision and for taking action to achieve it.

I do wish to clarify that although I'm using the visual reference, you may experience your inner strength through other senses or modalities. That is, you do not have to "see" the vision, you can hear the sound of success, or you can feel the results of success. So, please understand that your vision can be heard or felt or even smelled and tasted.

Wright

Okay Lyle, I understand that, but aren't you just using "vision" as another term for "goal"?

Johnson

I think not, yet at some level of abstraction, perhaps they do merge.

I endorse the setting of goals; they are valuable. On the other hand, I believe they have become mechanical. Furthermore, there does not seem to be much emotion attached to the failure to achieve a goal. There is a "so what" response to not meeting a goal.

Think about a business—your business. Sales and profit goals are set. They are written and everyone nods in agreement while secretly not believing them. The period for which the goals were set comes to an end and there is a substantial shortfall. The excuses begin—I thought the goals were pretty ambitious, etc. The excuses are accepted and the goals revised because to do otherwise would indicate accountability. This is commonplace in far too many organizations.

The inability to achieve personal goals is fascinating to me. I find it fascinating because of the creativity of the excuses. I have concluded that there must be a dog walking around that is absolutely stuffed with term papers and business reports that he ate. Hence, in my mind, the importance of goal achievement has been diminished in our society.

A vision, on the other hand, differs in that it possesses the passion for doing whatever it takes to manifest it. There is never a failure. There may be delays and diversions, yet ultimately the inner strength, triggered by passion, ensures the vision is manifested.

- Pursuing a goal, the question is: how *do* I get there?
- The question in a vision is: how *did* I get here?

This may seem a subtle distinction yet, to me, it is the key to personal and business success.

Wright

So, there is a difference. What can we do?

Johnson

Succinctly, what you can do is take action. Action is eloquence.

Cure yourself of paralysis from analysis. Stop the mechanical and plodding progress from the present and take action as if the future is now. Pull yourself from the present into your created vision of the future you want.

- Positive thinking is a good mental state to maintain, but has no value without action.
- Accomplishments are easy with vision, passion, accountability, and action.
- Action is the trigger to success.

There has been an abundance of literature of late about attraction—the Laws of Attraction, etc.—and I think these are great. However, most omit the essential element of taking action. It seems one can sit—Lotus position preferred I understand—and attract winning the lottery. Perhaps that works, I am not sure, but what I am sure of is that unless one takes action and buys a lottery ticket, the attracted winning will not be realized.

So take action and, with a passionate vision guiding you, the result will occur. Even if the result does not actually move you forward, it will be positive in that you will learn what does not work. (I guess I slipped in a bit of positive thinking there.)

Wright

You used the term "simple," Why, then, doesn't everyone use this technique?

Johnson

That is a critical question, isn't it? The answer is that very few people know what they truly want. Sure, if you ask them they will tell you what they want. Yet probe a bit and their uncertainties begin to surface. The most common result of the initial probing is that people are confused about what they really want.

- They are not sure if they want something or if they are acting upon something, they were told they should want.
- The goals they state to get their wants are mutually exclusive. They conflict and neutralize each other, hence when they are in conflict, those goals are neutralized and passion is diluted.
- The initial wants, easily verbalized, are ego/materialistic, whereas the hard-to-admit wants are at the emotional level.

Most people are only marginally, if at all, self-aware; they exist in a trace, a semi-hypnotic, state. On the other hand, it seems the majority of people do possess the ability to be honest with themselves and thus become self-aware. Unless one is self-aware, one cannot determine what a true, core, personal want really is.

The need for self-awareness is, in my perception, tantamount to accountability. Shakespeare targeted self-awareness when he wrote: "The remedies in ourselves oft time do lie." I take exception only to the use of "oft time" as I believe it should be always. Self-awareness will lead to awareness of your inner strength.

How do you become self-aware? There are many techniques; all have the common element of creating a relaxed, calm state of mind wherein one may separate true wants from externally imposed wants. You can do this yourself, yet some may need a bit of guidance to get started.

Let me give you a very minor yet extremely effective method to initiate your awareness. This method will enable you to take back control of a portion of your behavior. You can deprogram yourself and in doing so you will become more aware of you. You have yielded control and allowed yourself to be manipulated by others, so why not manipulate yourself?

Here is the technique and it is very basic. It is rooted in operant—classical—conditioning. I am sure most people recall Pavlov and his drooling dogs. Well, you can teach yourself to drool, figuratively, at a self-determined stimulus. Consider conditioning yourself to your desk as a place only for work, reports, analysis, etc. My experience has been that most managers are terribly inefficient at their desk with regard to work. They perform many non-work tasks—reading papers, trade magazines, socializing over coffee, conducting social telephone calls, and so forth.

Now I am not asking that you stop any of these activities, just no longer do them at your desk. If you want to read the paper, go to another location (chair) in your office. Same with coffee, go drink it somewhere other than at your desk. Discipline yourself to conduct only specifically defined work activities at your desk.

After you have consistently applied this discipline for a short period, you will find that you automatically begin working the moment you are at your desk. The result of becoming more effective is actually a fringe benefit; the real achievement is that you have become aware that you can control your actions. Also, as self-awareness grows within you (and it will seem to just happen because you have awakened your inner strength) you experience more and more benefits.

Most of us say and do things we wish we had not; we regret them. Consider how great it would be if you could ask yourself, "Why *do* I feel like saying that?" instead of regretfully asking, "Why *did* I say that?"

Back to your question. Once one devotes attention to one's true wants and creates a passionate vision, achieving results is simple.

Think about what I just suggested about a desk and work. It is very simple and very easy and absolutely works. However, it may not seem appropriate or relevant to some people and they will do nothing if they have no emotional investment in trying the method or think that it is too manipulative. These may be the same people who, when a commercial airs during a football game (stimulus), go to the refrigerator for another beverage (response). They have programmed themselves, albeit unconsciously, in the same manner I suggested in the desk example.

Wright

What is the single most important thing a person must do?

Johnson

The most important thing to do for making your life work is to stop listening to others and take action.

This book is about accessing—discovering—your inner strength and I have been talking about vision, passion, attention, and action. That is because I accept that we all have this sleeping giant within, we must just arouse him. I believe action is the key.

Thought follows action, but most people think action follows thought. If you need more sales, go out and make more sales calls. How many sales will you make if you sit thinking about who might be a true prospect, what they may need, etc.? Get out and do something. If it is a "no sale," you will have something to think about for your next call.

- If you don't like your job, quit.
- If you want to be in a relationship, stop thinking about the ideal person and get out and meet people.
- If you are in a disappointing relationship, sever it.
- Stop contemplating and act.

If you wish to gather excuses for not acting, do the following: tell people your vision and attempt to record all the reasons you are told why it is: a) impossible, b) impractical, c) cannot be done, d) you are not equal to the task, etc.

President John F. Kennedy stated a vision of a man on the moon. The vision was realized although it was impossible, impractical, and could not be done. He took action that caused the achievement of amazing results.

So, again, if you want to be comfortable (a synonym for unsuccessful) and want excuses for not realizing worthwhile goals and visions, then just ask others. They will provide you with all the success-inhibiting, negative commentary necessary and some great excuses.

Wright

All right, taking action—but what actions?

Johnson

Any action is better than no action.

I like to challenge my clients. I ask them to think of something that is totally out of character for them or something they feel would be impossible. Then I ask them to consider doing it, I do not care what it is, provided it is ethical and moral—just do it.

For example, most people believe it is impossible to walk on fire, yet there are many of us who are firewalkers. So, go walk on fire at an event near you. Maybe you don't think you could ever eat an octopus. Go try some at your local sushi bar (it tastes like chicken).

Stretch yourself; get out of your comfort zone. Ask yourself why you think it is comfortable to lead a predictable and boring life.

If you are an accountant, go sell something. If you are in sales, do a prior period adjustment to the books. Now, if you just thought, I can't do that, go directly to jail (your thought-created prison), do not pass go, do not collect two hundred dollars (an appropriate analogy using the game *Monopoly*).

Any action you take that you thought you could not take comes from accessing your inner strength. Envision your inner strength as a muscle you have not used much. As you begin using it there may be some pain, but as you use it more and more it will become easier and finally become a source of pride.

There needs to be a word of caution here. Don't devote a lot of time to thinking about what actions to take—they will come to you. When you think you could not possibly do something, that is the very action you must take. Sure, there is risk—a risk that you will appear foolish, that you will not succeed at the attempt, or, for example, that you will not able to keep the octopus in your stomach, etc.

Focus, instead, on the reward. Embrace the benefit of getting in touch with yourself and accessing your inner strength.

Wright

What techniques can you provide our readers now to begin accessing their inner strength to create visions leading to the outcomes they desire?

Johnson

The vision is the trigger for inner strength. Therefore, I believe techniques for creating the visions will be of greatest benefit to our readers.

The creation of your vision, again using the visual modality, is detail. The greater the degree of detail you create in your vision, the more effective it will be. Bear in mind, the brain does not distinguish between actually observed and intensely visualized or imagined events and/or information. It is very important, therefore, that you practice and envision exactly what you want.

Sports, rather than personal endeavors and business, were some first disciplines to accept and embrace this concept. Golf and tennis players realized that mental practice was as effective, even more effective, as physical practice. They also learned that the practice must be accurate; the correct stoke must be the one visualized.

Using tennis, the vision for the perfect return of a serve, would include: You are aware you are on a clay court, the sun is shining, glinting off the net, and the frame of your racquet; you feel its warmth on your skin. A gentle breeze is present and that, too, you feel. There is a smell of freshly cut grass from the lawn around the clubhouse. You see the ball coming toward you. It is green; you can detect the seams and even the fuzz on it. You are aware of the sweet spot on your racquet and begin your swing to precisely coincide with the arrival of the ball. As you return the serve, you follow through perfectly and the ball sails just over the net to touch down right on the line. (This is partial, there is more to imagine for strengthening your vision in tennis.)

If you want to have a highly successful, very profitable growing business the vision might be: You are approaching the building in which your company has its offices. The Rolls-Royce (silver over black, with silver gray glove leather upholstery) has just stopped at the curb. Then, as you walk up the steps, you feel the warmth of the sun and, as the glass door to the building opens, you feel the cooling effect of the air conditioning. You detect the light scent of cinnamon in the lobby. You begin walking down the blue carpeted, white hallway, trimmed with dark wood. (The preceding were truncated descriptions; the degree of detail is the critical element.)

The actual vision must be yours, and yours alone, and the detail is the requirement. It is the amount of detail that validates a vision; vagueness is a characteristic of a goal.

I suggest that you relax, focus on exactly what your vision will look like.

I want to share a technique I have used effectively for years. As you have probably detected from my comments, although I am at ease in the financial arena, my passion is sales. I will explain how I prepare for a sales call. The fact that I know my product or service and my company's unique selling propositions is a given, so there is no preparation there.

I arrive at the client's location. I take a couple of deep breaths to relax, and close my eyes. Then I decide what he or she will purchase and create a vision of the order being executed. Next, I see the meeting place, although I have never been there before. I visualize the décor, the colors, and my prospect. I mentally experience our greeting, some of the things we discuss, and how pleased the client is that I allow him or her the opportunity to buy from me.

There is an interesting sidebar to this technique. Many times, I find that the décor, colors, and even the client are exactly as I imagined them, even though this is the first meeting. This is an example of really tapping into inner strength and you have that strength in you right now.

That is my pre-call preparation. Try it.

In closing, remember that your ability to manifest what you want, passionately, is always there; it will never leave you and you should not leave it.

- Determine what you really want, passionately; not what you have been led to believe you want.
- Create a vivid vision, in great detail, of having what you want.
- Look back, from your envisioned success, and "see" the steps you took to get there.
- Take action.

- The vision is already realized, it just may take some time for it to fully manifest in the "Now."

Vision—a passionate vision—and taking action, leads to outcome-based thinking and outcome-based thinking is, in my opinion, the key to success.

About the Author

Lyle R. Johnson lives in Phoenix Arizona, having earned the right to enjoy the continuous sun through spending many winters in New York and Chicago. His two grown children live in Seattle, where he was raised, because they seem to prefer to be damp all the time.

Lyle has devoted the last three decades to assisting clients through advisory services, including coaching, to achieve their optimal performance. While adept in financial, production, and organizational areas for small to medium sized businesses, his true passion lies in the sales and marketing area (a passion realized in his own company as well as during his employment by Procter & Gamble, Quaker Oats, etc.) He provides "magical" sales training as "The Sales Wizard."

He was one of the pioneers of the commercialization of Biofeedback devices (alpha/theta monitors). Lyle has actively pursued motivational psychology—with primary application to sales training and coaching and training—and obtained his doctorate in that discipline.

Lyle has been a speaker for the American Management Association, Sales Executives Clubs, and various universities (Fordham, University of Washington, University of California at Santa Barbara, etc.)

Lyle is a member of the International Coach Federation (ICF) and Institute of Management Consultants (IMC).

Lyle is retired as a Lieutenant Commander in the Coast Guard (Reserve) in which his primary assignment was Finance Officer.

Lyle R. Johnson, PhD, MBA

L R Johnson, Inc.
5025 N Central, Suite 497
Phoenix, Arizona 85012
Tel: 602-938-7174
Fax: 602-938-8764
lyle.johnson7@gmail.com

Chapter Eleven

Using Strategy to Discover Your Inner Strength

An Interview With...

Brian Tracy

David Wright (Wright)

Many years ago, Brian Tracy started off on a lifelong search for the secrets of success in life and business. He studied, researched, traveled, worked, and taught for more than thirty years. In 1981, he began to share his discoveries in talks and seminars, and eventually in books, audios and video-based courses.

The greatest secret of success he learned is this: "There are no secrets of success." There are instead timeless truths and principles that have to be rediscovered, relearned, and practiced by each person. Brian's gift is synthesis—the ability to take large numbers of ideas from many sources and combine them into highly practical, enjoyable, and immediately usable forms that people can take and apply quickly to improve their life and work. Brian has brought together the best ideas, methods, and techniques from thousands of books, hundreds of courses, and experience working with individuals and organizations of every kind in the U.S., Canada, and worldwide.

Today, I have asked Brian to discuss his latest book, *Victory!: Applying the Military Principals of Strategy for Success in Business and Personal Life.*

Brian Tracy, welcome to *Discover Your Inner Strength.*

Tracy

Thank you, David. It's a pleasure to be here.

Wright

Let's talk about your new book the *Victory!: Applying* the *Military Principals* of *Strategy* for *Success* in *Business* and *Personal Life.* (By the way it is refreshing to hear someone say something good about the successes of the military.) Why do you think the military is so successful?

Tracy

Well, the military is based on very serious thought. The American military is the most respected institution in America. Unless you're a left liberal limp-wristed pinko most people in America really respect the military because it keeps America free. People who join the military give up most of their lives—twenty to thirty years—in sacrifice to be prepared to guard our freedoms. And if you ask around the world what it is that America stands for, it stands for individual freedom, liberty, democracy, freedom, and opportunity that is only secured in a challenging world—a dangerous world—by your military.

Now the other thing is that the people in our military are not perfect because there is no human institution made up of human beings that is perfect—there are no perfect people. The cost of mistakes in military terms is death; therefore, people in the military are extraordinarily serious about what they do. They are constantly looking for ways to do what they do better and better and better to reduce the likelihood of losing a single person.

We in America place extraordinary value on individual human life. That is why you will see millions of dollars spent to save a life, whether for an accident victim or Siamese twins from South America, because that's part of our culture. The military has that same culture.

I was just reading today about the RQ-1 "Predator" drone planes (Unmanned Aerial Vehicles—UAVs) that have been used in reconnaissance over the no-fly zones in Iraq. These planes fly back and forth constantly gathering information from the ground. They can also carry remote-controlled weapons. According to www.globalsecurity.org, the planes cost $4.5 million each and get shot down on a regular basis. However, the military is willing to invest hundreds of millions of dollars to develop these planes, and lose them to save the life of a pilot, because pilots are so precious—human life is precious. In the military everything is calculated right down to the tinniest detail because it's the smallest details that can cost lives. That is why the military is so successful—they are so meticulous about planning.

A salesperson can go out and make a call; if it doesn't work that's fine—he or she can make another sales call. Professional soldiers can go out on an operation and if it's not successful they're dead and maybe everybody in the squad is dead as well. There is no margin for error in the military; that's why they do it so well. This is also why the military principals of strategy that I talk about in *Victory!* are so incredibly important because a person who really understands those principals and strategies sees how to do things vastly better with far lower probability of failure than the average person.

Wright

In the promotion on *Victory!* you affirm that it is very important to set clear attainable goals and objectives. Does that theme carry out through all of your presentations and all of your books?

Tracy

Yes. Over and over again the theme reiterates that you can't hit a target you can't see—you shouldn't get into your car unless you know where you are going. More people spend more time planning a picnic than they spend planning their careers.

I'll give you an example. A very successful woman who is in her fifties now wrote down a plan when she was attending university. Her plan was for the first ten years she would work for a Fortune 500 corporation, really learn the business, and learn how to function at high levels. For the second ten years of her career she talked about getting married and having children at the same time. For that second ten years she would also work for a medium sized company helping it grow and succeed. For the third ten years (between the ages of forty and fifty), she would start her own company based on her knowledge of both businesses. She would then build that into a successful company. Her last ten years she would be chief executive officer of a major corporation and retire financially independent at the age of sixty. At age fifty-eight she would have hit every single target. People would say, "Boy, you sure are lucky." No, it wouldn't be luck. From the time she was seventeen she was absolutely crystal clear about what she was going to do with her career and what she was going to do with her life, and she hit all of her targets.

Wright

In a time where companies, both large and small, take a look at their competition and basically try to copy everything they do, it was really interesting to read in *Victory!* that you suggest taking vigorous offensive action to get the best results. What do you mean by "vigorous offensive action"?

Tracy

Well, see, that's another thing. When you come back to talking about probabilities—and this is really important—you see successful people try more things. And if you wanted to just end the interview right now and ask, "What piece of advice would you give to our listeners?" I would say, "Try more things." The reason I would say that is because if you try more things, the probability is that you will hit your target

For example, here's an analogy I use. Imagine that you go into a room and there is a dartboard against the far wall. Now imagine that you are drunk and you have never played darts before. The room is not very bright and you can barely see the bull's eye. You are standing along way from the board, but you have an endless supply of darts. You pick up the darts and you just keep throwing them at the target over there on the other of the room even though you are not a good dart thrower and you're not even well coordinated. If you kept throwing darts over and over again what would you eventually hit?

Wright

Pretty soon you would get a bull's eye.

Tracy

Yes, eventually you would hit a bull's eye. The odds are that as you keep throwing the darts even though you are not that well educated, even if you don't come from a wealthy family or you don't have a Harvard education, if you just keep throwing darts you will get a little better each time you throw. It's known as a "decybernetic self-correction mechanism" in the brain—each time you try something, you get a little bit smarter at it. So over time, if you kept throwing, you must eventually hit a bull's eye. In other words, you must eventually find the right way to do the things you need to do to become a millionaire. That's the secret of success. That's why people come here from a 190 countries with one idea in mind—"If I come here I can try anything I want; I can go anywhere, because there are no limitations. I have so much freedom; and if I keep doing this, then by God, I will eventually hit a bull's eye." And they do and everybody says, "Boy, you sure where lucky."

Now imagine another scenario: You are thoroughly trained at throwing darts—you have practiced, you have developed skills and expertise in your field, you are constantly upgrading your knowledge, and you practice all the time. Second you are completely prepared, you're thoroughly cold sober, fresh, fit, alert, with high energy. Third, all of the room is very bright around the dartboard. This time how long would it take you to hit the bull's eye? The obvious answer is you will hit a bull's eye far faster than if you had all those negative conditions.

What I am I saying is, you can dramatically increase the speed at which you hit your bull's eye. The first person I described—drunk, unprepared, in a darkened room, and so on—may take twenty or twenty-five years. But if you are thoroughly prepared, constantly upgrading your skills; if you are very clear about your targets; if you have everything you need at hand and your target is clear, your chances of hitting a bull's eye you could hit a bull's eye is five years rather than twenty. That's the difference in success in life.

Wright

In reading your books and watching your presentations on video, one of the common threads seen through your presentations is creativity. I was glad that in the promotional material of *Victory!* you state that you need to apply innovative solutions to overcome obstacles. The word "innovative" grabbed me. I guess you are really concerned with *how* people solve problems rather than just solving problems.

Tracy

Vigorous action means you will cover more ground. What I say to people, especially in business, is the more things you do the more experience you get. The more experience you get the smarter you get. The smarter you get the better results you get the better results you get. The better results you get the less time it takes you to get the same results. And it's such a simple thing. In my books *Create Your Own Future* and *Victory!* you will find there is one characteristic of all successful people—they are action oriented. They move fast, they move quickly, and they don't waste time. They're moving ahead, trying more things, but they are always in motion. The faster you move the more energy you have. The faster you move the more in control you feel and the faster you are the more positive and the more motivated you are. We are talking about a direct relationship between vigorous action and success.

Wright

Well, the military certainly is a team "sport" and you talk about building peak performance teams for maximum results. My question is how do individuals in corporations build peak performance teams in this culture?

Tracy

One of the things we teach is the importance of selecting people carefully. Really successful companies spend an enormous amount of time at the front end on selection they look for people who are really, really good in terms of what they are looking for. They interview very carefully; they interview several people and they interview them several times. They do careful background checks. They are as careful in selecting people as a person might be in getting married. Again, in the military, before a person is promoted they go through a rigorous process. In large corporations, before a person is promoted his or her performance is very, very carefully evaluated to be sure they are the right people to be promoted at that time.

Wright

My favorite point in *Victory!* is when you say, "Amaze your competitors with surprise and speed." I have done that several times in business and it does work like a charm.

Tracy

Yes, it does. Again one of the things we teach over and over again that there is a direct relationship between speed and perceived value. When you do things fast for people they consider you to be better. They consider your products to be better and they consider your service to be better—they actually consider them to be of higher value. Therefore, if you do things really, really fast then you overcome an enormous amount of resistance. People wonder, "Is this a good decision? Is it worth the money? Am I going the right direction?" When you do things fast, you blast that out of their minds.

Wright

You talk about moving quickly to seize opportunities. I have found that to be difficult. When I ask people about opportunities, it's difficult to find out what they think an opportunity is. Many think opportunities are high-risk, although I've never found it that way myself. What do you mean by moving quickly to cease opportunity?

Tracy

There are many cases were a person has an idea and they think that's a good idea. They think they should do something about it. They think, "I am going to do something about that but I really can't do it this week, so I will wait until after the month ends," and so on. By the time they do move on the opportunity it's to late— somebody's already seized it.

One of the military examples I use is the battle of Gettysburg. Now the battle of Gettysburg was considered the high-water mark of the Confederacy after the battle of Gettysburg the Confederacy won additional battles at Chattanooga and other places but they eventually lost the war. The high-water mark of Gettysburg was a little hill at one end of the battlefield called Little Round Top. As the battle began Little Round Top was empty. Colonel Joshua Chamberlain of the Union Army saw that this could be the pivotal point of the battlefield. He went up there and looked at it and he immediately rushed troops to fortify the hill. Meanwhile, the Confederates also saw that Little Round Top could be key to the battle as well, so they too immediately rushed the hill. An enormous battle took place. It was really the essence of the battle of Gettysburg. The victor who took that height controlled the battlefield. Eventually the union troops, who were almost lost, controlled Little Round Top and won the battle. The Civil War was over in about a year and a half, but that was the turning point.

So what would have happened if Chamberlain had said, "Wait until after lunch and then I'll move some men up to Little Round Top"? The Confederate troops would have seized Little Round Top, controlled the battlefield, and would have won the battle of Gettysburg. It was just a matter of moving very, very fast. Forty years later it was determined that there were three days at the battle of Gettysburg that cost the battle for the Confederates. The general in charge of the troops on the Confederate right flank was General James Longstreet. Lee told him to move his army forward as quickly as possible the next day, but to use his own judgment. Longstreet didn't agree with Lee's plan so he kept his troop sitting there most of the next day. It is said that it was Longstreet's failure to move forward on the second day and seize Little Round Top that cost the Confederacy the battle and eventually the war. It was just this failure to move forward and forty years later, when Longstreet appeared at a reunion of Confederate veterans in 1901 or 1904, he was booed. The veterans felt his failure to move forward that fateful day cost them the war. If you read every single account of the battle of Gettysburg, Longstreet's failure to move forward and quickly seize the opportunity is always included.

Wright

In your book you tell your readers to get the ideas and information needed to succeed. Where can individuals get these ideas?

Tracy

Well we are living in an ocean of ideas. It's so easy. The very first thing you do is you pick a subject you want to major in and you go to someone who is good at it. You ask what you should read in this field and you go down to the bookstore and you look at the books. Any book that is published in paperback obviously sold well in hardcover. Read the table of contents. Make sure the writer has experience in the area you in which you want to learn about. Buy the book and read it. People ask, "How can I be sure it is the right book?" You can't be sure; stop trying to be sure.

When I go to the bookstore I buy three or four books and bring them home and read them. I may only find one chapter of a book that's helpful, but that chapter may save me a year of hard work.

The fact is that your life is precious. A book costs twenty of thirty dollars. How much is your life worth? How much do you earn per hour? A person who earns fifty thousand dollars a year earns twenty-five dollars an hour. A person who wants to earn a hundred thousand dollars a year earns fifty dollars an hour. Now, if a book cost you ten or twenty dollars but it can save you a year of hard work, then that's the cheapest thing you have bought in your whole life. And what if you bought fifty books and you paid twenty dollars apiece for them—a thousand dollars worth of books—and out of that you only got one idea that saved you a year of hard work? You've got a fifty times payoff. So the rule is you cannot prepare too thoroughly.

Wright

In the last several months I have recommended your book, *Get Paid More and Promoted Faster* to more people. I have had a lot of friends in their fifties and sixties who have lost their jobs to layoffs all kinds of transfers of ownership. When I talked with you last, the current economy had a 65 percent jump in layoffs. In the last few months before I talked with you, every one of them reported that the book really did help them. They saw some things a little bit clearer; it was a great book.

How do you turn setbacks and difficulties to your advantage? I know what it means, but what's the process?

Tracy

You look into it you look into every setback and problem and find the seed of an equal or greater advantage or benefit. It's a basic rule. You find that all successful people look into their problems for lessons they can learn and for things they can turn to their advantage. In fact, one of the best attitudes you can possibly have is to say that you know every problem that is sent to you is sent to help you. So your job is just simply look into to it and ask, "What can help me in this situation?" And surprise, surprise! You will find something that can help you. You will find lessons you can learn; you will find something you can do more of, or less of; you can find something that will give you an insight that will set you in a different direction, and so on.

Wright

I am curious. I know you have written a lot in the past and you are a terrific writer. Your cassette programs are wonderful. What do you have planned for the next few years?

Tracy

Aside from speaking and consulting with non-profits, my goal is to produce four books a year on four different subjects, all of which have practical application to help people become more successful.

Wright

Well, I really want to thank you for your time here today on *Discover Your Inner Strength!* It's always fascinating to hear what you have to say. I know I have been a Brian Tracy fan for many, many years. I really appreciate your being with us today.

Tracy

Thank you. You have a wonderful day and I hope our listeners and readers will go out and get *Focal Point* and/or *Victory!* They are available at any bookstore or at Amazon.com. They are fabulous books, filled with good ideas that will save you years of hard work.

Wright

I have already figured out that those last two books are a better buy with Amazon.com, so you should go to your computer and buy these books as soon as possible.

We have been talking today with Brian Tracy, whose life and career truly makes one of the best rags-to-riches stories. Brian didn't graduate from high school and his first job was washing dishes. He lost job after job—washing cars, pumping gas, stacking lumber, you name it. He was homeless and living in his car. Finally, he got into sales, then sales management. Later, he sold investments, developed real estate, imported and distributed Japanese automobiles, and got a master's degree in business administration. Ultimately, he became the COO of a $265 million dollar development company.

Brian, you are quite a person. Thank you so much for being with us today.

Tracy

You are very welcome, David. You have a great day!

About the Author

One of the world's top success motivational speakers, Brian Tracy is the author of many books and audio tape seminars, including *The Psychology of Achievement*, *The Luck Factor*, *Breaking the Success Barrier*, *Thinking Big* and *Success Is a Journey*.

Brian Tracy

www.BrianTracy.com

Chapter Twelve

Bully Free at Work

An Interview With...

Valerie Cade

David Wright (Wright)

Today we are talking with Valerie Cade. She has earned worldwide acclaim as a speaker and consultant and she is committed to stopping workplace bullying. She has been a CEO of one of Canada's largest training companies, earned the Top Candidate award in Canadian Basic Military Training, and was honored with a

President's Award for Distinguished Service from the Canadian Association for Professional Speakers. Valerie has worked with all levels of business and her clients note that she is relevant, well researched, and delightfully insightful. She has been featured in numerous radio, television, and newspaper publications. Valerie has a genuine passion for helping people in organizations receive the respect and dignity they deserve.

Valerie, welcome to *Discover Your Inner Strength*.

Valerie Cade (Cade)

Thank you! Glad to be here.

Wright

So, how is workplace bullying different from working with difficult people?

Cade

First of all, if you ask people if they have experienced bullying, many will answer yes. I have found it helpful to define the term "bullying." Workplace bullying is deliberate, disrespectful, repeated behavior toward another for the bully's gain. The key here is it is deliberate behavior that's disrespectful, premeditated, and very intentional. Does the bully really know what he or she is doing? Yes.

The difference between a bully and a difficult person is that a difficult person's behavior is not intentional. Difficult people are not usually trying to sabotage communication. If they appear difficult, it might be because they are just trying to cover up their own needs and are unaware of what they are doing. You can usually rationalize with a difficult person, but you cannot rationalize with a bully.

Wright

Give us some important facts that we should be aware of about workplace bullying.

Cade

I like looking at the facts. People often will wonder if bullying really exists. Perhaps they have never been bullied. Workplace bullying occurs in every country in the world. One out of six people are being bullied at work. There is new research being conducted that indicates it can be as high as one out of four. A bully targets someone for his or her own gain. If you have a boardroom of twelve people, the odds are that two people are being bullied. If you have a department of twenty-four, probably four of them are being bullied.

Wright

Who is bullied more, men or women?

Cade

Seventy-seven percent of the time, a woman is the target of workplace bullying. Men might not feel comfortable admitting that they were targeted. Men are usually brought up to be strong and brave. Perhaps there is more of a denial factor in men reporting bullying.

Wright

What are the top triggers that cause bullying?

Cade

Well, that's a great question. Bullies actually target people they want to be like. The bully wants what the target has. The main driver behind a bully is a jealous and envious nature. Because of this, the bully deliberately tries to take the target's power away. The bully then has a false sense of security because the bully has power over someone. In fact, if bullies don't receive power over someone on a routine basis, they go into withdrawal. It is actually an addiction, and the behavior is repeated.

Wright

So is envy the only thing that drives a bully's behavior?

Cade

Research has shown that in most cases, during childhood those who bully have been severely wounded at an emotional level by parents, teachers, or some authority figure. This caused them to cut off their emotions; and when they grow up to be adults, they are incapable of empathy, remorse, and self-reflection. Bullies don't believe they have self-worth, so they try to take it from others in order to make themselves feel superior.

Wright

I've seen a few bosses bully in my time. What are the different types of bosses who bully?

Cade

There are five types of bully bosses. One type is the arrogant bully. What does "arrogant" really mean? Arrogant bullies are preoccupied with themselves and their own achievements. They believe with full confidence that others should admire them and show deep respect toward them. They have a huge need for admiration and affirmation and when they believe they're not having these needs met, they push others around in order to gain them. They put themselves in the limelight and break the rules and boundaries to achieve their desire to be admired.

How do you compete with somebody like that? The bottom line is, don't compete with them. When possible, you can show your admiration for them (as long as you don't compromise your integrity) and of course, do not be defensive. Understand that bullying is more about the bully than it is about you.

Another type of bully boss is what we call the manipulative bully. This is a secretive type of bullying that I have seen very often in most companies. Schoolyard bullying is very overt and physical in nature, but in the corporate arena that would be obvious. The manipulative bully resorts to singling out someone, often in private so that nobody else is a witness to it. It is two-faced in nature in order to show false support for appearance's sake. Manipulative bullies try to charm others with their overly charismatic persuasiveness. You can be deceived and think they actually care, but as soon as they get what they want from you, they disregard or ignore your needs. This behavior is very confusing to someone who's a target of a manipulative bully.

A third type of bully boss is the dictator. Dictators believe they know better than anyone else does. They tend to be unaware of other people's strengths and abilities, and therefore they will not be able to acknowledge others' accomplishments. Many employees go through much of their career waiting for their boss to acknowledge their efforts, but if they have a dictator boss, their efforts will seldom, if ever, be acknowledged.

The dictator boss will tend to micromanage and criticize what is wrong, as opposed to acknowledging what their employees have done right. Again, this is more about the bully than it is about others. The key here is to not point out any errors to your boss. If you do point out errors, be prepared for a fight. The dictator bully boss will use defensiveness in almost any situation in order to gain back perceived loss of control. When they "win" over you, they experience a rush of power.

Do not think you can enlighten a dictator bully boss; and furthermore, do not expect them to say, "Oh, I see what you mean. I'm sorry." Remember, the bully is more concerned about looking competent and in control than he or she is about connecting with anyone. Because bullies feel they lack personal power of their own, they project their inadequacies on others as if it is the target's fault, when in fact this is just another means of exerting power.

What can you do? First of all, knowing this about the bully is key. Secondly, decide not to take this personally—dictator bullies will try this with everyone. And thirdly, the confidence in really knowing that this is not your fault will help you to bully-proof yourself. In fact, the bully will probably pick up some "vibes" that, while you refuse to be controlled, you are interested and open to a win-win. This mature confidence is an excellent boundary to create between yourself and any bully.

Another type of bully boss is the victim bully boss. A victim bully boss tends to be negative, or whine when his or her needs are not met, rather than dealing with people in a win-win way. Bully bosses will complain about their "bad luck" and not being appreciated enough, and will often not admit mistakes or own a problem. Victim bully bosses believe that others are out to dominate and control them, so they often drag their heels in making decisions, even though you may have communicated the urgency for getting something done.

How do you cope with victim bosses? Do not count on them. Cover yourself with deadlines and commitments, and do not expect them to comply with your requests. Remember, it is not the task that is hard for them, it is the commitment to the task—they feel controlled in having to do anything on someone else's agenda or timing. Set clear expectations in all areas with solid documentation. Be clear that oppositional and negative displays of behavior are not appropriate, and give examples of what this behavior looks like.

The last type of bully boss is the suspicious bully boss. These bosses tend to be hostile, sarcastic, secretive, and argumentative; they do not trust others. They seek others who are compliant and who will not question their decisions. They perceive that others are "out to get them" and treat others with disregard and a lack of trust.

When this type of boss questions you and perhaps attacks your motives, be prepared for a blowup. Remember, suspicious bully bosses are behaving in this way for their own safety needs, not usually because of your incompetence. Remain calm and supportive, and do not get defensive—it will only make matters worse.

Wright

So what are some of the top bullying behaviors experienced by targets?

Cade

I've narrowed this down to three areas. The primary bullying behavior that we see the most is verbal abuse. Verbal abuse occurs when hurtful words are used at the expense of the target to somehow try to give the target a false sense of who he or she is, usually in the area of character. When this happens, the bully is preying on the target's good nature. The bully is counting on the target's kindness and forgiving attitude, hoping that the target will not challenge what is being said.

Verbal abusers are not interested in your responses. This is important to note because sometimes it is tempting to respond defensively in order to prove your point. Most people want to come to a resolution and move on, but verbal abuse is about power. The most powerful thing you can say to a bully is, "Your behavior is unacceptable." Use the word "you" instead of the phrase "I feel." When you say, "I feel this is unacceptable," you're implying that it is your opinion and therefore it's up for debate. When you say, "Your behavior is unacceptable," you're coming from a more powerful position.

Another form of bullying behavior is exclusion. It's very easy to exclude people from information. If the bully can use exclusion to keep information from the target, then the target is left scrambling. This is exactly what the bully wants. An example is sending out an e-mail regarding a meeting and excluding the target. Everyone shows up to the meeting except for the target. The bully then asks the target, "Where were you?" and argues with the target, saying that the e-mail was sent.

Exclusion may take more effort to detect because it is often performed secretively, where others are not able to witness the bully's tactics. If you feel you are being excluded, the best advice is to keep a journal, indicating the date, time, what happened, what you believe should have happened, who bullied you, and any witnesses. Lastly, include how this made you feel, and as a result, how it affected your work performance. Logging this over time can show a pattern of consistent occurrences. This helps you know you are not going crazy; and furthermore you will have professional data to share with someone in authority who can help create a more productive pattern. Also note: someone in an authority role is interested in job performance, so you are more likely to receive support when you can show how the behavior has hindered your productivity. There is no winning against someone who uses exclusion as a bullying tactic.

Creating a lack of clarity is also used as a bullying technique. For example, if job performance standards are vague or unclear, it is more difficult for an employee to "win" at work or create success. Instead, the reverse happens—the target works hard, but is left confused and off guard when the bully boss reprimands him or her for missing performance standards. Keeping the target wondering is a bullying technique. Targets should ask for specifics in order to clarify expectations.

Wright

Does everyone who is bullied suffer?

Cade

Seventy-five percent of the people who are bullied can muddle through it, but it's the remaining 25 percent who suffer greatly. This will happen for two reasons: the severity of the bullying or the level of coping skills of the target, or a combination of the two.

Wright

Are there different levels of severity of workplace bullying?

Cade

Yes, the levels of bullying are minor, moderate, and severe.

Minor bullying occurs when the bullying behavior is experienced as difficult, such as teasing and arguing. With clear, confident, and accountable conversations, this behavior may change. If a target does not say anything and proceeds to let this behavior get the best of him or her, this mild bullying behavior, unaddressed, may unnecessarily grow into dissonance.

With moderate bullying, the bully's behavior is experienced by most people as very difficult. When the target has good boundaries and stronger self-esteem, there is a chance of influencing the bully's behavior through discussions based in clarity, confidence, and accountability. If the target's self-esteem is stronger, the bullying is experienced as moderate. However, if the target's self-esteem is weaker, the bullying behavior is experienced as more severe.

In severe bullying, the bully's behavior borders on psychopathic, anti-social behaviors, where the bully is incapable of working out any type of conflict. The bully is not open to any win-win negotiations or discussions. The only way to control severe bullying is through an intervention.

Wright

Why do people put up with workplace bullying?

Cade

This is a great question. The main reason people put up with workplace bullying is that they don't recognize the behavior as bullying. They wonder why they feel so confused. As they feel worse and worse, they then develop a sense of lower self-worth. When you have low self-esteem, you start to believe it's your fault.

Another reason people tolerate bullying is fear of rejection and a loss of acceptance and harmony with the bully. The real fear is addressing the conflict, thinking that the bully will retaliate. This is a definite possibility; you can expect a push-back from the bully. Note, however, that you do not have to take on what the bully is doing to you—it is your choice whether or not to accept this behavior personally.

What grieves a target even more than the bullying itself is when the target asks a boss for help, and that person does not have the skills to help. The boss does not acknowledge the target's reality, and furthermore, tries to minimize the situation, mainly because the boss does not have the skills to address workplace bullying.

When people at work witness workplace bullying, yet are not empowered to help, this is called the bystander syndrome. A boss, by the authoritative power granted from the company or organization, often has more power to help than is realized.

Wright

Can you rationalize or negotiate with a bully?

Cade

The answer is no. Bullies are incapable of empathy and caring. They have diminished interpersonal relationship skills. With them, it's all about power.

When dealing with a bully in the workplace, there must be an intervention with the bully. Usually, in conflict resolution, we are taught to extend the olive branch; but with a bully, this is not an effective way to end the behavior. You can try the usual conflict resolution tactics. If they don't work, move on to being direct and firm about what you want instead.

If you're met with a spirit of noncooperation or there is no resolution, then you've really run out of influencing skills or influencing behaviors. Severe bullying always requires an intervention.

Wright

So what can one expect when confronting a bully?

Cade

Well, expect bullies to push back. Do not expect open arms or immediate cooperation. First of all, the bully will most likely deny what you're saying. You'll find yourself over-explaining and over-analyzing. Bullies will continue to deny their behavior and you'll never get any further.

Another tactic the bully uses is the counterattack. The counterattack occurs when the bully adds something else he or she is upset with you about. This serves to confuse your initial issue. Ignore the bully's additional comments and stay with the issue at hand.

The third thing to expect is that the bully will try to play the victim. Bullies who play victim will say how difficult things are for them instead of hearing out the issue you are trying to resolve. This is a diversion technique to minimize and ignore your needs, and thereby gain back control for the bully.

Wright

Goodness! So how do you approach a bully from the bottom line?

Cade

By confronting the bully, you will actually set a boundary for yourself. People want to know what to say. My suggestion is to think of short, simple comebacks such as, "That is inappropriate," or better yet, "You are being inappropriate." By saying something like this, you are letting the bully know that his or her behavior is unacceptable. Avoid anger, because that's what the bully wants. Don't waste your time.

You can also give short, one-word replies that imply you have heard what the bully is saying, but you're not agreeing with him or her, such as, "Interesting—" or "Oh—" Another phrase you could use is, "You might be right." This is different than saying the bully is right. A more powerful statement would be, "Stop! This is going nowhere, and I'm walking away." If you don't feel that you can say anything at all, look the bully right in the eye, use very firm body language, and leave.

Wright

Well, I think I've learned a lot here today.

Cade

It's intense.

Wright

I really appreciate all the time you've taken to answer these questions. I've taken a lot of notes here. I'm sure that our readers are going to recognize these problems and you've given them some things to think about and some tips about what to do about bullying.

Cade

It's definitely a pressing need. If we can help people get the respect and dignity they deserve, then mission accomplished.

Wright

Today we've been talking with Valerie Cade. She has earned worldwide acclaim as a speaker and consultant. She is committed to stopping workplace bullying. She has a genuine passion for helping people and organizations receive the respect and dignity they deserve. Our businesses really need that.

Valerie, thank you so much for being with us today on *Discover Your Inner Strength*.

Cade

You are very welcome; it has been a pleasure.

About the Author

Valerie Cade has earned worldwide acclaim as a speaker and consultant and she is committed to stopping workplace bullying. She has been a CEO of one of Canada's largest training companies, earned the Top Candidate award in Canadian Basic Military Training, and was honored with a President's Award for Distinguished Service from the Canadian Association for Professional Speakers. Valerie has worked with all levels of business and her clients note that she is relevant, well researched, and delightfully insightful. She has been featured in numerous radio, television, and newspaper publications. Valerie has a genuine passion for helping people in organizations receive the respect and dignity they deserve.

Valerie Cade, CSP

Suite 356, 1500 14th Street, SW
Calgary, Alberta, T3C 1C9, Canada
403.508.0678
Val@BullyFreeAtWork.com
www.BullyFreeAtWork.com

Chapter Thirteen
An Internet Pioneer

An Interview With...

Hillary S. Bressler

David Wright (Wright)

Today we are talking to Hillary S. Bressler, a recognized authority on Internet marketing and one of the nation's Web pioneers. In 1997, she founded .Com Marketing, a top 100 interactive marketing firm based in Winter Park, FL. She is a highly sought after speaker on a variety of subjects relating to the Internet. Hillary earned her degree from the University of Georgia, as well as studied in Aix en Provence, France. She currently resides in Winter Park with her daughter and chocolate brown poodle. In her spare time, Hillary enjoys international travel to far away places like Cambodia and Bracina Fasso; boating; and feng shui. Hillary, welcome to *Discover Your Inner Strength*.

Hillary Bressler (Bressler)

Thank you.

Wright

What was the key driver that prompted you to start your business?

Bressler

The early days of the Internet and all of the confusion surrounding it was what led to the creation of .Com Marketing. Like most early-stage products, the Internet grew at a very rapid pace, especially at the beginning. Our company has always been focused on the Internet as a marketing tool for businesses, so I was able to ride the wave at a time when the combination of Web *and* marketing expertise was rare. There are still many marketers today who have a top line understanding of the Web, but have not fully leveraged its potential. Hence, why so many people came to me looking for some guidance in the black hole of this new medium.

Wright

How did you brand yourself as an expert in Internet marketing?

Bressler

In December 1996, I practically spent the entire month surfing the Web and learning what was out there with regard to Internet marketing. I was working in the marketing department of The Golf Channel at the time, and all questions about the Internet came to me since I was one of the few people who understood the technology. Even though there wasn't much available information, I quickly discovered that I knew more than most people because I had really dove deep into the Internet and Web. This realization led me to strike out on my own to found .Com Marketing because there was a real need for the knowledge I had acquired.

Becoming known as an expert at age 26 fell into my lap due to all of my hands-on experience and a general lack of information in the marketplace. As the industry began to evolve, the mentality was, "If you build it they will come." Applying marketing principles to Websites was virtually unheard of at that time. But those who understood how to market on the Internet hit it big, as evidenced by sites like Amazon.com. They became popular because they combined novel ideas with brilliant marketing plans. In the beginning, many people thought the Internet was a fad, but I knew it was going to be big. I've always had a gift for anticipating what was going to stick around and be popular – with the exception of a few personal stock choices. As they say, "Stick with what you know."

Wright

How did you start your speaking engagements?

Bressler

As .Com Marketing grew, requests for speaking engagements started pouring in since I had fortunately become an expert in an area where so many people were so lost. I started speaking to small organizations, and then received invitations to speak at corporations and at large conferences. And because I was on the marketing side, I was able to speak in terms that people understood rather than in technical jargon. I quickly gained a nice following of people who recommended me for other speaking engagements, so that part of my business really grew.

I tend to give away a lot of tips and guidance that people can understand. "Geek speak" goes over most people's heads, so I learned how to teach CEO's and business owners about the Internet in a way that helped them increase sales. People come up to me after my speeches and say, "Thank you, I finally get it. You made coming to this conference worthwhile." Even today, technology continues to grow at a pace that far exceeds most peoples' learning curves, so I still receive requests to speak about the Internet and new online strategies like mobile and social media marketing. The Internet is really fascinating when you look at the trends it has created. I enjoy opening people's eyes to this amazing technology.

Wright

When you talk about Internet marketing, are you talking about how to get these companies recognized maybe higher up on the list than anyone else in there, or is it something different altogether that you do?

Bressler

A strategy to help Websites appear higher in search engines, called Search Engine Optimization, or SEO, is definitely one of our areas of expertise. With billions of Internet searches conducted each month by people looking for companies, products and services, clients coming to us often say, "Hey, I am not even on page five. Can you help me get my Website listed on the first page when someone does a search on Yahoo! or Google?" There are hundreds and hundreds of companies trying to get into that first position or at least on the first page, so it is very competitive, especially for popular search terms.

More or less, to answer your question, "Internet marketing" is marketing your Website and your business on the Internet. That involves other things like email marketing; designing a Website, if you don't have one; and updating the site to make it current. A few other advanced technologies also competing for your attention are worth mentioning here – Facebook, Twitter and YouTube. Companies can generate a lot of exposure by exploring those routes. It can be very confusing, but lucrative at the same time for those who understand and embrace it.

Wright

I thought that Facebook and those kinds of things were for younger generations?

Bressler

Facebook was originally developed for college students, but more recently has become mainstream. If you'll recall, "social media," or the use of personal networking sites, was a key strategy in the 2008 political election. You'd be surprised how many people are using Facebook to connect with friends and people from their past. Over 200 million people are registered users today. In the last six months, the volume of users has exploded, doubling on Facebook and LinkedIn alone. Part of the reason is the current economic situation, but I also believe social networking has simply reached the tipping point. Providers have done an exceptional job of adding functionality and benefits for their members, as well as for businesses. It's quite amazing. However, I always say, it's not about the technology; it's about the relationship. Don't be intimidated by the Internet. It's simply the medium used for communication, entertainment, networking and so much more.

Wright

Where do you see success on the Web?

Bressler

Most companies that have good, up-to-date Websites and are aggressively focusing on Search Engine Optimization (SEO) to appear higher on search engines are doing well. It's also important to keep your email marketing updated by emailing to current clients and those who ask to receive information from the company. Many companies have come to realize that the Internet is a very targeted, cost effective way of marketing. In fact, year-over-year projections show the Internet marketing business growing, while other marketing vehicles like radio, television and newspaper are flat or even declining, as in the case of newspapers.

To be successful, you must ensure your Website appears trustworthy. At one time or another, everyone has landed on a Website, scratched their heads and said, "Can I trust them? I'm not sure I want to give them my credit card because something looks shady?" Those companies most likely tried to save a little bit of money by doing it themselves or having a "friend of a friend" build their site rather than relying on an experienced professional. As the old saying goes, "You have to spend money to make money." I highly advise people who have businesses to hire professionals to design and maintain their Web presence. Oftentimes the impression you make with a prospect on the Web is the first, and may be the only one, if it is not well done. A professionally designed and executed site almost always pays off in the long run.

Wright

What are some of the life lessons that you have learned since starting your business so young? Didn't you say 26?

Bressler

Yes, I have been in business since 1997. I came from a family of entrepreneurs, so I think I had it in my blood. One of the lessons I learned from my father was how to spend money in the right places when you own a business.

I remember one Halloween I went out and bought some decorations for the lobby, just a pumpkin and haystack to give it a fun atmosphere. When my dad came in, he immediately asked, "How much did you spend on those decorations?" About $45, I said. He then asked, "Are you going to get any new business from it?" I said, "Actually, no. It was really just to make the office look fun." He said, "That's a lot of money to spend. If you are going to spend money, be sure that you are going to get business out of it." When I mentioned that I wanted to buy a $1,500 laptop, he quickly asked if it would be used to win new business. After explaining that it would primarily be used for presentations, he quickly said, "Then get the $2,500 laptop. Get the best one that you can find." I thought that was a really good lesson. Even when you only spend $40 or $50, it really adds up. So *always* spend your money in the right places.

Wright

What are some of the struggles and challenges that you have faced over the years and how did you overcome them?

Bressler

As far as the challenges, I really think that because the Internet and the Web were so new, I had to become an educator and teach people about the basics like Search Engine Optimization and Email Marketing. But fortunately business owners and decision makers trusted .Com Marketing and its expertise. Even though it was a challenge, spending a lot of time educating people before getting down to the nitty-gritty of the sales process meant that we typically won the business and made clients happy. That challenge has served me well because I discovered that my customers were able to trust and rely on us as valuable resources.

As a business owner, especially back in the early days when I was so young, I was challenged with developing and keeping good employees. I found interviewing prospective employees tricky because some people came across very well initially, but ended up being entirely different the day they started to work. Unfortunately, I don't think there is any golden rule to hiring. However, we're much smarter today and we better understand how the interview process works. We now include aptitude and personality tests to ensure that all employees can execute on what they claim to know. The personality assessments are especially beneficial as it helps us understand their core values and traits, as well as how they will fit in with the management team and their co-workers. Since our work is very time-sensitive and detail-oriented, a high performing team is critical to our success. Our longevity shows that we have cracked that nut. Our inventory is not a product, it is our intellectual knowledge. That takes an exceptional team of very smart people.

Wright

What is the biggest lesson that you have learned in running your own business?

Bressler

The biggest lesson I have learned is persistence. People often say, "Wow, I wish I could start a business." The fact that I have maintained a positive cash flow for 12 years is a good statistic for a privately owned company. The industry and economy have certainly had their ups and downs, but persistence and being conservative has paid off for .Com Marketing.

Wright

What advice would you give someone who is thinking about starting a business today?

Bressler

I think you should start a business in your area of expertise. It's about taking what you're good at and going for it. I knew the Internet inside and out, so that's where I started. I dabbled in real estate in the past, but was not successful because I didn't have the depth of knowledge. Most people have a lot of ideas, but you have to narrow your focus. You don't know what will really happen until you throw something against the wall and see what sticks. Keep trying until one really takes off. But definitely do what you know.

I think it is also good to look at the industry and do your research before starting. When I started, there was no research about the Internet industry. But if I were to start the business today, I would definitely spend a few months in the research stage.

Wright

How do you stay on top of the Internet industry? Just in my business, we have 13 computers running non-stop and always installing updates. I purchased a new system the other day that I'm still trying to learn. What is your advice?

Bressler

It is hard to stay on top of the Internet industry, not to mention other technologies, like mobile. It seems that when you buy a cell phone, two months later it's already out of date. Fortunately, I have a knack of predicting what's hot and what's not. In one of my most popular presentations, "The Latest and Coolest in Internet Marketing," I discuss the newest tools out there and how to leverage them for marketing purposes.

People often ask how I stay up to date. There is no way one person can remain current on everything, but I do read a lot and spend time online just playing around. I also take advantage of opportunities to learn from others. And don't forget to check out business magazines that publish yearly reviews of the latest technologies. One technology I read about some time ago was Websites that will emit smells through a little gadget hooked into your USB. Just imagine visiting a florist's Website and you suddenly smell roses or gardenias. While this technology has not yet made it to the mainstream, it is one of those interesting ideas that might have materialized. Who knows, perhaps there is still some potential in the future. Often many of these new ideas are just about timing.

Cell phones and mobile devices are the next hot technologies to watch. Asia and Europe are way ahead of us in terms of usage, but I do anticipate that we'll start seeing mobile devices morph into e-wallets very soon. Just imagine purchasing a Coca-Cola from your mobile phone and the charge automatically appears on your cell phone bill. I find new devices like the iPhone completely amazing, and it's exciting that there are new applications popping up every day. It even surprises *me* how fast this industry is advancing.

Wright

I've had a publishing company now for 18 years and you've got me worried. Should I use YouTube and Facebook?

Bressler

Should you as a publishing company use these tools? I don't know. I would have to talk to you a little more to determine if that's the right market for you. However, there is a way to market yourself called "social marketing." It's all about helping people connect with other people. .Com Marketing makes extensive use of social marketing techniques for our clients. Some companies have been successful using YouTube to get their message out there to millions of people…for free!

Companies are definitely finding smart, cost-effective ways to market themselves beyond traditional outlets like TV, radio and print. In fact, Electronic Word of Mouth and Consumer Generated Marketing are becoming more powerful than anything we can do as marketers. Anyone not embracing these trends will miss huge opportunities. Marketers are no longer in control. Those who survive are already adapting to this new environment.

Wright

Have you changed how you market over the years and what things do you do differently now?

Bressler

We really have found great success in the strategic ways we market our own business. Obviously, I think with any company, word of mouth advertising is still tremendously powerful. If our clients are successful and happy, they're more likely to recommend us to others. That's old school.

Even with a high-tech company like mine, I find that speaking engagements are very important in earning trust because it allows me to meet people and connect face-to-face. We also generate a lot of news in our company, so we issue regular press releases. Then there's email marketing, which we've done since day one. We built our own list, which currently contains between 6,000 and 7,000 names. That might sound small to a lot of companies, but I will tell you that we have had personal contact with each of those people on the list in some way or another. Obviously, that list is very valuable to us. Could it be half a million names by now? Sure, but we built it the right way based on relationships. We practice what we preach as far as keeping communication open via email and relationship marketing. Remember, the relationship is *always* more important than the technology.

Wright

What are you doing to drive your success in the future? Especially now in tough economic times.

Bressler

Actually, it's interesting. During times where the economy is not as strong, we find a lot of companies move their marketing and advertising dollars to the Internet. Decision makers are finding that the return on investment with the Internet is typically greater than more expensive types of advertising because we're able to target their audience with a greater degree of precision. We feel very blessed that our industry continues to grow with no end in sight. As with most companies, we're always working on new business development efforts during good times and bad. That's really the name of the game…keeping the pipeline full and making sure that your current customers are happy and satisfied.

Wright

What a great topic and what a great conversation. I've learned a lot today and I'm sure that our readers have as well.

Bressler

Good!

Wright

I appreciate you taking all this time with me today to answer all these questions. I really do appreciate it.

Bressler

Thank you so much.

Wright

Today we have been talking to Hillary S. Bressler. She is the founder and CEO of .Com Marketing, a top 100 interactive marketing firm. Hillary is a recognized authority on Internet marketing and one of the nation's Web pioneers. She certainly knows what she is talking about. To learn more about .Com Marketing, visit www.commarketing.com.

Hillary, thank you so much for being with us today on *Discover Your Inner Strength*.

About the Author

Hillary S. Bressler is a recognized authority on Internet marketing and one of the nation's Web pioneers. In 1997, she founded .Com Marketing, a top 100 interactive marketing firm based in Winter Park, FL. She is a highly sought after speaker on a variety of subjects relating to the Internet. Hillary earned her degree from the University of Georgia, as well as studied in Aix en Provence, France. She currently resides in Winter Park with her daughter and chocolate brown poodle. In her spare time, Hillary enjoys international travel to far away places like Cambodia and Bracina Fasso; boating; and feng shui.

Hillary Bressler

www.commarketing.com
bressler@commarketing.com
866-266-6584

Chapter Fourteen

Moving Beyond Fear

An Interview With…

Sharon Moist

David Wright (Wright)

Today we're talking with Sharon Moist. Sharon is the founder and CEO of Successfulosophy,® an international coaching and consulting company at the forefront of entrepreneurial and entertainment industry trends.

With more than twenty years of experience in the business world, she has worked in the corporate arena, the retail industry, the not-for-profit sector, and in the entertainment industry. After five years as head of television at one of the top boutique talent agencies in Los Angeles, Sharon left the agency to start her own coaching company.

Today she works with an elite group of private clients who are completely committed to living their life purpose and growing their business. Known for her innovative ideas and out-of-the-box thinking, Sharon's coaching provides her clients with the help and support they need to synergistically fuse their own personal "success philosophies" with their business brands.

Sharon, welcome to *Discover Your Inner Strength.*

Sharon Moist (Moist)

Thank you very much; I'm very glad to be here.

Wright

So let's get right to the point. What do you believe is the key for each of us to discover our own inner strength?

Moist

You know, David, I've spent a lot of time thinking about that question, and what I discovered was that for me, personally, and for the clients I work with, the key has been for each of us to overcome our fears. That is what has enabled both my clients and me to truly define who we are and what we're capable of being and doing in our lives.

Wright

Yet when we talk about the concept of inner strength, the topic of fear is not one that readily comes to mind. Why do you suppose that is?

Moist

We live in an amazing time in history. When you look at how technology has influenced our lives and the level of social consciousness that exists today, the possibilities are endless. A perfect example of this is the election of Barack Obama to the highest office in this country, President of the United States.

I have no doubt that Mr. Obama probably went into this presidential race with a lot of fear and trepidation about the whole process. Could he beat some of the other candidates who were far better known than he was to become one of the front-runners of the Democratic Party? And, if he was able to do that, could he really compete with Hilary Clinton's popularity in order to win enough votes to receive the presidential nomination? Then, if he was able to overcome all of those odds, was America even ready for an African-American president?

Whether you like him or dislike him, the truth of the matter is this: Barack Obama did not allow any fears he had about running for president to get in the way of actually stepping up to the plate and doing it. Instead, he faced his fears head-on in order to fulfill his life purpose—to become the leader of this country during a time of severe economic crisis, political strife, and international hatred of the United States.

I don't think anyone can ever truly discover what they're made of in order to live up to their potential until they're able to address those fears that are getting in the way of fulfilling their own life purpose—that unique contribution that only they can make in this world.

Wright

Would you tell our readers a little bit more about that last statement?

Moist

I'd be glad to. Most people have things they want to do or goals they want to accomplish in life, but when you get right down to it, they are unable to accomplish anything because fear is keeping them from moving forward. They might be able to achieve smaller goals, but it's usually the big ones that are elusive, and they're elusive because they cannot move past their fears in order to actually pursue those goals.

The big goals and accomplishments are the ones that develop character. If you look at any big goal you have accomplished in your life, it is often one that has helped you develop your character as a human being. Big goals are the ones that help us become who we're meant to be by enabling us to develop those special skills and talents that we're supposed to share with the rest of the world.

Wright

How do you think fear prevents us from discovering our true inner strength in order to accomplish those goals or dreams that we have for our life?

Moist

By keeping us stuck exactly where we are, with no ability to move forward.

Wright

From your experience, when does fear tend to rear its ugly head in our lives?

Moist

Usually when we're dealing with the unknown or when we have no guarantee of success.

Wright

Will you give us an example of how we allow our fears to get in our way?

Moist

Absolutely. I recently wrote an article on fear for one of my newsletters, and here's what I wrote:

One summer, when I was ten years old, my mom enrolled me in formal swimming lessons. Up until that time, I had always loved the water and was a bit of a fish, but now it was time for me to learn the proper way to swim.

The lessons lasted about four weeks and soon after that, the swim instructor came to my parents and asked them if he could put me on the swim team. By the end of that summer, I was the regional conference champion in Backstroke, and by age twelve I was training for the Olympics.

For the next seven years, I set swimming records and remained the regional Backstroke champion. No one could beat me. Then, at the age of eighteen (my last year of eligibility on this particular swim team), we were driving to the final conference championship when a single thought crossed my mind that had never crossed it before: "What if I lose?" For eight years straight I had won this event. And in those eight years, I had never even considered the possibility of losing this race.

It wasn't a good feeling, and I did my best to shake that fear as I swam the other two individual events in which I was entered. Then it came time for *my race*—the fifty-yard Backstroke. We got in the pool, the gun went off, and the race was on. The first forty-five yards of the race were fine, but as I took my final three strokes, the thought of losing once again crossed my mind. Sure enough, my mind took hold of that fear and I lost the race by .01 seconds. Unbelievable! After eight years of being the best swimmer in this event, all it took was one moment of doubt to find myself in the spot of "second best." I was crushed because fear had gotten in the way and kept me from winning a race I had won every year previously.

The power that fear can have over us can be enormous, if we let it be. The key, however, is that it can only have as much power as we give to it. If we give it a lot of power, it can keep us completely frozen and prevent us from moving forward. On the other hand, however, if we acknowledge that fear, but don't allow ourselves to dwell on it, and instead choose to continue moving steadily forward, 99 percent of the time we can get past it.

Wright

Let's take a look at some other well-known people who have moved past their fears when dealing with the unknown. Who comes to mind for you?

Moist

You know, the first person who comes to mind, and I'm a huge fan of hers, is Dara Torres, the forty-year-old swimmer who recently won an Olympic silver medal in the fifty-yard Freestyle. (She also lost her race by .01 seconds, so I'm in good company!) When you look at the fact that her first Olympics was twenty-four years ago, when she was sixteen years old, and the fact that at the age of forty she chose to come back and compete again in an event that's really a young person's game, I admire her courage enormously because there were no guarantees that she would even qualify for the Olympic team, let alone win a silver medal. Dara is a great example of someone who chose to step beyond the boundary of fear because she challenged herself to really discover how much inner strength she had and she went for it.

Obviously, swimming is my thing because Michael Phelps is another person I think about who chose to move beyond any fear he may have had when he made the decision to try and set a record of winning eight gold medals at the Olympics. And, when you consider the fact that some of those medals were completely beyond his control because he had to depend upon his relay teammates to do their part, you realize that it was a huge risk for him. Also, when you look at the amount of media coverage and publicity Michael was receiving about this potential record-making opportunity, I'm sure there were many times when he was very afraid of not living up to everyone's expectations, especially with all of the hype that was surrounding him. But, at the end of the day, Michael's goal, vision, and commitment was to himself and his God-given swimming talent, and he just went for his dreams regardless of the fact that there was no guarantee he would actually win eight gold medals.

The last person who comes to mind is Lance Armstrong, the seven-time Tour de France winner who recently made the decision to come back and compete in his eighth Tour de France race this year. When you consider that he left the sport when he was on top, by winning the tour seven times previously, and now he's choosing to come back with no guarantee of anything, you realize that it takes a very courageous man who can say to himself, "You know what? I'm going to do it anyway. I've done it before, so let's see what happens this time."

Wright

It's all downhill for him.

Moist

Exactly. But, by the same token, could I do it? Absolutely not! You know, if I knew that I went out on top, I'm not sure I could turn around and say, "Well, let's try it once more and see what happens." I think I would feel completely embarrassed if I lost. But that's just me at this stage in my life. If I were actually in a situation like that, maybe I would feel differently. Either way, however, I admire Lance's courage and his decision to go for it one more time.

Wright

So how do you deal with fear in order to get to the other side? What steps can we take to do this?

Moist

Well, I have a little system I use with my clients that I'd like to share with you.

Step One of the system is to acknowledge your fear, because you can't deal with it until you actually acknowledge that it's present in your life.

Step Two is to list your fear, in order to know exactly what it is. Is it fear of failure, lack of money, or maybe making the wrong decision? This step is about making a list so you know exactly how many fears and what fears you're dealing with.

Step Three is to name those fears. That's right—give each one of your fears a personal name so that every time it rears its ugly head, you can call it by name. Afraid of making a wrong decision? Call it George. Then, when you're in the decision-making process and that particular fear comes up, you can say something like: "Oh, that's just George, stopping by to say Hello. Hi George! Bye George."

Step Four of the system is to create a personal phrase or mantra for yourself (mine is "Cancel That") so whenever you feel fear coming on, you can tell yourself to "cancel that" (or whatever your mantra is) until the fear goes away. It may take fifty times of saying your mantra, but eventually that particular fear *will* go away. And, as time goes on, it will become easier and easier to eliminate the fearful thoughts that cross your mind.

Dealing with fear will take some work on your part. And while it won't happen overnight, you *can* find a way to start taking control of your fears and letting go of them. Acknowledge each fear, list it, name it, and give yourself a mantra to deal with it.

Wright

How is the process working for your clients?

Moist

It's been working really, really well. Now, that's not to say it's easy in the beginning, because sometimes it's very easy to get stuck in a negative thought pattern or get frustrated by a situation over which you have no control. However, my clients have found that the system actually does work—if they work the system. Things don't happen overnight, but with time and practice, it will get better.

Even I have had to use it at times! In fact, I recently had a situation happen that was really frustrating for me because I couldn't control the outcome of it, so I had to use my own four-step process to deal with it until the situation changed!

Wright

Why is dealing with fear such an important part of discovering inner strength?

Moist

I think dealing with fear is such a key element in the process because it will enable you to live a complete and fulfilling life, so that at the end of every day, and at the end of your life, you will know that you lived your life with no regrets and there's nothing you would have done differently. I view it as a way to completely live the life you were meant to live.

Wright

A wise man once told me that if I were ever walking down the road and saw a turtle sitting on a fencepost, he didn't get up there by himself. When you look back on your career, and I know that you have had tremendous success, who was there for you? Who do you think helped you to become who you are and have the mindset that you have?

Moist

I would have to say that my parents and my grandmother were the people who have had the most influence on my life in terms of who I've become and how I view the world.

My grandmother was an entrepreneur who was way ahead of her time. She and I were kindred spirits, and she's played a huge part in my success.

Both of my parents had their own businesses, as well, and they have always believed in me, no matter which career path I followed. And, as you can see from my work history, I went in many different directions until I found my own life purpose! My parents also taught me a lot about learning to trust my own intuition, as well as how to work with people and how to run a successful business.

Wright

So what's next for Sharon Moist? Any future plans, dreams, or goals, either personally or for your business?

Moist

My first book, *101 Tips for Actors,* just sold out of its first printing, so I've been spending some time editing the second edition, which will come out this spring. I'm also in the process of developing some new products and coaching programs for my business, so that's keeping me very busy, as well. And, because I spent so much time traveling this past year, I'm actually looking forward to just sitting down in my favorite chair and reading a book!

Wright

Sounds exciting. It also sounds like you're able to help a lot of people and that's always nice.

Moist

I love what I do. I truly have a passion for helping people believe in themselves and in their own potential, so that they, too, can fulfill their own life purpose, whatever that may be.

Wright

Well, I appreciate all the time you've taken to answer these questions this afternoon. I've learned a lot, and I'm starting to view fear a little differently from the way I did before we spoke.

Moist

Well, that's always nice to hear!

Wright

You've given me a lot to think about, and I think our readers will have a lot more to think about, as well.

Moist

I've enjoyed our conversation immensely, so thank you very much.

Wright

Today we've been talking with Sharon Moist, founder and CEO of Successfulosophy,® an international coaching and consulting company. Sharon works with an elite group of private clients who are committed to living their life purpose and growing their business. And, after our conversation this afternoon, I tend to believe that she knows exactly what she's talking about, and I think our readers will, as well.

Sharon, thank you so much for being with us today on *Discover Your Inner Strength*.

Moist

Thanks a lot, David. It was my pleasure.

About the Author

Sharon Moist is founder and CEO of Successfulosophy® LLC, an international coaching and consulting company at the forefront of entrepreneurial and entertainment industry trends. With more than twenty years of experience in the business world, Sharon has worked in the corporate arena, the retail industry, the not-for-profit sector, and in the entertainment industry. Sharon's background includes:

- Outlining two product ideas for a Fortune 500 company, which has resulted in sales revenues of more than $460 million dollars in seven years.
- Accepting a position as an assistant at one of the top boutique talent agencies in Los Angeles and being appointed as the Head of Television *one month later*. (The average length of time for this kind of promotion is seven to nine years.)
- Producing one of the top-rated radio talk shows in Los Angeles, taking it from having no rating to the number two-rated show in the Los Angeles market in eight months.
- Serving as a member of Trend Forecaster Faith Popcorn's *BrainReserve*, an exclusive group of experts who "collaborate with clients on the process of weaving the future into the everyday texture of their companies and brands." Past and present *BrainReserve* clients have included: BMW, American Express, McDonalds, Kodak, and Bacardi, among others.

Today Sharon works with an elite group of private clients who are completely committed to living their life purpose and growing their business.

A member of the International Coach Federation, Coachville, American Women in Radio and Television, and Women in Film, Sharon is also the author of the book, *101 Tips for Actors: Secrets for Success Every Actor Must Know*.

When she's not traveling on business, Sharon divides her time between Montana, California, and Florida.

Sharon Moist

Successfulosophy® LLC

www.SharonMoist.com

Chapter Fifteen

Retirement with Attitude: How Boomers Reinvent the Wheel

An Interview With…

Kim Kirmmse Toth

David Wright (Wright)

Today we're talking with Kim Kirmmse Toth. Kim is a licensed clinical social worker and a certified life coach. A Baby Boomer herself, she works with those between the ages of fifty-five and seventy. Kim has a strong background in positive psychology and is considered a strength-based coach, encouraging people to use their strengths on a daily basis to lead the lives that they desire. Most of us will have another twenty, thirty, or even forty more years left in our lifetime. Kim encourages Boomers to enjoy this unique stage of life and offers programs to support them on this road less traveled.

Kim, welcome to *Discover Your Inner Strength.*

Kirmmse Toth

Thanks, David.

Wright

So would you tell our readers why everyone is making such a big deal out of the Baby Boomers these days?

Kirmmse Toth

Well, there are seventy-six million of us so I think we're hard to ignore. We are the group that was born between 1946 and 1964, so we're post World War II babies. Compared to generations before us, most of us have higher educations and we have many different expectations about how we live our lives and how prosperous we think we should be. Other generations before us would probably say that we have a sense of entitlement that they didn't feel they had. As Boomers, we have a real history of doing things differently and making waves. We were idealists back when we were younger and I believe there is a large number of us who are still idealists. We were once known as a counter culture—if you think of hippies and events such as Woodstock. I think that as we age we are still idealists. It's still really important to us that social and personal improvement is a part of who we are in our everyday lives. That part of who we are hasn't changed much.

Wright

The word "retirement" has been around for decades. Why is everyone trying to change it to something different?

Kirmmse Toth

Well, that's just how we do things—we don't want it to be what it always was before. If you look up "retirement" in the dictionary, you probably wouldn't be too pleased with what you saw. Basically, the definition is to go to bed, stop engaging in daily activities, withdraw, and go to a place of less activity. And, quite frankly, that's not something that most Boomers want to do at all. So the retirement that our parents and grandparents had is probably going to be very different from what we're going to create. We have tried to change the word "retirement." I think AARP worked on that for quite a while. There are a lot of different terms out there but none of them seems to really be sticking as far as I've experienced. I think it's more about redefining the word "retirement" instead of finding a new word.

Wright

"Partial retiree" almost sounds like a conflicting term—retirement has always meant stop working, don't ever work again.

Kirmmse Toth

Right, and now you just have this image of a rocking chair. We are simply not like that. This is not to say that we don't want some of that once in a while, but we don't want that 100 percent of the time.

Wright

So how do you think our retirement will be different from that of our parents and grandparents?

Kirmmse Toth

I believe we are a lot more active—our expectations are higher, we want to travel, we want to do things that we've been putting off because we were working and raising families. I think we look at it as a time to really spread our wings in way that we haven't been able to do. This may be especially true if you worked in a corporate level job where you worked at least forty hours, maybe sixty or seventy hours a week and are ready for that to change.

Wright

So why do Boomers talk about reinventing themselves?

Kirmmse Toth

Think about what we've been talking about. The retirement age used to be sixty-five. You got your gold watch and they had a big retirement party for you. That was it—you were gone. At sixty-five today, we have a good ten, twenty, or thirty years ahead of us, so that rocking chair is really unattractive. I think it's a time when most of us really want to re-evaluate who we are and how we live our lives. We don't want to just work for money; we want to work for something that we're passionate about. It really means taking a look at what we've been doing with our lives. We can keep what's working for us, change what isn't, and move on to something different. That's where the term "reinventing" comes from.

Wright

So do you think Boomers will ever be able to afford to retire?

Kirmmse Toth

With the way the markets have been lately, that's hard to know, isn't it? Again, it depends on how you want to define retirement. There are many people who retire and it doesn't work out the way they thought. You may feel that you failed retirement so you go back to work. Hopefully, you are doing something that you really are passionate about—something you really do love and can sink your teeth into.

Part of your decision will depend on what kind of lifestyle you want to live. Some people's expectations are really high and they want to travel the world in first class. That's great! For the majority of people, you may cut back on your work, if you don't quit entirely, and during those first five or ten years of that period of your life, you may be active and busy doing things you love to do. The reality is that things slow down after awhile. And retirement may not cost as much if we're not flying around the world or buying expensive boats or other extravagances. So everybody has to make his or her own decision about that, obviously, but I think a lot of us will be working a lot longer than we intended to. That's why it's so important to change how we are doing things if it's not working for us 100 percent.

Wright

So what is this talk of re-crafting or re-careering about?

Kirmmse Toth

I think those are new terms, and I think that they have evolved because we do want to do something that we're thrilled and excited about. There's a real good chance the job we've had for the last ten years or more isn't something that we want to continue to do. So we make choices around that; maybe we still want to work or financially we need to work.

If you want to re-craft your career, take the career you're in already and make changes or tweak it enough so that it's something that is more to your liking—something you can wake up in the morning and be excited about doing. My experience is that there are a lot more ways to re-craft our careers than we think there are. We really need to think out of the box sometimes and be creative in looking at what's available to us.

As far as re-careering goes, there are many people who really do change careers. They go from whatever they were doing to something that possibly stands on the shoulders of their first career. Or maybe it's something totally different. My experience is many people who have worked for big companies and corporations want to work for themselves. Then there are people who have worked for themselves say, "You know what, I don't want the responsibility anymore, I'm going to go work for somebody else."

Wright

I think with most of the people that I've talked to, it's almost as if they think when you retire, then your second job might be a Wal-Mart greeter, but that's not what you're talking about is it?

Kirmmse Toth

I've been to Wal-Mart and the greeters are very friendly people. I want to assume they are there because they want to be, not because they have to be. If they are, they're there because they have to be I hope they're also enjoying it—it's something they look forward to and it's fun for them. But maybe these are people who have had real careers before that. I have no idea, but that really isn't totally what I'm talking about.

Wright

One of the things I think would concern our readers is if we're going to live so long, what will our health be like?

Kirmmse Toth

It's funny you should ask because I was just reading an article that was talking about just that! There's a term that's been coined for us called "boomeritis." I think it was coined from an orthopedic doctor. As a group, we don't want to stop—we want to keep skiing, playing golf, riding our bikes, and running marathons. The reality is that our body parts do wear out. It's no big deal anymore to get a hip replacement or a knee replacement. They have figured out ways to do this because I think we've demanded it. We want replacements for the parts of us that are wearing out, and there's probably good and bad about that.

I'm a big skier and you can go to Vail and see people skiing who are seventy-five, eighty, and eighty-five years old, and I want to be one of them! (I don't know how many parts I'll have to have replaced for that to happen!) The ski resorts don't even have senior packages anymore. You used to be able to ski for free if you were past sixty-five, then they made it seventy, then seventy-five. Now it doesn't even exist because there are too many older skiers. But we're going to push it and ski whether they charge us or not!

Wright

What exactly is the "sandwich generation"?

Kirmmse Toth

That was something that obviously coined by us also. The word evolved in the 1980s. It came about because many of the women in our generation had children later in life than previous generations. The result is we have children at home and we may be caring for our elderly parents. Whether they're living with us or they're living somewhere else, almost doesn't matter—we're still caught in the middle of taking care of parents and raising children at the same time. So basically, we are "sandwiched" between those two generations.

We also have a new situation that's been happening with us and it's called "boomerang children." Many of our children graduate from college and come home to roost. When I was in college, that would be the last thing I ever would have done—you just didn't do that. Now kids do come home, and some of them come home to stay for a long time. That can create issues in and of itself, in areas such as finances, privacy, and expectations. It's like things have never changed—our children left and they came back, but they don't want us to "parent" them anymore. That's another kind of a new phenomenon also.

Wright

So how do we keep our family together when everyone is all over the world?

Kirmmse Toth

That's the good or bad news, right? That we're all over the world? I remember when I was in college—we called home once a week from the pay phone in the hallway of the dorm and we called collect. That certainly doesn't happen anymore! Everybody has cell phones and most of the plans have free long distance. We have e-mail that is also free where you can be connected to anybody at any time. I don't know what the statistics are as far as who has computers, but you would be very unusual if you didn't have one. People have family blogs to keep connected.

I know that my family has done planning for family reunions using a teleconferencing line where we all call in on a bridge line and it's possible to have fifteen to twenty people on it easily. We would meet every week to talk about what we were going to do and we were very far away—we were all over the place. So it's just really pretty simple.

Wright

Well, I thought I was a Baby Boomer, but you said 1946 to 1964. I was born in 1939.

Kirmmse Toth

Maybe you have a Baby Boomer attitude and are one at heart!

Wright

You're scaring me, I have a twenty-year-old daughter—she was just twenty this month—and she's a sophomore at Belmont University in Tennessee. Do you mean I can look forward to her coming home!

Kirmmse Toth

Well, there is that chance. For some parents that's a wonderful thing. Remember, we parent differently than our parents parented us. I know many of the universities around here in Colorado are concerned because as parents, we are too involved in our kid's lives— we're "helicopter" parents. We want to go to college interviews and job interviews with them. We want to have such a strong influence and say in their lives that maybe a lot of us haven't allowed our kids to be independent enough and make bad decisions as we probably did.

Wright

Right!

So how do I create a legacy for my family and myself? How will people remember me?

Kirmmse Toth

You know, this is something that has become very important also to people. Since families are more distant than they used to be, in spite of easy contact, it's become even more important—it's more of a need for people.

One of the things that I love to do with families is Ethical Wills. They're not legal documents, but they're important and of great value. It's a very heartwarming process. You write to either one person or two, all of your children, or whoever else is important to you.

People write Ethical Wills for a variety of reasons. You may write about how you love them, how you want them to remember you, and what values are important you that you hope they carry forward. Some look at it as a way to pass on family stories. You might do an audio or possibly a video ethical will. Many people have kept journals. These are some items we need to treasure. Many of us aren't journal-keepers as our parents may have been, but the storytelling and getting our stories on paper or on audio are really important because these are the stories that are passed down—it's our heritage. People don't want to be remembered just for the job they had or the Christmas presents they received and gave. They want to be remembered for special things they did or important things they did with their grandchildren. Leaving that kind of emotional legacy is very, very important. I think we really need to be careful to not discount that and just look at a legacy as financial.

Wright

Well, what an interesting topic, and an interesting conversation. I really appreciate all the time you've taken to talk with me today.

You said there were seventy-six million Baby Boomers in the United States today?

Kirmmse Toth

Yes, that seems to be the general consensus. That's a lot folks!

Wright

It's got so many implications, both financial, political—almost everything. Is most of the money spent in this country by those seventy-six million?

Kirmmse Toth

I think that for the most part we're a pretty affluent generation. I know that one of the concerns big companies have is Brain Drain. "Brain Drain" is the term often used for people who retire and leave the workforce. There are thousands and thousands of Baby Boomers who are retiring so what do companies need to do to keep these them there? There's a term called "phased retirement." People leave their jobs over a period of time. It avoids people being there one day, sixty hours a week, and the next day they're gone. I think it would work beautifully for companies and corporations and for the employees to have that happen in a slower fashion. It might be another example of re-crafting your career—doing the things you do best that are fun for you, but that your company also needs from you.

Wright

You mean as a phased retirement, working from forty hours and then dropping down to thirty, then twenty, and then ten. Is it something like that?

Kirmmse Toth

It might look something like that. It would be something you would negotiate with your company—a schedule that would work for both of you. There is a lot of concern about all of us walking away and leaving Gen Y and Gen X to pick up the pieces. So, that is where the term "Brain Drain" comes in. I think that companies, big and small, may really want to take a look at that if they haven't already. It's going to be a real issue to be dealt with.

Wright

Well this was very, very interesting. I really do appreciate your time, and I think this is going to be great information for our readers.

Kirmmse Toth

Well, thank you, David, I appreciate it.

Wright

Today we've been talking with Kim Kirmmse Toth. She is a licensed clinical social worker and certified life coach. Kim is a strengths-based coach who helps her clients create a blueprint for their future. Her biggest emphasis is that we need to take the time to plan this time of our lives and not expect it to fall into place by itself. Kim offers programs to support you along this road less traveled.

Kim, thank you so much for being with us today on *Discover Your Inner Strength*.

Kirmmse Toth

Thank you, David. You're most welcome.

About the Author

Kim Kirmmse Toth has an expertise in empowering women to tap into their strengths throughout their lives. She encourages continual growth with a non stop optimism in helping women reach even the loftiest of goals. She works primarily with Baby Boomer women 55-70, on the non-financial side of retirement planning. The "what are you going to do with the rest of your life?" piece. This is also a stage of life that is full of transitions, which can be challenging as well as exciting.

She has over 23 years experience as a licensed clinical social worker in private practice and is a Certified Life Coach. She is an author, trainer, live group and Teleclass leader.

Kim is an International Trainer with Mentor Coach. Kim is a member of the International Coach Federation, the Denver Coach Federation and NASW.

Kim is privileged and honored to work with women who choose to live their lives as growing, compassionate women, who balance themselves well and love who they are.

Kim Kirmmse Toth

Positive Aging, Inc.
Littleton, CO
720.922.1201
kim@positiveaginginc.com
www.positiveaginginc.com
www.redhotretirement.com

Chapter Sixteen

Who Gets Your Best?

An Interview With…

JoAn Majors

David Wright (Wright)

Today we're talking with JoAn Majors who is often described as a team member who has temporarily left the office. She is a professional speaker and author whose highly sought-after presentations are known for their authenticity, humor, and level of engagement. JoAn's area of specialty is working with teams from traditional industries like banking, real estate, healthcare, education, and her favorite, dentistry, to help individual team members recognize their value to the final product or service of any company, no matter the size. Two-time business founder and author of the *Open the Door Series,* JoAn is a team leader who not only knows how to motivate others but moves her audiences to action as well. Her unique storytelling style of teaching allows her to create a meaningful connection to the teams with whom she works.

JoAn, welcome to *Discovering Your Inner Strength.*

JoAn Majors (Majors)

Hello and thank you, David, for having me.

Wright

As a member of the National Speakers Association, you have had the opportunity to see many of these collaborative book projects over the years, yet you have never chosen to be involved in one. Why is this project different?

Majors

You know, David, that's a great question. When I saw the title, *Discovering Your Inner Strength,* it immediately resonated with the things that I share with audiences. We all have talents and strengths within us that are unique to us as individuals. What often happens when we get in touch with the core of our inner being is that life, love, and labor become a lot more fun. For one thing, that inner strength helps us connect with and develop our own natural talents. And secondly, the talents that we have to work at to make our own, the ones coaches, trainings and books help us improve upon become so much easier to learn. What I speak about when I am at the podium is helping team members understand what their inner strength is and to use that to create change for others.

Wright

It is obviously very important to you to encourage others to discover their inner strength. Who are the people who have served as your role models for discovering and drawing on their inner strength?

Majors

I have to give credit to two great parents. Very early on, I discovered what most people wouldn't want to discover about inner strength! I had a wonderful mother who had a stroke at the age of twenty-nine. She also had small children and was divorced (she had been in an abusive marriage). She married my father, had a stroke, and was told that she would never walk, talk, write, or ever speak again. It was devastating to my family.

My mother was one of those people who just never gave up. I was able to learn this from the people who knew her because I had not been born at that time. She never quit. She had an inner strength that just radiated outward in all directions when someone told her that she couldn't do something.

Through all that, she battled cancer twice in her life and came back. Even though she was told that she would never walk, talk, or write again, she had another child. My husband would tell you that this child is very challenging, because that child is me. Fortunately, I was not physically challenged as the doctors thought I would be. My mom always believed that she could, so she did. She was raised on little else than inner strength, having quit school as a very young girl to raise her family. I was the youngest of seven children. It was amazing to watch her get by on her inner strength, not intellect. Her inner strength guided her at all times. The same was true for my father.

Wright

Would you tell our readers how you might teach them to discover their inner strength?

Majors

Again, I'll go back to a core principle: I believe that you work to develop your talents, both the ones that come naturally and are God given, and the ones we go to school to learn. We have to dedicate some time to reflect on the things that we do naturally that make us feel better about ourselves and that cause others to feel better about themselves when they are around us.

My mother was certainly someone who drew people toward her; they always felt better about themselves when they were around her. Let me put this in context. This was a woman who spoke Spanish, had a stroke, and had to learn to speak again.

When she finally did regain her speech, she spoke in very broken English with a limited vocabulary. But I never met anyone who didn't clearly understand what she was about because she was such a natural empathizer. Years later, I learned that 93 percent of all communication is nonverbal; but in my mother, I watched a master at communicating her unbelievable inner strength. We all have that buried within us, but being around her brought it to the surface for me.

Wright

Clearly, you are a storyteller as evident in your seminars and books. Why do you feel that storytelling is such an integral part of a successful presentation?

Majors

If someone offered me the chance to lead a workshop or present a seminar but without telling any stories, I wouldn't board the plane, David. The material that I teach *comes alive* when I share with audiences the smart and inspiring things that teams I train with have done. The examples that I draw upon illustrate to teams that they too can feel confident to learn these valuable new skills. It's in the application of principles that are tried and true that teams come to own these principles for themselves.

As professional speakers, whether it's five people in a small business roundtable or crowds of thousands in the rafters, we have a responsibility to mean what we say and live what we teach. Sharing stories keeps the learning experience human, which makes the teaching more credible to my audience.

My greatest mentors—people I have learned from in this industry and others—are all people who share their stories of success. The ones I have really learned from are the ones who also share their stories of failure. It is not the amount of failures we have that matters, it's how we turn the no of failure into the yes of success that people yearn to know. And that's a very humble and very human tale to tell.

There is a tendency in some of us to put inspiring speakers on a pedestal. However, storytelling allows my audience to recognize me as one of them—I live where they live, in the trenches and not in some ivory tower. I often joke with my audiences, "Whatever you do, please don't call me a consultant!" It has been my unfortunate experience with many consultants I have worked with in business, that they shared with me what I ought to do but they weren't necessarily doing it themselves. It's better to walk the talk and storytelling, as long as it is my own story and is authentic to me, is one of the greatest ways that I can share a truth.

Wright

A wise man once told me that the definition of a champion is someone who gets up one more time than he or she gets knocked down. You prefer to be called an action-oriented speaker rather than a motivational speaker. Would you tell our readers why and what is the difference between the two?

Majors

Most speakers have to motivate an audience—to find something that stirs an emotion in them. For myself, when I'm sitting in seminars or learning from mentors, the issue that I continuously confront is that I really want what I teach to make a difference. I don't mean just when I'm at the podium—I mean after I'm dead and gone. That desire has helped me drop the ego thing and recognize that my presentation is really not about me; it's all about the audience and what new tools they will return home and put in their toolbox. Because my success is really about my audience's success with the material, I wonder what happens to them on Monday, their first day back after the seminar. What's going to be different for that person with his or her team as well as the person's family?

There is a quote by Frank Teboat that I love, "We should be taught not to wait for inspiration to start a thing. Action always generates inspiration. Inspiration seldom generates action." One of the things I do in a training seminar or lecture is to set up systems that are action-oriented. I want the audience to make a difference afterward. It's not just a "feel good" thing. I want them to take that difference home and make a difference where they live and work. I want people feeling better after our time together. After all, they are the ones who must take action.

Wright

You've been described as a team member who has temporarily left the office. What, in your opinion, is the significance of being considered a team member?

Majors

In one word, *credibility*. I have worked with many teams in dentistry and in other industries. They go to a seminar, lecture, or workshop where someone tells them all these great things to do and shares with them how they can do something differently. For such a speaker to be most effective, however, it is imperative that he or she knows what every member of the team is going through, and the only way to know is to have been there and done that.

Although I am a business owner, the fact is that I was raised with a team mentality. Because I've been a team member in so many different capacities, I recognize that teamwork is the process that creates the final product. Take dentistry, for example. The final product—that beautiful smile the patient walks away with—changes his or her life for the better. It's contagious. The doctor and team know and are proud; they feel really great when their patient smiles. But how was that final product achieved? My goal is to demonstrate that teamwork is our greatest strength.

It's all connected, from the team members in that dental practice to the lab that created the porcelain and the manufacturer that came up with the product that built the porcelain, and so it goes all the way back. So many times, the long chain of people involved in the process do not get to see or share in the end result.

I love this quote, "There is no limit to what success we can achieve when it doesn't matter who gets the credit"—Laing Burns, Jr. I live by that. So my job description includes doing a lot of research on a team before I do a program with them because I need to understand the dynamics of how this team best works together. This way, my recommendations are not coming from "on high" but are more eye-to-eye. I find this helps team members to do Job Number One: learn how to manage their own morale on the job. A work environment free of gossip, personal pettiness, and excuses is an ideal way to discover the amazing results we can produce when we work as a team.

Wright

You often share with businesses—both small and large—the importance of taking the negative and reframing it or repositioning it. Would you explain what you mean by this and why it is so important?

Majors

I'm happy to do that. Let's call a negative thought "the elephant in the room." If I'm working in dentistry, the elephant in the room might be that I am married to a doctor. Team members may wonder any number of things: how did she get here? Does she really know anything about dentistry? Did she marry her husband by first working for him? Many possible distractions go through their heads that cause them not to be able to pay full attention. So I hunt out the elephants and reframe them up front.

My mentors told me early on in my career to take what the audience is thinking about and bring it up before anybody else does. Now I am free to change that possible minus into a definite plus. If I wait until the audience brings it up, I have to defend being the wife of the doctor. In my last book, there's a chapter called "Information or Excuse: Everything Falls into One or the Other Category." If you tell me before anything actually goes wrong, we call it information; if you tell me after, we call it an excuse.

Let me illustrate the value of addressing the elephant in the room. Several years ago a *Reader's Digest* article came out that basically said in no uncertain terms, "Buyer, beware: all dentists are crooks." It was an interesting phenomenon because I worked with many of my dentistry clients who took that particular issue of the magazine out of their waiting area so patients would not be exposed to that negative connotation. Well, we didn't do that. In fact, we did quite the opposite. As a matter of fact, we made many copies of the article—one for every patient. On the copy, we put a section saying, "Please sign your name to the bottom of the article so we know that you have read it. We feel it is so important for you to know what is out there and how bad it can be to better recognize the care you get when you come to our practice." It was just a pro-active response, but my husband's short report to his patients, *Ten Ways to Choose a Great Dentist*, ended up reprinted in the *San Antonio Express News*. He was then invited to appear on television in a morning news show. Inside the perceived adversity, we had managed to find the real opportunity to raise the town's dental IQ.

Wright

In articles that you have written and in your seminars, you encourage companies to consider transformation, not change, for long-term measurable success. What is the difference?

Majors

That's an excellent question and it goes right to the heart of the matter. Change happens when one is told something new, but transformation happens when the entire team acts on implementing the new. So many times leaders of businesses call me and say, "My staff is not up to par and our profits are down. We want you to come in and motivate our staff." In other words, by the time that I hear about it, the finger is already pointed! Sometimes I'm told, "I'll send some of my key team members over to hear you. If they feel that your input is good, then they will have you in." But I wonder what does the term "key team members" mean? Are those the ones with executive washroom keys? Are those the only ones management wants to keep or cares to invest in? I have never really understood making that distinction.

For most groups or organizations, change happens from the outside in. The key team members say, "Okay, this is how we are going to do things differently now that we heard such great things at this seminar." But the team members who were not invited to the seminar are often lost, confused, uncertain, and afraid. They often feel left out and expendable. So I recommend to management that they bring their entire team to my presentation. If long-term success is the goal, then everybody must play an important role in making that happen. You might say that by bringing the entire team together management is making their commitment clear. By including everyone, change begins to happen from the inside out, not because of a seminar but because the team collectively looks toward improving their performance. When that happens, transformation is truly possible. This way, when new ideas are shared, the team leader can ask, "Who would like to be accountable for that implementation? Let's get a plan." There is clearly a difference in the success quotients.

Wright

Obviously, action plays an important role in your programs. In the programs themselves, you stress how important it is to anchor a moment in the seminar to the story that the action is shared. One particular anchor that caught my attention was the yellow note card that simply asks, "Who gets your best?" Will you share with our readers the importance of this question and how it works as an anchor?

Majors

Yes, I am happy to, David. We live in a society where there are often two income earners in a household. The bottom line says that we need to give our best at work. Faith and family sometimes are not the first priority.

Let me illustrate with a story. Several years ago, I had gone away to lead a program. I had hoped to return on Friday night because I have a small son and three grown daughters. But my husband said, "Why don't you stay until Saturday because if you come back sooner you will invariably need the rest of the weekend to decompress, to make notes, and enjoy some alone time." Not only was this true, but I thought about how I preach to my audiences to give their best to their clients, whoever they may be. So I came up with a yellow note card that just simply says, "Who gets your best?"

I shared it with my audience that evening and asked them to put that yellow card on their steering wheel, their labs, in the lounge, and at different places in their own homes as a reminder that the people you are with *in that moment* are the people who get your best. We hear people all the time say, "I gave 110 percent at the office!" That means that the people we go home to only get what is left over. This goes back to a quote from Nido Quebein, "We don't teach values; we model values." So I often ask myself, what values am I actually modeling? So now I use note cards to remind my audiences of things to ask themselves regularly.

Even when you are on top of your game, life is not always easy. Different things happen every day. People of all ages get sick, some pass away or are never the same again, families split up in divorce, and people lose their homes, jobs, and pensions. A lot of things happen that are not predictable or pleasant. So in my presentations I often quote my mother, "If we could greet each person each day as if it were the first time we ever met but knew it could be the last, wouldn't we act differently?" I think that at some point we have to hold ourselves accountable for our own actions. I always go back to one of my favorite books, the one that says, "Love your enemies..."—Matthew 22:39. If we could just learn to love our neighbors, we would be on our way.

Wright

You often talk about reading and developing a quest for learning. I recently saw a bookmark that you give out at your seminars. On it is a quote from you: "Success is often about making the money. Significance is always about making the difference." Will you tell me what that means?

Majors

There is a great periodical called *Success Magazine*. I read every issue cover to cover and recommend it for many of my clients. We are in such a success-driven society. Search the Internet for book titles with the word "success" in them. It's an amazing number! We have success on the brain.

In fact, let me tell you a story to illustrate my point. I had gone to a mentor a couple of years ago and said, "After I do these seminars, I get these great evaluations but something is missing." She simply said, "You've been successful and you've proven it, but are you ready to become significant? Now is when you are ready to truly make a difference, but you've got to choose between being a success and being significant."

Many of us in business enjoy success. At every seminar I ask my audience, "How many of you feel that you have had some level of success in the business you are in?" Everybody raises his or her hand. But far fewer hands go up when I ask, "How many of you have actually enjoyed some level of significance?" In other words, when it wasn't about your success anymore—when it was all it about the other person—did you make a significant difference? It's a huge wake-up call for many to see that the money is a byproduct and that it's not the only thing driving us to work in the morning. Let's call it significant service.

My dad often reminded me, "If the intent is right, the reward will come." In today's world, with its struggling economy, it is crucial to remember that if our intent is right and we get back to serving others we can be significant and make a difference in their lives.

Success says, "Here I am! Do you know who I am?" Significance says, "There you are. I am so glad that you are here. I couldn't do what I do if it weren't for you." That's why I like to be out in the audience meeting the group before I speak. Then they are always surprised to see me at the front of the room, leading the charge. We have to go be significant, not just successful.

Wright

Your private speaking practice, JoAn Speaks, offers what you call "immersion events." What is an immersion event?

Majors

For the businesses with whom I work, I do some standard straightforward programs that create change and action and new thought processes. Several years ago, someone said to me, "We do a yearly planning meeting and we want you to join us. We want your energy and enthusiasm but moreover we want your thought process. We want to be with you for a few days to see if you ever turn off." The guy laughed when I said, "Well, I'm not called *the chihuahua on caffeine* for nothing." So I began to spend greater amounts of time with teams. One thing I already knew was that team members who are primarily women have an awful lot on their plate when they go home. A great advantage for the team is to be able to get away to a hotel or a resort and spend two and a half days having fun while learning new skills. It is an immersion event in which the team is truly immersed in the material. No one need leave or shop for the milk or stop by the cleaners or drive anyone to cheerleading practice. It's just quite different.

Wright

That's fascinating. Well, JoAn, I really do appreciate all this time you've taken with me this morning to answer these questions. I have learned a lot and it has just been pleasure learning from you. I am sure that our readers are going to feel the same way.

Majors

Well, thank you. It has been great to be with you.

Wright

Today we have been talking with JoAn Majors, a member of the National Speakers Association and the International Federation for Professional Speakers. JoAn delivers to her audience a contagious enthusiasm, as we have found today. She is grounded in practical applications and marketing savvy. She can be reached at www.joanmajors.com, a private practice dedicated to custom presentations, seminars, keynotes, and immersion events. In addition, she is one of the most respected trainers in the dental industry and the founder of Dentistry by Choice, a dental training LLC, and the author of the *Open the Door Series*. Happily married to a practicing dentist, JoAn and her family reside in Texas.

JoAn, thank you so much for being with us today on *Discovering Your Inner Strength*.

Majors

Thank you and have a fantastic day!

About the Author

JoAn Majors is often described as a team member who has temporarily left the office. She is a professional speaker and author whose highly sought-after presentations are known for their authenticity, humor, and level of engagement. JoAn's area of specialty is working with teams from traditional industries like banking, Real Estate, healthcare, education, and her favorite, dentistry, to help individual team members recognize their value to the final product or service of any company, no matter the size. Two-time business founder and author of the *Open the Door Series*, JoAn is a team leader who not only knows how to motivate others but moves her audiences to action as well. Her unique storytelling style of teaching allows her to create a meaningful connection to the teams with whom she works.

JoAn Majors

Dentistry by Choice, LLC
www.JoAnMajors.com
www.DentistryByChoice.com
866-51-CHOICE
P.O. Box 880
Caldwell, TX 77836

Chapter Seventeen

Recognizing Your Rainbows

*"Life's not about waiting for the storms to pass...
It's about learning to dance in the rain."*—Vivian Greene

An Interview With...

Karen Phillips

David Wright (Wright)

Today we're talking with Karen Phillips, a motivation and leadership coach, author, and speaker. I had the opportunity to meet Karen at a conference and hear her speak and I'm pleased to say that she possesses a dynamic personality and displays a professional presence. She has nearly thirty years experience in the area of education. As a classroom teacher, she has taught in the fields of health, physical education, and reading. She retired as a school building administrator after sixteen years of leadership. She has had the opportunity to lead and learn from individuals with diverse backgrounds, beliefs, and motivations. Her creative aspect allowed her to start a small business, which, after three years, she sold, but the business continues to date. In her retirement phase, she accepted a job in the business world and became senior vice president of an established company. This experience afforded her greater vision and clarity, solidifying the concept that great leaders are needed in all walks of life.

As an amazing tribute, Karen leads a positive and blessed life as a Professional Certified Life Coach in her own Christian business called Empowered Potential. What strikes me most about Karen is that she serves as an inspiration to those who face adversity, because she has lived with the everyday challenges of Multiple Sclerosis (MS) for more than twenty-six years.

Karen, welcome to *Discover Your Inner Strength.*

Karen Phillips (Phillips)

Thank you, David. It's nice to be with you today.

Wright

So you have a disease about which very little is known. That in itself is a little scary. No pun intended (knowing that you are from Las Vegas), do you feel that you've been "dealt a bad hand?"

Phillips

When we talk about being "dealt a bad hand," I just think of statistics regarding the health of Americans today. A study by Chronic Health in America has projected that by the year 2020, one hundred and fifty-seven million people in America will have one or more severe health issues such as diabetes, heart disease, asthma, etc. Can you imagine what the percentage would be if we added obesity into that picture? When reading those numbers, a profound statement my parents said to me during an early hospital stay rings true. They told me, *"Everyone has their own cross to bear; this one just happens to be yours."* So I've never really viewed myself or my condition as unique, in fact, I feel blessed.

To go back to your question, David, as far as being "dealt a bad hand," I like to remember the words of John Wooden and Steve Jameson, *"Things turn out best for those who make the best of the way things turn out."*

Wright

It's interesting that you feel you've not been "dealt a bad hand" and that you feel blessed to have MS. For those of our readers who may not know what MS is, would you mind giving us a brief explanation?

Phillips

Wow, to give a *brief* explanation is difficult, but I'll sure try. MS stands for Multiple Sclerosis, which is an autoimmune disease. It is where the body's own defense systems attack the myelin, which is the fatty substance protecting the nerve fibers in the central nervous system. Those nerve fibers themselves can also become damaged, and the damaged myelin forms scar tissue called sclerosis, which gives the disease its name.

Did you know MS affects more than four hundred thousand people in North America? It usually affects more women than men; approximately two hundred new cases of MS are diagnosed every week. Worldwide, MS affects about two and a half million people.

Another unique characteristic of MS is it usually starts between the ages of twenty and forty; however, we're starting to see more young children with positive diagnoses of MS. I believe that's due to more doctors becoming educated to the signs and symptoms of the disease in addition to the advances in medical testing and technology.

Wright

Now that describes whom it affects, but what does MS actually do?

Phillips

MS affects the Central Nervous System (CNS), which is made up of the brain and spinal cord. It's like a computer that keeps us in touch with the world or like a train that runs on a track. If part of the track is damaged, the train gets derailed.

When any parts of the myelin sheath or nerve fibers are damaged, nerve impulses traveling to and from the brain and spinal cord are distorted or interrupted, producing a wide variety of symptoms.

The CNS picks up signals from the outside world through our senses: sight, sound, smell, taste, and touch. It coordinates all our conscious and unconscious activities such as moving, talking, thinking, remembering, and our reflex actions that happen without our thinking about them.

Wright

So how can MS affect people?

Phillips

That's a really great question David, but it's a broad one because the symptoms vary from person to person. MS is truly a very strange disease. I guess I'd call it a rebel without a cause. This disease has an unknown origin, which makes it difficult for researchers to find a cure, thus doctors can only *try* to manage patients' symptoms.

The symptoms vary in all individuals, from changes in sensations with numbness and tingling, to extreme muscle weakness, vision problems, difficulty in controlling the bowel or bladder, or sexual problems. Others may have difficulty with balance and coordination; they may be extremely tired, they might have problems with speech and swallowing, mood changes, and possibly cognitive problems such as memory and even speed of thinking. MS can bring a wide, wide path of destruction.

Wright

I never really knew the extent of the damage MS could do. What were your initial thoughts when you were diagnosed?

Phillips

Of course, I was very frightened because I didn't know what was wrong with me. When I was in the hospital and going through testing, initially my doctors told me that I could have diabetes, a tumor on my spine, a brain tumor, or MS. By the next morning, they had ruled out diabetes. Not knowing what I should ask the doctor, I pulled from my knowledge base the only information I had. My comment to the doctor was a question I had heard patients ask their doctors many times on the television soap opera *Days of Our Lives.* "If it's a brain tumor, is it operable?" My question seemed appropriate, but the doctor's answer really terrified me. He said, "It depends on where it's located!"

His comment forced me to face the reality and seriousness of my situation—I was only twenty-six years old, married with two children (ages three and five) and I was working full-time as a physical educator. This just couldn't be happening to me!

Since this diagnosis took place years ago, results were not readily available—patients had to wait. In my case, the neurologist called me at home and told me the results over the phone. At the time, the results still didn't really have a whole lot of meaning for me—they were just words that he was speaking.

Wright

I don't know that I understand why the results wouldn't have had meaning for you.

Phillips

Well to me, I still had a life to lead with kids to raise and a husband to enjoy. What the doctor had said to me were just words. He told me that he'd send me a disability note and that I should stop working. I must admit, the thought of being a stay-at-home-mom sounded great, but I knew it wouldn't work for our family. I agreed that I probably needed to rest and that I would take the remainder of the week off. I would relax over the weekend, but Monday I planned on going back to work.

I tried to think of follow-up questions for the doctor while we were on the phone together. The best I could come up with after hearing I had this disease that I knew absolutely nothing about, was a very simple question, "When should I come and see you again?"

Great question, or so I thought! I asked a simple question and I got a simple answer. He said, "Well, when you're blind or paralyzed." Now, that answer stopped me in my tracks. There was no way I would accept that answer. I did ask the doctor why he would make such a bold statement. He politely told me that from the reading of the MRI, I had lesions on both my brain and spine and blindness and paralysis would be the result. He also said he had no idea as to when.

Wow! Blind or paralyzed! So I politely told him that I heard what he was saying but he shouldn't plan on seeing me in his office anytime soon. I prayed a lot, changed my diet, rested more often, and was more grateful for what I did have. I didn't go back to that doctor for many years. I have been very, very fortunate and blessed.

Wright

Strength to endure life's shortcomings takes special handling. How are you handling your disability?

Phillips

Each and every one of us handles problems in different ways. I believe I'm doing quite well, but I've never really done it alone. I am extremely fortunate because I do have family and friends who are supportive of me. Most importantly, I believe that God is with me on this long journey. In general, I try to maintain a positive attitude about life.

Wright

When most people receive a diagnosis that's not favorable, they go through a grieving process. Did you experience anything like that?

Phillips

That's a really good question. In looking back at that time, I'd now have to say that I did go though my own grieving process—I'm no different from anyone else. Although I didn't curl up and die when the neurologist said that I'd be blind and/or paralyzed, those words always remained on my mind. I always remembered what he had said, but I didn't let it stop me from going forward with my life.

Wright

How did you combat your grief? What did you do?

Phillips

As a family, we loved taking our kids on various outings such as boating, hiking, and camping. It felt great to show them how absolutely gorgeous things were right in and around where we lived. Everything looked so beautiful that I never wanted to forget what it all looked like and the good times that we had. So I bought a nice camera to capture all the memories.

My goal was to create visual memories so I would always have them. This was not a cheap new hobby. By the time I bought interchangeable lenses, various filters, and film processing, my simple desire turned into a major expense. My father was a professional photographer, so growing up with photographs around the house felt like a normal process. I never realized how expensive my new hobby truly was.

Finally, after a Sunday dinner, when my family was sitting around the dining room table, an amazing thought entered my mind. I looked at everyone and I said, "Why are you guys letting me spend all of this money, taking all of these photographs? Did anybody think of what the doctor told me—that one day I was going to be blind or paralyzed?"

Here I was taking pictures so I could look back and reminisce of the places we'd gone with the kids and it just hit me—if I were blind, I wouldn't be able to see the pictures anyway. They just laughed and said they had thought of that a long time ago. So I suppose that was my first realization of my non-acceptance of my diagnosis. Honestly, it did make everyone chuckle, even me!

I think the next crazy thing I did in my grieving process was to prove to myself and others that I really could enjoy life and be free. This disease was not going to kill me. I would say that to friends. They would laugh and tell me, "You want to feel free? Great! Get a Harley [Davidson]." Since I'm only five feet tall and we lived on a budget, a Harley Davidson wasn't in my plans or pocketbook, but a moped was. I convinced my husband of the benefits of owning a moped and promised to ride it to work daily. Remember, I was a physical educator, so riding it to and from work would be feasible. I could wear shorts or something comfortable and I wouldn't need to take a change of clothes. I could park that darn thing in the locker room and I promised to wear a helmet. So with arguments like that, who could resist? We found the perfect moped—white with royal blue accents.

After about four weeks, I was driving home from work and I had my second epiphany. "I'm not going to die from MS—I'm going to die if I keep driving this moped on the streets of Las Vegas!" I came home and told my husband about the crazy drivers on the road. Needless to say, we sold the moped.

So whether my grieving involved taking pictures that I might not be able to view in the future or driving a moped on the streets of Las Vegas, I appreciate that my loved ones let me do what I thought I needed to do at the time and just supported me; but they were always ready to catch me if I fell.

Wright

I'm sure you've heard about the "why me syndrome." Did you ever wonder why you were diagnosed with MS, versus those who were not?

Phillips

Yes, initially I think I did. I remember briefly praying to God and saying, "God, I accept this disease of MS that you've given me, but please let me live long enough to help my husband raise our children. And P.S., could you please not give me cancer?" As soon as I said that, I immediately prayed again asking for forgiveness. I realized that He doesn't make any deals and that He already had a plan for my entire life. This was part of the plan—my life plan from God and I just needed to view it as a gift and unwrap it. So the why-me question turned into a why-not me question.

Wright

When you were a classroom teacher and administrator, did your students or teachers know about your battle with MS?

Phillips

Some did, some didn't. It was more on a need-to-know basis. Early on, I think that some people knew I had the disease even before I knew I had it. Believe it or not, I'm pretty certain an eighth grade student of mine in physical education was the first person to recognize I had the disease. Unbeknownst to me, her father had MS. He was wheelchair bound, and she was quite knowledgeable about what happens to one's body and how situations could aggravate or alleviate symptoms.

One day I was teaching volleyball outside. In Las Vegas, the black asphalt can get so hot that you can fry an egg on it. Needless to say, I often felt dehydrated, sweaty, and totally drained. This student, whose name is Tina, came out to class with a cloth bandana she had rolled up. It was soaking wet. She just threw it around the back of my neck and tied it on me. She was laughing and so were the rest of the students.

At first, I couldn't figure out what was going on. Then Tina quickly said with a polite smile, "Hey, I thought I would put that around your neck to keep you cool." She passed it off as being a joke just because it was so hot outside and she was making a nice gesture. After I was diagnosed with MS, I realized that heat exposure is one of the triggers that people with MS could have. I didn't know that, but Tina did.

Another day, she had talked to the other teacher in my office and got my teacher's chair (the one with wheels) and she actually rolled that chair outside to class. I said, "What are you doing with my chair?" She said, "Well it's so hot out here! I don't see how you can stay out here for six hours a day. So after you do roll call and we do everything we need to do to start class, and once you get our games started, how about if you just take a seat and watch us? You can get up when you need to; but man, I don't even know how you can have any energy by the end of the day." So to me little Tina was wise beyond her years.

Then there was the time around Easter when Tina ran into the locker room in between classes and dropped off a flyer from the local mall. The mall was going to hold a benefit event doing photographs with the Easter Bunny. Tina said, "Hey, why don't you stop by and bring your kids over and have their photos taken? Ya know, kinda like with Santa but with the Easter Bunny. I'm working there. I'm a volunteer for the MS Society." I politely accepted the invitation and made my way to the mall that weekend.

That was the true starting point for Tina to indirectly talk with me about the disease I would be living with for the rest of my life. She began talking about her family and what life was like living with her father and his MS. She told me of all the positive things they did together, even how they did the labeling on the MS newsletters that were mailed to the Society's database. She would hand-deliver a monthly newsletter to me, give me a hug, wish me a good day, and go on about her way.

Tina was my teacher. She taught me not to be afraid and how important it is to give to others. For someone that young to be placed in my life was a true blessing. The diagnosis of MS is a very long road and still is my journey in life. Tina educated me about the disease—she educated me about life.

Wright

You're right! Tina was quite remarkable student. Are there any other stories like that that you would like to share with us?

Phillips

When teachers have concerns about students, they generally send them to the counselor's office. Counselors achieve amazing results. On the rare occasion when counselors can't really get through to a student or need another perspective, they may keep moving up the ladder for help, and heaven knows that I was the top of our ladder.

There was a high school student named Brittany who quit doing her class work. Her teachers were frustrated and her counselor was at a loss. The girl would not tell anyone what was going on, so they sent her to me. Let's be real—being sent to the principal was never the place anyone went "just to chat." Think about it, what student is sent to the principal's office and feels that he or she wants to sit down and shoot-the-breeze?

I welcomed her to my office and prefaced our meeting by telling her she didn't need to talk to me if she didn't want to. I offered her some water and crackers and asked if she'd mind if I continued with my work, but I was here to listen to her if she wanted to talk. She accepted my ground rules. She then slowly started asking me questions about my job, things on the wall, and photos of my family on a shelf.

Suddenly she shouted out, "You just wouldn't understand!" I told her to try me, and she did. She started to cry and said, "My mom is dying!" With that, I silently thought she was absolutely right. I would never be able to fully understand her feelings—I was lucky because I still have my mother, although my dad had passed away. So maybe there was little connection there.

I listened and when the time felt right, I asked what was wrong with her mother. She kept her head down and told me her mother had Multiple Sclerosis. Chills went up and down my spine. I looked at her as if she could have been one of my own kids reacting to my diagnosis. I asked her if she knew anyone with MS and she shrugged her shoulders and shook her head no. I assured her that she did—she knew me.

After sharing my story with Brittany, her head lifted up and her tears slowly stopped. She came around the desk and gave me a great big hug. She cried again saying, "It's possible then that my mom may be okay!" We sat and talked and I answered her questions about MS that she had been too afraid to ask her parents.

Brittany got her schoolwork back on track—and her life too! She realized that just because there were changes that might make her life situation unlike others, it was her attitude that would make her strong and make the whole difference.

A warm feeling came from Brittany's hug, along with the knowledge of why I might have this disease of Multiple Sclerosis. I didn't know I was going to help Brittany simply with my common story or even that our paths would cross, but they did. I'm so fortunate that they did because Brittany, just like Tina, taught me things about myself and life that I could not have learned anywhere else.

My last story is similar to Brittany's but involves a frustrated father with his daughter. She had never missed school without an excuse and now she was in trouble for truancies and her academic grades were falling.

At our parent conference, I started painting a picture for the father about his daughter's failure to attend her classes, her tardiness, and her lack of responsibility concerning her schoolwork. The father agreed, immediately assuming all the responsibility for his daughter's failing school performance. "We're having family problems," he said. Needless to say, that was not the typical conversation I would have with parents in a first meeting.

I told him that I truly appreciated his honesty with me and I would be happy to work with him to help his daughter through these troubling times. He proceeded to tell me they had just found out that his wife had MS and they decided not to tell their daughter. He confessed that neither he nor his wife knew that much about the disease, but he felt that his daughter may have overheard them talking and crying about the situation. He felt her truancies and not turning in classwork and homework were all a direct result of the tension, anxiety, and uncertainty in the house.

Once again, I told my story about having MS and I was glad I had Kleenex in my office for the father and me to share. Together, I helped him make his first call to the local Multiple Sclerosis chapter. He was able to get enough information about the disease and how to discuss it with their daughter, that he was very comfortable when he left my office. The best part was that their daughter was able to pull everything together, to cope with Mom's new way of life, to adjust to changes in her family's routines, and get caught up in all her classes. It was great! She ended up graduating with honors.

Memories like these have become part of my uniqueness. Maybe that's part of the reason why I have MS. Maybe that's what makes me different from others.

Wright

You amaze me that after twenty-six years with this disease you can still be so positive. That's great! So what makes you different from others who have this disease?

Phillips

That's really hard to say. I don't see myself as truly different from others, just that my attitude and the respect that I have for the disease may be slightly unique. For example, I look for the positive in everything. I'm optimistic and upbeat. I feel blessed that I have MS because of the people I've met, the knowledge I've gained, others I have helped, and for my spiritual growth.

Wright

I agree with you that a positive attitude is one thing, but is there anything else that makes a difference for you?

Phillips

I try to maintain a sense of humor, that's for sure. I usually try to find humor in different situations and I laugh at myself all the time. I think humor and laughter are the best medicines that anybody can have.

For example, just recently my MS has advanced from relapsing-remitting into the secondary progressive stage. Now I'm not walking with great coordination and balance, so I have to use a cane. I was the type of person who had high heels that matched everything and now I have to wear flat shoes. That was okay because I got to buy new shoes, even if they were flats. But I wanted to have some class, so I told my husband and doctors, "Just as a woman can never have too many shoes, a woman in need of a cane can never have too many canes." I also decided that since the canes were a big part of me, they were going to take on a personality of their own. They should all be named.

I have a clear cane that's made of Lucite and her name is Lucy. She has a brother—a blue cane—and his name is Blake. They have a sister—a bronzy colored cane—and her name is Amber. Having different canes makes it easy—when my husband asks me which cane I'm taking with me, I just call them by name. It sounds so therapeutic if you say, "Which cane do you want?" But if I'm asked, "Who are you taking out with you today?" it makes every outing feel a little more personal and special for me.

Recently, my mother and I went to the grocery store and I had Lucy with us resting in the shopping basket while we looked around. We had yet to put any items in our basket and the store was quite crowded. When we turned around, our basket was gone. Someone had mistakenly used our basket as his or hers. Immediately I said, "Mom, where's Lucy?"

People shopping around us heard my panic. Now *we* knew Lucy was my cane, but people were thinking Lucy was a small child. They started coming up to me saying, "What's Lucy's description? How old is she? Don't worry, we'll find Lucy."

At that point, I didn't quite know how to explain the situation to the concerned shoppers that Lucy was the personal name I had given my cane. About that same time, a lady came down the aisle toward us with Lucy silently hiding along the inside of her basket. Lucy was found—the amber alert was off.

I just think that we have to maintain a sense of humor. We need to look at turning our misfortune into a victory and taking our pain and turning it into purpose.

Wright

How hard do you think it would be for others to implement what you do in your life and your way of thinking?

Phillips

It's not that difficult at all, but it would depend on how committed that person is. There are a few simple principles that everyone could practice to live a healthier and happier life. First, we need to put others before ourselves, live right, eat healthier, and exercise to our own abilities. Can you imagine what our society would look like if we followed these basic principles?

Wright

Absolutely. We'd all look great, feel wonderful, and be much healthier. But how do you take your basic principles and put them into practice?

Phillips

Believe it or not, I've been asked that question before. People have wondered how I might summarize putting these principles into practice. I finally put them into writing and I've developed what I call the "*Keys 2 Success.*" It's simple to do and anyone can alter the steps to fit his/her own lifestyle.

There are seven simple steps; can you believe it? The seven tips that I've come up with in leading a better life could work for anyone. I use an acronym—SUCCESS. I'll go through what I do for each letter and give an example of how I apply it to my life.

Wright

Let's start! I've spelled out the word SUCCESS and I'm ready to make my notes.

Phillips

Great! Here we go.

- **S** = Start each day with spiritual solace and give thanks for the blessings in your life. Some possibilities might be to take a moment to read a daily devotional; maybe you're a journal-writer and you want to write down your private thoughts or even take time to meditate. I know all of us could probably make of list of things that are wrong in our life, but if we turn those thoughts around and list everything that's right, it will make a huge difference in how we feel each day. Our problems may not change instantly, but it's amazing how our perspective can.

- **U** = Unlock the fullness of your life through gratitude. It's a way to bring inner peace and you can turn darkness into light; you can turn a house into a home. Gratitude is your readiness to show appreciation and your act of returning kindness. You can even turn your enemies into friends. I'm sure you've heard the saying before, "Have an attitude of gratitude."

- **C** = Commit to faith. This would include deeply believing in oneself, others, and a much higher power. Faith can inspire faith. When you believe, your rate of return is going to be substantial. When you have faith and believe that change is possible, you can envision the endless possibilities. These possibilities can truly become realities—if you believe.

- **C** = Circumstances do not define you, but your attitude and actions sure can. You're much more than a "bad situation" or "a person of ill health." Your character will shine through any circumstance regardless of your health, the amount of money your have, the type of car drive, or where you live. So you need to change the way you look at things and you need to demonstrate a positive attitude daily. In other words, "You need to walk the talk!"

- **E** = Everything in your life is for a purpose. So live your life, love your life, and feel blessed with the life that you do have. Don't forget to be thankful for the small stuff.

- **S** = Save your energy and emotions for a time when you may really need them. I know it sounds very basic, but anger, jealousy, and self-pride can needlessly consume all of us. We need to practice forgiveness and appreciation and being a good strong person. Save your energy for the situations that really matter. I used to say to my own children when they'd cry as they tattled on one another, "What if you need those tears later? What if you use them all up right now?" So don't sweat the small stuff; and remember, in the big picture, it's all small stuff.

- **S** = Stay silent and still and listen to your inner voice. We must be open to changes. Things may not always be going the way that we think they should, but that doesn't mean they aren't in alignment with our big picture of life. Sometimes changes or outcomes are small or unplanned but in time, you may recognize their overall significance. Be silent and listen.

Those are the *"Keys 2 Success"* that I incorporate into my daily life, along with my basic principles of putting others first, living right, eating healthier, and exercising.

Wright

Great information, Karen! I really do appreciate all the time you have given me this morning; I appreciate your candor. I really celebrate the life that you have and what you've been able to do, not only for yourself, but also for others.

Phillips

David, I've truly enjoyed our conversation and the time we've spent together.

In closing, I'd like to share one of my favorite quotes with you. I feel it summarizes everything that we've talked about today. It's a quote from Dr. Wayne Dyer. He said, *"When you change the way you look at things, the things you look at change."* So I hope that if we have changed just one person's perspective in the way that they view their situation, maybe they will have a better life tomorrow. If we've done that, then I've accomplished my goal.

David, thanks so much for this opportunity.

Wright

Today we've been talking with Karen Phillips, a Christian motivation and leadership coach, author, and speaker. Having spent thirty years in the educational field as a classroom teacher and administrator, she is well-versed in successful training methods. She also started a small business that she sold three years later. In her retirement, she accepted a job in the business world and was the senior vice president of an established company. Today she is the president of her own coaching/consulting business called *Empowered Potential.* So much for MS stopping people. It certainly hasn't stopped Karen.

Karen, thank you so much for being with us today on *Discover Your Inner Strength.*

Phillips

David, it's been my pleasure.

About the Author

Karen Phillips is a native of Las Vegas, Nevada. In first grade she told her parents she wanted to be a teacher and when she grew up, she realized that goal.

After attending Northern Arizona University in Flagstaff, Arizona, she transferred to the University of Nevada Las Vegas and completed both a bachelor's and master's degree in Education. She then completed her administrative endorsement. Karen is also a Professional Certified Life Coach.

In 1976, she married her husband, Eddie, who was also an educator. Together they raised two children, daughter Krystal, an experienced educator, and their son, Erik, a firefighter/paramedic. They have been blessed with six grandchildren. Karen is a member of the Citizens Advisory Board for the Nevada Chapter of Multiple Sclerosis and serves in a leadership role in an internationally based women's Bible study group.

Karen and her husband reside in Henderson, Nevada—a suburb of Las Vegas— enjoying family time, outdoor activities, and relaxing at their Utah cabin with their two dogs.

"One hundred years from now it will not matter what my bank account was, what kind of house I lived in, or what kind of car I drove. But the world may be a little different because I was important in the life of a child."
—Dr. Forest E. Witcraft

Karen Phillips

Empowered Potential
2509 Antique Blossom Avenue
Henderson, NV 89052
702-269-7979
Karen@EmpoweredPotential.com
www.empoweredpotential.com

Chapter Eighteen

The Third Entity

An Interview With…

Faith Fuller, PhD, PCC & Marita Fridjhon, MSW, PCC

David Wright (Wright)

Today we're talking with Faith Fuller PhD, PCC, and Marita Fridjhon MSW, PPC. They are co-directors of the Center for Right Relationship and authors of the Organization and Relationship Systems Coaching Program. They have over twenty years of working with relationship systems including teams, organizations, families, and community groups. Their training program is designed to foster excellence in relationships of all kinds. It's useful to remember that we are always in relationship. Faith and Marita believe that we are only beginning to uncover the power and potential inherent in successful relationships. Their life mission is to inspire and equip change agents who work with relationship systems of any kind.

Dr. Fuller, Ms. Fridjhon, welcome to *Discover Your Inner Strength.*

Marita Fridjhon (Fridjhon)

Thank you, David.

Faith Fuller (Fuller)

It's great to be here.

Wright

So what do you do at the Center for Right Relationship?

Fuller

David, as you mentioned in our introduction, we know that there is never a time when we are not in relationship. Every moment of our lives we are in relationship, and even when we are alone we are still in relationship with ourselves. What we do at the Center for Right Relationship is foster excellence in those relationships, which means that people can have the most powerful, productive, and joyous relationships that they can, whether that's at work, in private life, with friends, or within our communities. So, it's about being in right relationship, which means conscious and intentional relationship with all the different connections in our lives.

Fridjhon

I'll just add to that a little bit. There are a lot of really, really good relationship and organizational development theories out there—Peter Senge, Arnold Mindell, Ken Wilbur, and folks like them. One of our core competencies is to take sophisticated systems theories and operationalize them. We develop practical and applicable relationship tools based in theory and research and we train people to use those tools to create relationship excellence.

Wright

So what are your backgrounds?

Fuller

Well, I'm a psychologist with a lot of experience in working with relationships of all kinds. I've worked with communities, organizations, families, couples, and groups. I am trained through the Coaches Training Institute, so I'm also a Certified Coach.

Fridjhon

As we talked about earlier, I'm a social worker who specializes in medical and psychiatric social work—that was at the beginning of my professional career. I'm trained as an organizational development consultant, I'm a mediator, and I am a certified coach. Just about everything that Faith and I learned in our years of professional and academic training came together and was integrated within the coaching paradigm. I'm a trainer for the Coaches Training Institute as well in our work. The two of us bring a very broad professional, clinical, and applied background to this work.

For me there is also cross-cultural work. I am from South Africa originally and I've lived and built companies in seven different countries, so I have a strong interest in cross-cultural work.

Wright

Tell me, what is the connection between relationships and discovering inner strength?

Fuller

I think the simplest answer to your question is that since our whole life revolves around relationships, we encourage people to develop what we call "relationship intelligence." The world already knows about emotional intelligence. Recently Goleman and others have coined the term "social intelligence." We prefer the term relationship intelligence. Relationship intelligence is the next developmental step. Relationship intelligence involves knowing how to navigate your way successfully through the complexities of relationships. Relationship intelligence is a profound inner strength to have. It means that regardless of where you go in the world you know you have within you the skills, the awareness, and the knowledge to work with systems and people of all kinds. The ultimate inner strength is to be in excellent relationship, first with yourself and then with others.

Fridjhon

I'm going to take it very briefly to street level—a more radical perspective. I believe that you cannot know yourself unless you are in a relationship. We actually need somebody across from us to discover our own edges, our own strengths; it's very difficult for me to do it by myself.

Fuller

That's great Marita. Just to play off that, it's very easy to be skillful and self-aware when you're living alone in a cave. However, part of what we believe is that relationship actually is the ultimate spiritual path. It's only when people push your buttons and you see your response that you really are on the path of self-awareness. It's easy to be self-aware when you are on your own, but when your spouse or your business partner triggers you in some way, that's when you really need to have some knowledge and tools to bring to bear.

Wright

You both say that you take a systems approach to relationships. What does that mean?

Fuller

Well, maybe we can start with a very simple definition. We're talking here about human systems—relationship systems. We define a system as being a set of interdependent people with a common purpose or identity. Marita, how about taking a moment to play with the "virtual string exercise"? That usually helps people to understand what we mean by a relationship system.

Fridjohn

Sure. We will ask you to imagine some things while we're talking since we are not in the same room.

Fuller

David, imagine that I have a short piece of string in my hand and I'm going to pass the other end of the piece of string to you. So do you have your end?

Wright

Yes.

Fuller

Okay, good. So now what I'm going to do is pull gently on that piece of string, what do you find your hand doing?

Wright

Being tugged toward you.

Fuller

Yes, and you have a choice there don't you? As I pull on the string, what are your choices?

Wright

Well I could pull back or I could just let you pull me.

Fuller

If you pull back, what will happen with the string?

Wright

Either you're going to drop it or you're going to come toward me.

Fuller

That's right, and the string itself will have what?

Wright

A lot of tension.

Fuller

Yes, lot of tension. Now suppose I yank that string, what will happen?

Wright

First, I'd be surprised, but it will probably come out of my hand.

Fuller

Yes, either it will come out of your hand or the string itself might break.

Now let's expand the visualization a little bit more. I want you to imagine for a moment that we have six people holding on to a piece of string woven together like a web. In other words, we have a team—six people holding a web of string. Just like when the two of us were holding the string, all kinds of things are being communicated in the team web. Sometimes you have the perfect tension in the web so everyone can feel each other. However, if somebody lets go of the string, then the other team members have to compensate to keep the web whole. If somebody yanks on his or her string or breaks his or her connection, everyone on the web is going to feel it and will have to adjust accordingly to keep the web integrity. That is what a system is—interdependent. The point we want to make is that a system is like the string, and at the Center for Right Relationship, our job is help people work on their string. Our focus is less on the individuals and more on the relationship between them.

Fridjhon

In the work that we do, our focus is very much on that connection of energy between people. It doesn't help the team to focus just on the person who dropped the string; all the team members are involved. How do we, as a team, pick up the dropped string or compensate or not compensate? The system response is what is important. From the system perspective it's not about who did what to whom, it is about what is trying to happen. What's trying to happen with our web—with our set of strings—rather than focusing just on the person who dropped it. We hold that whatever happens with one individual in a system actually belongs to the system itself. Every individual is a voice of the system. It's personal but it's also not personal since it belongs to the whole system.

Our focus is very much on working with the entire web or system. Each system, whether it's the three of us or a pair or a team has its own unique, energetic signature like a personality. We call that the Third Entity. In other words, there are the three individuals in this interview and then there's the relationship between us— our Third Entity.

Wright

So why should our readers care about this systems approach?

Fridjhon

Oh, that's such a great question, David. Let's think about one-on-one work— individual work—for a moment, whether it is coaching or therapy or whatever. Individual work is important work; there will always be a need for individual development. However, whatever changes the individual client makes will ultimately affect the systems that the client is a part of. Every individual is embedded in multiple relationship systems. That means that individual work can have unintended effects on the systems that client belongs to.

Fuller

The individual and the systems they are a part of will impact one another. Most of us have had the experience of working with an individual who then returns to his or her team or family. Because the individual has changed, the person will affect the team/family differently—his or her part of the web has changed. Other times you can do great individual work, but when the client returns to the system, those changes are rejected by the system and all your good individual work is compromised. So you're never really just working with one person. When you work with one person, the person's changes affect every one of their relationships and vice versa. As change agents, we need to be aware that we are indirectly influencing, and being influenced by many systems when we work with an individual.

Fridjhon

Another reason we want more people to take a systems view is because when it comes to global or social change, those changes are most effectively created through working with larger groups and systems. It's a very powerful way to promote change.

Fuller

Another way of saying that is, by working with a system you leverage your influence. If you're changing people one at a time, that's fantastic, great, we need that, but when you work with a system—when you work with the string—you are affecting a much broader group of people. Your influence in the world is much greater. Therefore, if you want to be a change agent, one of the most powerful ways to leverage maximum change is to address the system—the whole system—rather than just the individuals.

Fridjhon

Now here's the thing: we are not unique when we talk about a systems approach. The systems approach has been around for a very long time; there are many fabulous systems practitioners and applications. Our contribution to systems work is the capacity to work directly with the Third Entity. We strive to develop tools that will allow us to work directly with the system rather than doing one-on-one work within the team. For us the system itself is the client. We think that this is our biggest contribution.

Wright

So what is a Third Entity?

Fuller

The Third Entity is the relationship or the relationship system itself. We assert that whenever there are two or three people together, there is also another entity—the relationship itself that lives between the people. We treat that Third Entity as a living presence. If you asked me if there actually is something scientifically detectable there, I would answer, probably not; but we reify the relationship in order to be able to work with it.

Fridjhon

The work of Rupert Sheldrake points to this when he refers to morphic fields. We are talking about relationship as an organizing field that affects and shapes the individuals involved with it.

Fuller

We treat the Third Entity—the system—as a living thing that has its own wisdom, knowledge, and understanding. Working with the relationship itself simplifies things because the client is the system, not the individuals within it. If you work with individuals, inevitably you're going to be pulled more toward one individual than another. You are going to like one person more or dislike someone because he or she reminds you of your ex-boss; but if your client is the relationship, then you're much less likely to be biased. A systems coach sees each individual as one important voice of that relationship. Your perspective is about what will serve the Third Entity—what will serve that relationship?

Fridjhon

Again, that ties into systems intelligence or relationship intelligence, which is a newly developing field. There are a number of people writing about social intelligence. One example is Daniel Goleman. What we mean by relationship intelligence is that the system itself has wisdom. Our job is to find more and more ways that we can directly tap into that intelligence. Individual voices tend to focus on "who did what to whom"? Relationship intelligence looks at what's trying to happen in the overall system. So the question is: how do we work directly with the relationship itself?

Wright

So how does someone actually work with a Third Entity?

Fuller

Well, there are a number of things we teach about this. The bottom line is that we need to encourage people to change their focal length view from the individual to the system—to move from the individuals to the string between them. There are a variety of ways we can do that. One way is to consider each individual, not just as an individual, but also as a voice of the system. Take a team for example, sometimes in teams, people don't speak up that much; but from the systems perspective, every person on that team is a voice of the system. Each voice is not just personal—it's an expression of the system.

So if you imagine for moment, David, that your voice on your team at your company is a voice of the system, how might that influence whether you speak up or not? Imagine you're sitting in a meeting at your company, and four or five people are there, and you hesitate to speak up about something. Yet if you really believed that when you speak up, you're not just speaking for David—you're speaking as a voice of the system, and speaking one truth of the whole team. If you really hold that belief, how would it affect your communication with the team?

Wright

Well, I certainly wouldn't hold back if I felt that way. I would feel a responsibility to give the entire team that truth and I would want everyone to have it.

Fuller

Absolutely. Because it's not just your personal perspective, it is also a voice of the system.

Fridjhon

Exactly. One of the things that we train as we work with teams and facilitators is a concept called "deep democracy." Deep democracy is a term coined by Arnold Mindell. Deep democracy holds that in order to know the total reality or truth of the team, all voices must be heard, even the unpopular ones. Unless we can at least listen to the unpopular voices—the marginalized ones—we're not working with the whole reality of the situation, so deep democracy is really important. This is the attitude we want the team to hold—that when David says something, even if it's unpopular, it actually belongs to the whole team. That creates a completely different sense of trust and confidence.

Fuller

So basically, we only have one rule and that is: "Everybody is right—partially." In other words, because of deep democracy, David has a piece of the truth, Faith has a piece of truth, and Marita has a piece of the truth. So we're all correct, but only partially.

Fridjhon

There is an exercise we do to access the Third Entity; it is one of our introductory tools. It's about meeting the Third Entity and giving it a voice. We'd love to walk you through it. Are you willing to play?

Wright

Absolutely.

Fuller

David, we'll be working with a real relationship in your life, but you're not going to have to share the details, most of the work will happen inside you. So there will be sections of silence while you are doing your thinking internally. At the end we'll talk about the impact of the exercise.

Fridjhon

Anyone reading this chapter can just follow Faith's instructions as well and do what we're asking David to do. That way everyone who reads this can have his or her own experience of the exercise.

Fuller

David, step one is to think of a relationship in your life that's important to you—that you care about and that relationship has a conflict or a hotspot or something troubling it. Again, choose a relationship that's important to you that has a hotspot. Do you have one?

Wright

Yes.

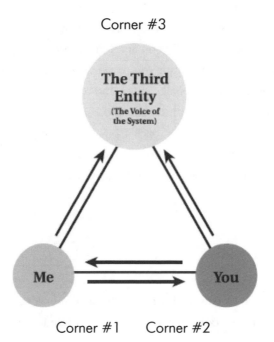

Fuller

Okay great! David, I'm going to ask you to move around a bit now. You will actually be moving through the three corners of a triangle. So step into one corner of the triangle, and that corner of the triangle is your corner, it belongs to you and your position on the issue. Across from you in the second corner is the person with whom you're having the hotspot or the dispute.

As you look across at that person opposite you, I want you to really let the person know how you feel about the issue. You can do this in your head quietly. State your position on this hotspot, your side of the argument. You don't have to be skillful; it's more about how you feel than the logic of the argument, so I want you to tell the person how you really feel about your side of the argument. Go ahead and do that, and take a few minutes. Those of you reading this chapter go ahead and do the same thing.

Wright

Okay.

Fuller

Great, I'm going to ask you now to move over to corner number two—the corner of the person to whom you were just speaking. For the sake of simplicity, I am going to call that person "Joe." (You and I know that your person has a different name.) As you get there, I really want you to allow yourself to become Joe. Find your way into Joe's body, the way he walks, talks, and moves, and the way that Joe thinks. Let yourself become Joe. Take a moment and really get a feel for him. Now, from Joe's shoes you're going to answer back from his side of the story. What is Joe's position? What is important to Joe about his side of the argument? So be Joe talking back to David. Talk back to corner number one. Go ahead.

Wright

Okay.

Fuller

Great, we're going to repeat this sequence once more, so go back to your own corner—corner number one. You're going to continue the next round of the argument from David's perspective. Again, it's about what's really emotionally important for you, less about logic, more about feelings. What would you say back to your opponent?

Wright

Okay.

Fuller

David, now one more time you're going to go back to the second corner and respond from your opponent's voice. Become Joe and let him respond, from what's important to him.

Wright

Okay.

Fuller

Great, so next we're going to move to a new spot—the third corner of that triangle. As you move there, you're going to find yourself in the corner that is right between the other two, right? So this is a completely new place and this is the voice of the relationship between you and Joe as if the relationship were a living, breathing entity. As you stand there, you are in the voice of the relationship. To help you experience this, I encourage you to put your arms out as if you were putting one arm around person number one, and another arm around person number two. You are the voice of the relationship now—the Third Entity—and these are your people, they belong to you!

So really let yourself feel that you're not either one of these people, but the relationship between them. Give yourself a few minutes to feel your way into being the relationship as if it were an entity.

Wright

Okay.

Fuller

My first question to you—the relationship—is: how do you feel about seeing these two people—your people—in conflict? As the relationship, what is it like to watch their dispute? Silently feel your way into that. Get a sense of how the relationship feels about what's going on. Do you have a little bit of a sense of it?

Wright

Absolutely.

Fuller

Good, okay. As the relationship, you actually have wisdom of your own and so the next question for the relationship is, "What is it that you know that maybe these other two people don't know?"

Wright

Okay.

Fuller

Great. And the final question to the relationship is, "What do you, the relationship, need from the pair of them?"

Wright

Okay.

Fuller

Great, thank you. So now we're going to go back to David's corner of the triangle—corner number one—so please move now. Once you are back in your corner, David, check in with yourself. What is different as a result of doing this exercise for you?

Fridjhon

I have to tell you, David, I'm sitting over here dying to know your discoveries. Is there anything you can share?

Wright

Well, the other person is someone I care a lot about—someone I also work with. I used a real problem—a real hotspot—with the person. As I stepped into the corners, I was able to empathize back and forth between myself and the other person. When I got into the Third Entity, which was really fascinating for me, I realized that the most important thing was the caring in the relationship. I said to myself, "No matter what the outcome of this issue, I will walk away with that part of the relationship intact, no matter what I have to do." Actually, I ended up in a compromise that was not so much of a compromise as it was a better idea than either of the two individuals had.

Fuller

That's great! It sounds like from the Third Entity perspective you could feel the importance and the power of the connection between the two individuals. Was the Third Entity able to give you some information about how to actually work with the issue?

Wright

Yes, the Third Entity was not encumbered by the opinions of the first two.

Fridjhon

There you go. A funny thing is, David, having done this hundreds of times, we have yet to find a Third Entity that's a jerk! Usually, the Third Entity holds a metaview—a bigger picture—and often it has a lot of wisdom and compassion.

Fuller

Here is the final step, David. If you were to take one action step for that relationship, as result of what you've learned today in the Third Entity Exercise, what would it be? It's okay if it's a small step, and it's fine to keep it private since this is a public interview.

Wright

Yes, I already know what it would be.

Fuller

Okay, great.

Fridjhon

You're a fast learner. To do the Third Entity Exercise there is a prerequisite for some emotional and relationship intelligence. To be able to do the exercise, you must have the emotional intelligence to know what your experience is, and relationship intelligence to formulate the experience of the other person. Once you can begin to do that, it becomes possible to step to that third place and listen to the voice of the Third Entity.

Wright

So how does Third Entity or voice of the system apply to teams?

Fridjhon

I did some work in South Africa recently with a large consulting organization where some of the partners were splitting off on their own. The company was dividing, and there was a lot of hostility, anger, and pain. We had the partners spend some time in that first position—their own position. People got short sound bytes to ventilate their frustration, pain, and anger. We spent time getting some of that first position experience—"This is why I'm upset, this how I feel, this is how I experience it." We didn't do the second position, since as each person was talking about what was going on for him or her, all of them could hear each other. So we spent some time in that first position.

Then I set a chair in the front of the room and did exactly what Faith did with you just now. I said, "That chair belongs to the relationship among all of you. It's the voice of this team. We invite you to get up from your personal corner and go sit in the team voice chair one at a time. However, when you are in the team chair, you are not using it to express your own personal opinion—you are listening for what the team needs and for what the team has to say. If you think you know what you are going to say before you get to that chair, then that is not the voice of the team. You must first let go of your personal agenda in order to be able to listen for the Third Entity of the team."

People were able to get up, walk over, sit there, and speak for the organization. Some spoke their empathy for the team's difficulties, others spoke about the connection they had as partners, and some spoke about compromises. Several times one of the team members would get up and start walking toward the team chair, and halfway there would turn around and say, "Nope, I'm still coming from my personal opinion. I'm going back to my chair."

We wrote down all the things that came from the Third Entity of the team and helped the team explore what was said. After that, the emotional field of the team was much softer, and from that softer space we created task forces and made some planning around what was going to happen next.

Fuller

If you do the Third Entity exercise with a pair, we recommend you have them walk through the three corners just as we did with David in the example in this chapter. You can also use this form for a team. Each person walks his or her own triangle directed by the coach just as we did above, and each does it silently, without interacting with each other. That way, each has his or her own experience without triggering another team member by what he or she might say. Then the coach can debrief the experience with an emphasis on the voice of the Third Entity.

The great thing about systems work is that it doesn't matter what the size of the system is. Regardless if you are working with your own internal personal set of voices or whether you're working with a pair or with a team or a community—the same principles apply. The Third Entity is just bigger, that's all. The beauty of systems work is that it's holographic—the same principles apply regardless of how large the system is.

Fridjhon

Tools that allow the individual to get beyond his or her personal ego and tap into the larger whole will help that individual become bigger as a person. The systems approach and relationship work helps the individual grow.

As a result of connecting with that Third Entity, David, you know a little bit more about yourself and have a little bit more of yourself available to the relationship than you had before.

Wright

So who do you think would benefit from the systems approach?

Fridjhon

Everybody.

Fuller

Here's why. Everybody has important relationships in his or her life. There is never a time when we are not in a relationship. We aren't born with great relationship skills and not all of us had good role models for relationship. So, on the most personal level, everybody can benefit from learning some skills. On the professional level, if you work with systems involving pairs, couples, teams, communities, or organizations, training in systems work will leverage your influence. This would apply to coaches, therapists, HR personnel, consultants, managers, team leaders, CEOs, and so on. You need to understand how to work with relationship systems because that is the most useful way to work with the string. Therefore, it's really helpful to get some training and knowledge in how to work very directly with systems.

Fridjhon

Research supports that one of the key qualities for great leaders is their relationship capacity and ability. That doesn't mean people have to stop doing their one-on-one work and become systems workers. It simply means that even as I work with an individual, I will have an eye on the system from which my client comes and to which he or she will return.

Wright

Well, what a great conversation! I really appreciate the time both of you have taken answering all these questions. I enjoyed the exercises and I actually learned a lot from them.

One of the things that I learned was an offhanded comment that one of you made. It was about the fact that I'm also always in relationship with myself and I really appreciate your pointing that out to me—I hadn't thought of that.

Fuller

Well, if you have ever had a fight with yourself, or been of two minds about something, then you know that there are many different Davids inside and they don't always get along.

Wright

That's right! Well, I really do appreciate this time and thank you both so much.

Fuller

Our pleasure, thank you.

Wright

Today we've been talking with Faith Fuller, PhD, PCC, and Marita Fridjhon, MSW, PCC. Faith and Marita are co-directors of the Center for Right Relationship. Their training programs are designed to foster excellence in relationships of all kinds. I don't know about you but I think they know what they're talking about.

Thank you so much for being with us today on *Discover Your Inner Strength*.

About the Author

Faith Fuller and Marita Fridjhon are co-directors of the Center for Right Relationship and authors of the Organization and Relationship Systems Coaching Program. They have over twenty years of working with relationship systems including teams, organizations, families, and community groups. Their training program is designed to foster excellence in relationships of all kinds. It's useful to remember that we are always in relationship. Faith and Marita believe that we are only beginning to uncover the power and potential inherent in successful relationships. Their life mission is to inspire and equip change agents who work with relationship systems of any kind.

Faith Fuller & Marita Fridjhon

Center for Right Relationship
111 West C Street
Benecia, CA 945910
866.435.5939
marita@centerforrightrelationship.com
Ffuller446@aol.com

Chapter Nineteen

Learning Orientation to Learn, Innovate and Succeed

An Interview With...

Dr. Margaret Martinez

David Wright (Wright)

Today we're talking with Dr. Margaret Martinez, CEO at the Training Place, Incorporated. She's worked extensively in instructional psychology and design, information, and technology for over twenty years. She has a PhD in Instructional Psychology and Technology and was previously Director of Worldwide Training,

Certification, Conferences, and Courseware at WordPerfect. Martinez's professional focus has been to pioneer personalized learning research. She is nationally recognized for her Learning Orientation Research based on her study of the neurosciences and contributions to the field of individual learning differences. She publishes, presents at international conferences, and pursues work on innovative learning solutions that support those who would want to learn more successfully.

Dr. Martinez, welcome to *Discover Your Inner Strength.*

Margaret Martinez (Martinez)

Thank you, David.

Wright

So tell me why you began your fascinating Learning Orientation Research Program.

Martinez

Well, David, my discussion about discovering your inner strength begins with a brief look at the Learning Orientation Research and then the neurosciences.

It started out with my interest in pursuing a doctoral degree at Brigham Young University in Utah. It was my honor and great pleasure to work with my friend and colleague, Victor Bunderson. He has a highly regarded history and reputation in cognitive psychology, education, and measurement. It was my great fortune to have found a mentor with such an extensive background in my own area of interest. More importantly, he willingly embraced, supported, and guided my quest as my PhD committee chair. When I met him, he already had more than thirty years in the field of education, so you can see he really gave me confidence and helped me achieve greater academic success. He generously offered his own experience, expertise, and very high standards to support my research program.

Wright

Tell me how you got started with your Learning Orientation Research Program.

Martinez

At the very beginning, I began with my own personal learning experiences; I've always loved learning and reading. As a child, I even asked teachers to give me extra projects so I could keep learning passionately. However, I would often get frustrated when the pace of the classroom was too slow for me and I could not go faster. I was often held back to keep pace with the average student.

Flash forward many years later and I was ready to pursue my PhD in 1997. I was searching for a dissertation project. When you pursue a doctoral program, you are supposed to make a contribution to the field. I felt my contribution would be to design an instructional system on the Web that would ideally support those learners who are more passionate about learning and wanted to learn faster at their own pace with their own learning goals. As my advisor, Vic Bunderson convinced me that my instructional system should be adaptive and help everyone else, not just the fast learners.

Wright

So what happened next with this broader challenge of supporting all learners who learn differently?

Martinez

I knew that if I was going to design an instructional system that helps all learners, I was going to need to understand how and why people learn differently. I knew that I had to start with a theory about learning, so I began with the Successful Learning Theory. The theoretical basis for the Successful Learning Theory and Construct Hypothesis was developed from a careful review of the many contributions of key researchers working in the area of psychology and developmental educational research. These contributions included discussions about intentionality, metacognition, learning efficacy, expertise-building, intentional learning, meta-learning, conation, cognition, achievement, intrinsic motivation, constructivism, and self-regulated learning. Additionally, because I recognized we needed to know more about emotions and motivation, my research relied heavily on foundations stemming from the neurobiology of learning and memory research.

The neuroscientific research particularly emphasizes the fundamental affect of emotions on thinking, learning, and living. It also emphasizes the human capacity for fear, stress, and pleasure and the need for individuals to learn, improve, and feel empowered.

After a year of study and research and a lot of statistical analysis, in 1998 I developed what is called a Learning Orientation Construct. This construct or model describes how three primary factors affect intentional learning success and influence individual learning differences. The three factors are: self motivated learning or the desire to learn, learning autonomy or independence, and committed strategic learning effort and persistence.

The first factor refers to an individual's desire or striving to learn, which are primarily conative and affective factors. It considers a learner's will, commitment, intent, drive or passion for improving, transforming, setting and achieving goals, taking risks, and meeting new learning challenges. It describes the individual's emotional response to the process of learning regardless of content, environment, resources, or course delivery. Naturally, learners will be more intentional and enjoy or apply greater effort in a preferred course or topic or in situations that interest or appeal to them and then motivate them to learn. The opposite can also be true.

The second factor—learning independence or autonomy—considers locus of control and refers to the individual's desire or ability to take responsibility, make choices, or control, manage, and improve their own learning. It describes how a learner will self-assess, reflect, and self-motivate and then make choices independent of the instructor in the attainment of personal learning goals.

The third factor—committed strategic learning effort and persistence—refers to the degree that learners persist and commit deliberate strategic effort to accomplish learning and achieve goals. Successful self-directed learners place great importance on passion, striving, and committing and continuing to persist as they apply focused strategic planning, hard working effort, and high principles and standards to learn. Holistic thinking skills are an important influence. The three factors correlate highly.

Less successful learners generally lack the insight, for example holistic thinking and critical thinking skills, that passion, autonomy and strategic planning and committed effort is a contributing factor for achievement. Research shows that less successful learners overlook the importance of setting challenging goals and sheer effort, and think that luck plays a far greater role. This is not new. Successful people generally suggest that the secret of success is practice and hard work.

Wright

Why are you highlighting the research that shows the importance of emotions on learning?

Martinez

David for most of the 1900s, education researchers focused most of their studies on how people think when they were learning. Even in the nineties, social, emotional, and conative factors were overlooked or demoted in conventional research. Fortunately, with recent advances in medical measurement technology, we are finally able to see what is going on in the brain. Researchers are discovering the incredible affect that emotions have on learning, communication, and memory. The research is revealing that the sometime dominant power of emotions and intentions on guiding and managing cognitive process is incredibly important to understand.

Wright

What do you do with the Learning Orientation Construct?

Martinez

The three factors in the Learning Orientation Construct (LOC) help me to be more precise about discussing learning ability. For example, people understand when you discuss that a learner is more successful because he or she is really self-motivated or the learner is persistent in achieving challenging goals. So the LOC is useful in describing learning orientations or an individual's disposition to approach, manage, and achieve learning intentionally and differently from others. The LOC identifies the key characteristics for learner differences and serves as a foundation for discussing successful learning. The LOC also provides a foundation for the Learning Orientation Questionnaire or the LOQ. The LOQ provides measures to assess learning ability, expectations about learning, and readiness to learn.

Wright

So tell me more about the Learning Orientation Questionnaire.

Martinez

It is important to know just how prepared an individual is to learn and how that individual can learn. This is the purpose of the LOQ. The LOQ is a twenty-five-item survey that measures learning ability and describes dispositions and readiness to learn. It is particularly effective in an online learning environment where many students may find the transition from classroom to online learning environments difficult or troublesome. How often do you hear someone say that he or she prefers to learn in a classroom versus online? The LOQ provides scores that are unique indicators of an individual's approach to learning. It describes attributes that influence learning success. Scores offer explanations for individual differences in learning and performance, including ideas about expectations, beliefs, preferences, strategies, skills, values, and approaches.

Course or curriculum designers and developers can use the scores to guide the more sophisticated use of instructional and assessment strategies. Educators or trainers can use the scores to improve teaching strategies or help individuals improve learning and study strategies. Organizations, institutions, or schools can use the scores to reduce attrition rates, improve engagement or retention, and predict academic and business outcomes. For example, student time to degree completion or workplace productivity and team management.

Once students take the LOQ and get their scores, they are provided with information about their learning and are offered special strategies for learning improvement and readiness.

Wright

So how are learning orientations different from learning styles?

Martinez

Learning styles are remnants of the research of the seventies and eighties. Learning style theories were developed before the medical measurement technology allowed us to look inside the brain and see and understand what is going on inside. New technology allows us to better understand the affect of emotions on learning and memory.

Additionally, research for disorders, such as schizophrenia, autism, and depression highlights the special importance of emotional influences on learning, thinking, and communication. In other words, today's more current research suggests that we really need to understand what emotions are doing in our brain. In contrast, learning styles typically overlooked the particularly powerful influence of emotions. We simply didn't have the technology back then to understand the affect of emotions on learning differences. Today we do.

So in contrast to learning styles, the learning orientation research uses the neurosciences to explore how learners approach and manage different learning environments and instructional presentations. It considers a more comprehensive set of key psychological factors, such as emotions and social factors, that influence how learners expect and want to learn—more or less successfully.

Wright

How would you define inner strength?

Martinez

Inner strength is everybody's ability to be the best he or she can be each day. Inner strength is taking care of your body, mind, and spirit to contribute something more worthwhile each day. Inner strength is surrounding yourself with good people, setting challenging goals, making good responsible decisions, and contributing great acts of kindness. Inner strength is knowing that with exercise, discipline, and commitment you can responsibly and positively change your brain. Finally, inner strength is understanding that the brain is capable of achieving many things, and, like a muscle, you must exercise it, take care of it, and use it well. The greatest measure of inner strength is reflecting on how well you mindfully achieve these goals every day.

Wright

What do we know about how people change or develop their inner strength?

Martinez

The neurosciences are helping us learn more about inner strength too. It has only been recently understood that people can change. We used to think our brains were pretty well developed in childhood. With new medical measurement technology, we are learning about what is often call brain plasticity or neuroplasticity. This refers to the neuronal changes that occur in the brain as a result of genetics, experiences, environment, stimulation, and influences. Today we know that our brain is changing every day with every stimulation and experience. Each of us has the ability to manage our brain more actively and mindfully with good nutrition, mental and physical exercise, good stress management, and healthy, spiritual living.

Recent studies of aging adults, particularly those with Alzheimer's disease, dementia, or loss of memory are highlighting the importance of brain fitness. Improving brain fitness is very similar to avoiding physical decline. Most studies are reporting that activities that stimulate and exercise the brain have excellent results, especially with memory loss, stress, attention, and other cognitive functions. If you challenge yourself with learning something new every day, the stimulation triggers your brain from passive to more active cognitive functioning. This is important because we know that people have the opportunity to improve their inner strength.

This is where the Learning Orientation research comes in. The LOQ is useful for brain fitness because it helps with identifying targeted interventions for improvement (e.g., improving intellectual skills). It's a pretty exciting time to be alive to experience the advances in the neurosciences. These are advances that can help others be the best that they can be as they discover and develop their own inner strength. As we learn more we will begin to see the brain fitness market grow rapidly in the future.

Wright

What are examples of how people can improve themselves?

Martinez

I think that everyone already knows the first step—you have to want to improve and discover your inner strength. Like physical or spiritual exercise, brain fitness requires the passion to want to change and make improvements to your life. Each person has to find important reasons to make changes in his or her life. Too often, you can let emotions sabotage your best intentions.

Finding a mentor or coach is also important. Mentors or coaches who are passionate and already leading the way with excellent life examples are wonderful if you have them around. Being around great role models help you to find ways to improve. But generally, being disciplined about learning challenging new things is how people can improve and discover their inner strength. Having good discipline, good habits, learning new skills, learning not to procrastinate, exercising regularly, these are all good things. I think everyone knows how to be good and exercise regularly, it just isn't always fun.

Using the LOQ, people can learn about ways to think more holistically, creatively, or critically. Once you learn your LOQ scores, you can learn more about how your brain works and find strategies to improve. Other examples are to set increasingly tougher goals, practice, practice, practice, use better time management skills, or simply just persist—don't give up—and find help if you need it.

Discovering your inner strength is a lifelong journey that requires constant awareness of where you've been, where you are, and where you want to go next. Improving inner strength means you are always setting challenging short-term and long-term goals and strategies.

Wright

So what's next?

Martinez

David, I'm really excited about all the recent advances in the neurosciences. New technologies are making such a difference to the speed of discoveries about learning and everything that affects our lives. For example, we are learning more about mirror neurons and neuromodulation. The Wikipedia describes a mirror neuron as a neuron that fires both when an animal acts and when the animal observes the same action performed by another. In other words, a mirror neuron helps us copy or imitate each other. Thus, the neuron "mirrors" the behavior of another animal, as though the observer were itself acting. In humans, brain activity consistent with mirror neurons has been found in the premotor cortex and the inferior parietal cortex. It's very important for us to understand this because it's helping us learn more about learning and communication. It is also helping us learn why the brain sometimes doesn't work as well as other times.

Also of interest to me is the topic of neuromodulation. The Wikipedia describes neuromodulation as the process in which several classes of neurotransmitters in the nervous system regulate diverse populations of neurons. This is important because the neurotransmitters are chemicals that trigger brain activity and interactions that influence neuronal development. So if we can better understand these chemical interactions, we can also better understand how people learn, especially how people want and expect to learn differently.

The neurosciences are also helping us learn about how technology is changing our brain. There are university labs discovering how the affect of today's media is influencing our brains, especially our younger generation. An example of this is how high-action video games can improve vision. Social networking communities and collaborative technologies are not only affecting our economy, they are affecting our brain development. We are obviously going to be able to use all this research in the field of education to help understand how people can learn more creatively, holistically, and critically.

People who want to understand how to use their brain more effectively can learn to be more innovative about developing their inner strength. Harnessing all this research and information to deal with rapid changes is definitely a challenge. Discovering our inner strength with so many distracting changes coming at us daily is also a challenge.

I am grateful that neuroscience research will continue to help Learning Orientation Research. I'll be following this type of research to support the Learning Orientation Research and provide and validate evidence for the Learning Orientation Questionnaire. Most importantly, I hope this research will help me make further contributions to the world of more mindful learning and education. My research will continue to focus on improving skills for holistic and critical thinking, innovation, creativity, and non-verbal ability. This research will also continue to contribute to brain fitness and helping others in their discovery of inner strength. In closing, you can find all of this research at www.trainingplace.com/source/research.

Wright

Well, what an interesting conversation. I guess this is going to be new for many of our readers, as it is for me. You sure have enlightened me. I appreciate all the time you've taken to answer these important questions for us.

Martinez

Thank you, David. It was my pleasure.

Wright

Today we've been talking with Dr. Margaret Martinez. Dr. Martinez is the Chief Executive Officer at The Training Place. She is nationally recognized for her Learning Orientation Research based on her study of the neurosciences and contributions to the field of individual learning differences. She publishes, keynotes, presents at international conferences, and pursues work on innovative learning solutions that support those who want to learn more successfully.

Dr. Martinez, thank you so much for being with us today on *Discover Your Inner Strength*.

Martinez

Thank you again.

About the Author

D r. Martinez has a PhD in Instructional Psychology and Technology. She has been a researcher and professional speaker in the academic and corporate world for over 20 years. Martinez is also an accomplished writer having been published numerous times in magazines, books and academic publications. Her research expanded years ago to include topics about how people learn, the neurosciences and self-discovery. She combines her vast experience in helping others determine their inner strength as they pursue their own personal self-improvement goals. Dr. Martinez offers a unique perspective and understanding found nowhere else. She uses the neurosciences as a foundation to offer tips on effective communications, learning and self-discovery skills. Her research appears at: http://www.trainingplace.com/source/research. The Learning Orientation Questionnaire is used worldwide. More information appears at: http://www.trainingplace.com/loq/loqinfo.htm.

Margaret Martinez, CEO

The Training Place, Inc.
743 West Bougainvillea Drive
Oro Valley, AZ 85755
520-877-3991
mmartinez@trainingplace.com

Chapter Twenty

Strength Through Negotiation: The Basics

An Interview With...

Laura Leezer

David Wright (Wright)

Today we're talking with Laura Swanson Leezer. Laura is a corporate and professional trainer with over twenty years of experience in sales and marketing. She has held management positions in the business field including sales, buying, and training. She is currently Vice President and Director of Marketing in the finance industry. Laura specializes in image and public relations as well as customer service. She holds a master's degree in Education and teaches classes in Marketing and Business. Ms. Leezer is certified in diversity and women's issues by the Professional Woman Network and serves on the International Advisory Board.

Laura, welcome to *Discover Your Inner Strength*.

Laura Leezer (Leezer)

Thank you so much. I'm very excited to be here.

Wright

So what does it mean to negotiate?

Leezer

It means that you are communicating to agree—to get what you want or solve a problem.

Wright

So when folks enter into a negotiating meeting or whatever it is, what is the main goal?

Leezer

If you're a good negotiator, you want both parties to achieve their goal. That would be a win-win situation.

Wright

What types of situations require negotiating?

Leezer

Practically anything that arises between two or more people that requires them to agree on something. I find that I have to negotiate with my six-year-old when he wants to wear his cowboy boots to bed or have a brownie for breakfast. I also negotiate with my eight-year-old daughter when she insists she needs her ears pierced. Both of my children are very good about communicating what they want and how it's going to benefit them and me if I give it to them. I give my reasons for not accepting this and the negotiating begins.

Negotiating takes place in marriages when spouses are making compromises on a daily basis. People negotiate every day in business when they need to make money or achieve a quota while still making their customers happy so they'll continue to do business with them.

Wright

So how would I know what I wanted prior to negotiating and how would I set objectives and goals?

Leezer

You need to understand your primary goal and secondary goal. What is the number one thing you want or need from this negotiating session? What are you willing to compromise on? It's important to remember that you don't always have a clear understanding of what the other person wants, so it's good to be adaptive.

It's important for a good negotiator to create a plan or outline with points that need to be covered. You want to start with a target position—the best you hope to achieve. An example would be: You're a salesperson and you're making a sales call on a current customer you have a great relationship with. Your primary goal, or target position, would be to make another sale. Your secondary goal may be to ask for a referral.

Wright

So how do people resolve conflicts in negotiation?

Leezer

The best way to resolve conflict is to communicate in a positive manner. Building a good rapport and understanding who you're negotiating with is important. We all have different backgrounds, so we all have different styles of dealing with other people. Understand the other person's position or goal clearly. Try to be flexible and think of alternatives that will make you both happy. You need to be a good listener and have a positive approach. Ask for clarification if necessary. Remember your goal—Win/Win!

Wright

In your experience, do you ever get the opportunity to talk to the two negotiating parties beforehand so they will understand that this is a negotiation?

Leezer

That's a good point and yes, sometimes you do, especially in the business world when you know you have an appointment set and you are going to be sitting down with a group of people. Maybe in a business you will have a board of directors you will be addressing. You can gather information prior to the meeting from all parties and inform them of the goal of the meeting. Understand the industry and understand the companies involved. If you're doing international negotiation, understanding the culture will help as well. If there will be multiple languages spoken, you will want to have an interpreter if you are not fluent in those languages. To be in a positive negotiating position, evaluate your needs and options.

Wright

Are there other types of guidelines that a negotiator can use?

Leezer

The best steps include goal-setting, research, and preparation. Set guidelines regarding your presentation: Is it realistic? Is it measurable? Is it achievable? Being in a position of strength helps you to reach your target position. What's your minimum position or what's the very least you're willing to walk away with? Many times, when you are sitting in a negotiation and you have an opening statement or an opening position, that's basically a starting point. The people you're negotiating with have an opening position as well. In their mind, they have a target position as well; that's when the negotiation starts. Be prepared to start compromising and making concessions.

Wright

So you start with the opening position and then you move to a target position—a minimum position. What about the adaptive plan?

Leezer

The adaptive plan, once the negotiation starts, is when you start saying, "Okay, this is what I'm willing to concede on; this is what I'm willing to work around." The adaptive plan is the path that's going to get you from point A to point B. You're going to be willing to work with that person and make concessions so both parties reach their goals. Remember, the ultimate goal is a win-win situation. You want to walk away with what you want, and the other party should walk away with what he or she wants so you can work together in the future. You're trying to build strategic partnerships.

Wright

So why would our readers need to know how to be good negotiators?

Leezer

When we're in business, we need clients or customers to stay in business. We want to make sure we help others achieve their needs so we can achieve ours. Being a good negotiator takes place in all aspects of business, even with your employees. If you're interviewing a candidate for a position in your company and you are negotiating the salary, as an employer you can use the fact you provide health insurance as a benefit of working for you. If you're talking to a company that is coming into the community and you want its business, but the company is used to doing business in a different way, you're going to have to change your way of thinking to adapt to what the company needs.

Wright

Would anyone need to know how to negotiate, even if he or she is not in a business situation?

Leezer

You can get into negotiating situations and not even know you're negotiating. I believe that anyone who communicates with others can benefit from being a good negotiator. Communicating with knowledge and a positive attitude can usually make everyone happy. If you communicate through greed or stubbornness, chances are there's going to be conflict that might not be resolved.

Wright

So what characteristics does a good negotiator have?

Leezer

I think that being a good listener is an important attribute. If somebody doesn't agree with what you're saying, I think that it's important not to be defensive. Being patient and articulate help as well. One also needs to be honest. Being assertive can be a positive attribute as you work toward your goal.

It's important to be informed regarding your subject of negotiation. Being organized helps with negotiating because once you start discussing your issues, you need to document what has been agreed upon. if you're a details-oriented person, you will help the process proceed smoothly.

Wright

So how could I become a successful negotiator?

Leezer

To become a successful negotiator, develop good communication skills. Listen to others as they communicate with you and truly understand their message. Stop and define how you are feeling during your conversation. Do you need clarification? Do you need more information? Practice helps develop our skills.

Stephen Covey, in his book, *The 7 Habits of Highly Effective People,* included a chapter on win-win situations.

Wright

What types of situations would require negotiation?

Leezer

Many types of situations in business and everyday life require negotiating. How a husband and wife plan a vacation destination is an example. The husband wants to ski and the wife wants the beach. They start to communicate what they want and why. They each talk about the benefits of each of their choices and the compromises begin. The wife will go skiing now if they can go on a cruise in April.

Here is a business example. A business customer is having a difficult time with a bank service fee and he or she wants it waived. Both parties sit down and start talking. What are the options? Is the bank willing to waive the fees without getting anything in return? Or, is there a concession that can be made? The bank might decide to lower the fee for the customer as a compromise while the customer's business will increase usage.

My eight-year-old daughter negotiated quite well regarding an increase in her allowance. She was willing to take on more responsibility if I would increase the money and we both ended up being very happy walking away from that negotiation. So I feel that negotiating can take place in every facet of your life.

Wright

My daughter, who's in college, negotiated last year with her mother. She wanted to move out of the dorm and into an apartment on campus and she used a slide presentation. I wish I had been more prepared; I wish you and I had talked before.

Leezer

Your daughter sounds very impressive! She also had a specific goal she was willing to work toward.

Wright

Actually, she proved it.

Leezer

So she was well prepared. She provided you with appropriate information. It sounds like you were in a collaborating mode, which means you wanted to find a suitable solution for both of you. Maybe you came into it with a win-win attitude and she had a specific need. She really took it seriously.

Several modes can occur when negotiating. The accommodating mode is where your needs become secondary to others' needs. Then there are people who are in an avoiding mode where they're uncooperative but not aggressive. People tend to not get their needs fulfilled when they take the avoiding mode—they don't' want to engage, they don't want to get into the process.

In a compromising mode, you're in the middle—you're cooperative and somewhat assertive while still being a good listener. You're making compromises and you might neglect your own goal. Maybe you didn't want your daughter to move into the apartment for safety reasons. But it sounds like she proved to you that her solution was the best for her.

Wright

That's exactly what happened.

So what preparation needs to be done prior to negotiating?

Leezer

Good question. Preparation is necessary before a negotiation to achieve the optimum result—Win/Win. Start with research. Find out who's involved. What information can be obtained regarding the company/people you are meeting with? For example: You have been asked to meet with a philanthropist to discuss giving a sizable donation to his cause. As a business owner, you ask yourself, "What's in it for me?" What do you want for your donation? Do you want press coverage and a photo opportunity that will be placed in all the local papers? You could do research online, ask for information, brochures, and ask what other contributors have received for their donations. If you do your research before the meeting, you'll be well prepared and able to negotiate for what you want as well as make a contribution to a worthy cause. Understanding and being committed to the process is key.

Wright

So how does one make concessions during the negotiating session?

Leezer

After you have decided what your needs are and you clearly understand what the other person wants, try to meet the person's needs without sacrificing your own. This is when concessions are made. Be sure to keep accurate notes. A skilled negotiator remembers what has been discussed and agreed upon. Once you've made a concession, you should write it down. Have a firm position that this is accepted and make it clear that "My understanding is that you and I are going to do XYZ. Is that correct?"

Concessions are made so all parties involved can continue to succeed; communication with a positive approach promotes a win-win outcome. The other alternatives are win/lose or lose/win.

Wright

It's terrible when you're in a business situation where both parties just won't concede. Negotiation skills can really help.

Leezer

That's a good point. Sometimes, when you do find yourself in a communication standoff and you find that the person is just not going to budge, it's time to step away. It's time to say, "Let's take a break." Come up with other tactics or do more research to uncover options. You could take the attitude that it's going to be a win-win, but just not yet. One party may have made concessions, but the other party doesn't feel he or she has received enough, so you might want to and re-evaluate to get to that win-win point.

Wright

Well, what a great conversation. I appreciate your answering all these questions for me. It's been very interesting and I've learned a lot; I'm sure our readers will also.

Leezer

Thank you so much. This is a wonderful project and I appreciate being a part of it.

Wright

Today we've been speaking with Laura Swanson Leezer. She is a corporate trainer in the professional development field as well as sales and marketing. She specializes in image and public relations, as well as customer service.

Laura, thank you so much for being with us today on *Discover Your Inner Strength*.

Leezer

Thank you.

About the Author

Laura Swanson Leezer consults professionally in the areas of marketing and public relations, and in personal and professional development. She has held management positions in the retail field, sales, buying, and training. She is currently a vice president in the financial industry and teaches at the university level. She holds a master's degree in Education, is certified in diversity and women's issues by the Professional Woman Network, and serves on the International Advisory Board.

Laura Swanson Leezer

10680 East 1000th Street
Macomb, IL 61455
309.837.2325
lauraswanson3@yahoo.com

Chapter Twenty-One
Purposeful Living

An Interview With...

Philip Guy Rochford

David Wright (Wright)

Today we're talking with Philip Guy Rochford. Philip played a key role after Trinidad and Tobago's political independence in August 1962. By September 1964, Philip returned from the United Kingdom as a business economist, he functioned as a staff assistant to the minister of Finance and Treasury's Representative on Public

Accounts Committee of Parliament. In September of 1967, Philip was appointed Corporate Secretary of Central Bank of Trinidad and Tobago, and by July 1970, he became the first and youngest Chief Executive of a commercial bank operating in Trinidad and Tobago. Philip is now a personal growth coach and he has written five books including his autobiography.

Philip, welcome to *Discover Your Inner Strength*.

Philip Rochford (Rochford)

Thank you, David.

Wright

What do you remember to be outstanding as a young child?

Rochford

My first recollection is at the age of four, when I had my first cruel experience—a teacher ignored my raised hand when I had to go to the bathroom. Perhaps this has subconsciously made me more sensitive to the needs of people, and to be more aware of my immediate environment.

As I grew older, what struck me was the central part that my mother played in our neighborhood. You see, Mama (as we called her) was the first female druggist in Trinidad and Tobago. In those days—in 1937—there were not many medical doctors, so the neighborhood relied on the druggist of the area to deal with their health issues.

While out of sight, sitting in an easy chair behind the counter with its raised display unit, I would hear a conversation like this, "Amy, what can I do about this nagging headache?" My mother replied, "Take this medication that has been working wonders for headaches." What upset me was the requirement to spend so much of my childhood time tied up in helping out in the pharmacy. Of course, I didn't realize then that this formative part of my life—between the ages of seven to thirteen—provided a foundation of knowledge that would be germane to my own health and those around me. While in the pharmacy, I was continuously exposed to health complaints and remedies to correct them.

There were also bounteous opportunities and possibilities. As a young person I realized there was sports, in which I participated, there was education that was mandatory, there was war that changed our style of living, there was religion that was foundational, there were beautiful relationships with my peers, and there was some excitement and entertainment.

Finally, when I think in terms of my childhood, one of my interesting memories was winning a competition, among my siblings, organized by our grandfather. This was for the child who had the best shined shoes during a particular month, with the prize being a sumptuous Chinese food dinner. This accounts for my fetish of having shiny shoes, and for Chinese food being one of my favorite dishes.

Wright

So what principles did you use for your success?

Rochford

Well, this is a very interesting question because there are three definitions that I have for success, and they are all interrelated. The first is internationally acclaimed; it states that success is the progressive realization of worthwhile goals. The second is more esoteric and claims that success is your growth in happiness, and the third definition, which is my definition, simply states that success occurs when you achieve your desires. My preference is to consider myself successful when I achieve what I really want.

The various definitions have one thing in common—success is related to your values and perceptions, and not necessarily to how people see you. For example, a brilliant medical doctor may decide to become a contemplative and withdraw to the Himalayan Mountains to achieve union with God. He will spend many years and eventually find what he is looking for. In his terms, he is successful. However, someone else may feel that the doctor wasted his life and was not a success.

In my success journey, I had the courage of my convictions. My family and friends did not always agree with what I was doing, but I decided my course of action and stuck with it. For example, in 1970 I had to choose between my public service job at the Central Bank, completing my final bar examinations in the U.K., or accepting an appointment as Chief Executive at a commercial bank. Some people felt that I should not give up the security of the Central Bank; others said I should establish my independence by qualifying as an attorney-at-law. Still others believed that I should accept the challenge of indigenous banking. I decided on the commercial banking option as being a challenge and opportunity.

In fact, I used the joining of the three success definitions I referred to earlier. The first requirement was to clarify and establish what I wanted. This is sometimes referred to as a vision. I have desires. I want to experience happiness. The basket of desires continues to grow, thus the concept of progressive realization of goals. In the first definition of success, the question is who determines whether your goals are worthwhile. My view is that this is dependent on the mores or values of the society in which you live. For example, in some neighborhoods a drug lord is considered a success, while in other places this would be deviant behavior.

One of the key elements I believe necessary for success is that you must have the will to succeed. It is not sufficient to have vision, passion, desire, goals, and action. You must *want* to win. This means that you have to do whatever, ethically, morally, and legally, it takes to succeed at winning. There is sacrifice. There is delay of instant gratification. There is disruption in your social relationships. There is the financial cost. But in the end, it is worth it to achieve what you set out to do.

The other principles I used for my own success were:

- Rigorous preparation
- Consistent and relevant action
- Honesty and integrity
- Managing my activities properly
- Having balance in my life
- Polishing my communication skills
- Keeping abreast of new trends and developments
- Working on my spirituality
- Maintaining a healthy lifestyle
- Ensuring that positive material flooded my mind
- Associating with persons of a similar mindset
- Minimizing contact with energy vampires

My secret weapon of success is preparation. Whatever the task at hand, it is tackled with massive preparation. Every conceivable requirement is researched and followed. All options are considered. Country viewpoints are analyzed. An example of this was that my preparation was so thorough and pressure-proof, that after one of my negotiations with an international corporation, I was invited to sit on the board of directors of one of their subsidiaries.

Wright

So who are your mentors and success role models?

Rochford

I would like to first point out the significance of mentors of success and success role models. They have traveled the road of success, they have gained the experience of the success chase, and it is beneficial to take advantage of their experience and wisdom. It is smart to build on what has already been achieved, rather than attempt to "reinvent the wheel." This is particularly true, as so many advances have been made in the world. Additionally, there is such a diversity of skills and technologies that one mentor is not sufficient to cover all the needs of the modern man. For example, I selected different mentors for career planning, book authoring, online Internet business, and banking. There were different mentors and success role models at different times in my life.

My definition of a mentor is someone you admire, and you aspire to be like that person. Quite often, the mentor is not even aware of his or her mentoring. You may not have even met your mentor. You may have selected your mentor from observation or reading about his or her success, or through another person who knows the mentor.

Initially, my mentors were some of my favorite teachers from primary school, such as Hugh Beckford, who continued giving me sound advice after I graduated from the university, including the admonition to study Spanish to be relevant in my career in the South American region. Mr. Clibert Anatol, another teacher, whose daughter (since deceased) became my first wife; and Dr. Charles Vernon Gocking, a secondary school teacher who prepared his students for life and even gave tips on cooking. Dr. Gocking later became the Chief Education Officer in the Ministry of Education.

In my work career, mentors were Victor McIntyre, one of my primary school teachers who became my boss in the Chief Secretary's Office, and later was appointed Trinidad and Tobago's Ambassador to Washington.

McIntyre's admonishments to me were, "Rochford, in your decision-making, observe principles and not personalities," and, "If you play office politics you will get office licks." These were two key steps that I followed assiduously over the course of the years. From following these precepts, family and friends were highly annoyed when I did not give them preferential treatment when it was not deserved. For example, there was a case when one my nephews applied but was not employed in the bank where I was Chief Executive. He did not pass screening by the employee selection panel, and therefore could not be employed. He was highly critical of me, and felt that I should have overridden the selection panel.

I held Dr. Alexander McLeod, governor of our Central Bank, in high esteem for his honesty, competence, and humanity. My leading success model is Dr. Anthony Sabga, foremost Caribbean philanthropist and czar of ANSA McAl, one of the largest conglomerates in the Caribbean.

Apart from the mentors who lived in Trinidad and Tobago, I adopted many overseas mentors and read their books, autobiographies, and listened to their audio tapes, CDs, and videos. Much of my success ballast comes from them. They provided the success mindset that I was looking for. Some of these overseas mentors are Dan Kennedy, Les Brown, Jim Rohn, Brian Tracy, Dr. Wayne Dyer, Stephen Covey, Anthony Robbins, Philip Humbert, Glen Dietzel, Scott Armstrong, Tom Hopkins, and other incredible personalities. These were my mentors and models.

Wright

So what part has spirituality played in your life?

Rochford

Spirituality has been very central to my life—my adult life has spirituality as its foundation. Perhaps I should clarify. There is a distinction between religion and spirituality. To my mind, religion is a human administration of spiritual principles and concepts. Religion is expressed through rituals, formalities, places of worship, and preaching of dogma. Spirituality, on the other hand, is the exercise of core religious principles and concepts in the exercise of your daily life. For example, my approach to spirituality is observance of the golden rule—to love God and to love my neighbor as myself. In exercising the golden rule, I have found that the word "love" has been abused, misunderstood, and misinterpreted in many different ways. For instance, there is divine love and human love that are decidedly quite different, and these have further subsets.

Thus, I have approached my own spirituality by operating on the basis of kindness toward others. I find that being kind triggers empathy, compassion, truthfulness, integrity, and generosity among other qualities. Moreover spirituality for me includes being in touch with my higher self. This allows me to keep centered on what is right and needed in any set of circumstances. You normally breathe, eat, and sleep on a daily basis. Similarly, you have to keep in touch with your spirituality on a daily basis. My methods of keeping in touch have been principally by prayer and meditation. These daily quiet moments allow me to shield my persona, and prepare me to receive the energies necessary to support my purpose in life, which is to learn to grow and to be fulfilled.

Being steeped in spirituality without making a public display about it positions me to follow the best course for my life from moment to moment. Of course, I am human and therefore I am not always in a receptive state to follow the better judgment of my conscience. However, my entire adult life has been guided by the concept that I am subject to a higher divine order and I that I am my brother's keeper.

In conclusion, I can say that a central value in my spiritual quest is forgiveness. When you forgive, you are not giving a benefit to the person who hurt you. This misconception leads persons to withhold forgiveness, as they do not want the person who hurt them to get the benefit. But when you forgive, you release yourself from the burden you're carrying. For example, imagine holding the back of a chair and dragging it along as you walk about the room. The chair represents the hurt that you're carrying. The chair—the hurt—keeps you from moving freely and quickly. Now release the chair and you will enjoy a greater freedom to move about. Forgiveness is the equivalent of releasing the chair. When you exercise forgiveness, you are helping yourself and not the person who hurt you.

Wright

How did education affect your life?

Rochford

Education is a prime element in anyone's life. An education is more than the formal training that you get in primary, secondary, or tertiary education. Education is broad and covers programming that you receive in the family and community generally. Also, education is what you distill from the information and knowledge that you receive, and what you convert and draw out from within yourself.

My first level of formal education took place between the ages of four and eighteen; this was the foundation for preparing me for life. At eighteen years I left secondary school, Queen's Royal College, and ignorantly believed that was the end of my education. At that time, I thought I had sufficient schooling, and that was the end of my pouring over books. Within four years, as I gained experience in the world of work I understood that my education had only just begun, and that learning was a lifelong event.

Trinidad and Tobago was only just then becoming politically astute and, led by our prime minister, Dr. Eric Eustace Williams, tertiary education was seen as an important factor to develop the region's human resource to support transformation of the economy. This concept fitted in with my own desire to be independent in business. I took advantage of the opportunity in 1960 to accept a government scholarship and pursue a first degree in business economics at Hull University in the United Kingdom.

During my latter years as a teenager, I read many books. In particular, I read autobiographies of successful people. This gave me a great impetus to look forward to leading a life of contribution to my society. This experience also provided me with speaking opportunities and training in life and street skills.

By the time I finished my first degree, I understood that to whom much was given, much was expected. I became aware of my great obligation to return to the community the social cost it bore to nurture me to that point in my life. Thus, while there were opportunities to receive better financial rewards in more developed countries, I opted to be part of the economic transformation process in Trinidad and Tobago.

Although I had read a great deal and educated myself on many matters, I understood that academic and professional certifications were still required as formal evidence of education. This led me to become a chartered secretary, chartered accountant, chartered banker, and to graduate with a Master of Science degree in

Accounting from the University of the West Indies. There were other educational activities I pursued that I considered important to my life. I became certified in mediation, and I undertook communication and coaching programs with Landmark Education of Canada. I attained ATM bronze certification with Toastmasters International, and pursued certification in lateral thinking with Dr. Edward DeBono, international "creative thinking guru."

So in conclusion, this range of education made it possible for me to exist in a fast-changing world, and positioned me to assess situations that continuously confront me. The things of the world are all interrelated in some way, so this broad spectrum of knowledge helped me to deal creatively and effectively with matters in my life. I'm still learning and being educated day by day, and it is a wonderful experience.

A few autobiographies that I've read were those of Sir Patrick Hastings, a great English criminal lawyer, and master politician, Sir Winston Churchill, Mahatma Gandhi, Jimmy Carter, Lee Iacocca, Anthony Robbins, Jim Rohn, Erhard Werner, founder of EST, and billionaire Sir James Goldsmith.

Wright

So why did you pursue the careers that you chose?

Rochford

My careers have included public service, banking, and success coaching. While these careers were consciously chosen, there were events and circumstances that influenced the choices.

After graduating from secondary school there was a choice of either going into the private sector petroleum industry or the public sector's civil service. Through my mother's influence, I chose the civil service. The deciding factor was her experience in the great depression in the 1930s when she witnessed the drove of people who lost their jobs in the private sector. My influencing factor was thus the job security element and, in any event, jobs were scarce and our schooling did not train us to become entrepreneurs.

My first career in civil service started at eighteen years of age. Within a short time, it was clear to me that I wanted something different. My free spirit and sense of self were not comfortable within the confines of the civil service bureaucracy. Therefore, I started looking for other career opportunities.

The legal profession seemed to be a career that I would enjoy. You needed to be a good speaker, with a logical mind, a sense of justice, and a commitment to diligent preparation. This exemplified my own mindset. However, this was one of my major goals that never materialized. The short story is that the year I received my government scholarship as an administrative cadet, law was no longer an approved subject for that scholarship. Nevertheless, I pursued law on my own, and when I had arranged to go to the United Kingdom in 1970 to complete the final bar examination, the opportunity to become the first local to be appointed Chief Executive of a commercial bank in Trinidad and Tobago was offered to me. This put me on the horns of a dilemma. Apart from the legal profession, my love was in the area of money and banking. I was drawn to this area when I was studying advanced level economics. Additionally, this was a career growth area because at that time there were no local chief executives in any of the seven international commercial banks operating in Trinidad and Tobago.

In September 1967, I was appointed Corporate Secretary of the Central Bank of Trinidad and Tobago. This gave me the opportunity of understanding commercial banks from the regulatory standpoint of the Central Bank. In July 1970, I accepted the appointment of Chief Executive of the National Commercial Bank of Trinidad and Tobago, and became, at thirty-seven years old, the youngest Chief Executive of a commercial bank ever to be appointed in Trinidad and Tobago (that has not yet been broken). I saw this bank appointment as confirmation that there were citizens of Trinidad and Tobago who could manage the affairs of the country in the various segments of the economy. This was a big responsibility and I stepped up to the plate. When I left the bank, at the compulsory retirement age of sixty, much had been accomplished. The bank grew from one to eighteen branches, thirty-five to eighteen hundred employees, and from having assets of thirteen million to over two billion dollars. Profits were generated in each of my twenty-three years in this job.

After formal retirement in 1993, I looked for a way to utilize the experience and training I had accumulated over many years. The answer came in the field of lifestyle coaching where a leaf was taken from coaching in sports, and applied to life situations. At that time, this was a relatively new career internationally, and it had not yet reached Trinidad and Tobago. This was ideal for me, as I loved to pioneer new things. I had been part of the pioneering of the national commercial bank, the Central

Bank, BWIA (International) Airways, the National Petroleum Marketing Company, and our international industrial merchant bank.

My coaching career has included individuals as well as corporations. This was a natural extension of using my accumulated experience and training to support the solutions required by people in their quest to be the best they could be. My success coaching career revealed that my experience could be distilled and reduced to a form available to posterity. Hence, I authored four books and co-authored two books. I'm still open to new career possibilities.

Wright

So what message do you have for people who want greater success in their lives?

Rochford

Well, first of all, I think it's natural for everyone to want something better in his or her life. Moreover, at any point in a person's life, some success would have already been achieved through following, either consciously or unconsciously, a defined success system. What may be necessary now is to become more aware of the system, and follow it more consciously and systematically. I would say that there are seven fundamental steps to follow if you want to generate greater success:

1. Establish the results you want.
2. Set a program of goals to accomplish your results.
3. Be focused and do not scatter your energies.
4. Keep your information up to date in the areas you want success.
5. Associate with persons of a similar mindset.
6. Review your progress regularly.
7. Celebrate intermediate success.

So the big question is whether you are clear on what you want. Most people are hazy about the precise details of the success that they want. Thus, the first key is to bring clarity to the improvement you want in your life. When you have established your goal of greater success, then there are some action steps you can take and core values to be adopted and pursued.

When you identify what you want, ensure it is something that you will enjoy and that will make you happy. If it is something that you are passionate about, you will overcome all obstacles and setbacks. You will have the energy to keep on going in the face of difficult circumstances. Put another way, your desire for what you want to be successful in must be strong and continuing.

However, strong desire alone is not enough. Your desires must be converted into a program of goals and sub goals that will deliver your results. For your goals to be effective, there must be these minimal elements:

- Written as specific as possible
- Have a timeline by which each is to be accomplished
- Be measurable
- Have an emotional commitment to it
- It must give you great joy when it is accomplished
- Be willing to make sacrifices necessary for its accomplishment.

Focus is very important if you desire greater success. You're multi-talented so there are many things you can pursue. However, an abundance of ideas is the enemy of success. Greater success requires you to have greater focus. If you direct the rays of the sun through a magnifying glass, creating greater focus of the rays, the result will be such energy generated that it burns paper or dry leaves that gets in its way. That's the power of focus. It generates greater energy to produce enhanced results. Focus allows you to finish the things you start. Keeping your attention with a laser-like focus will produce the greater success that you envision. You will fail to generate greater success when you do not keep pace with technology and new information in your fields of endeavor. If you do not keep up-to-date with new developments in your field, you can be sure that you'll be left behind—your competitors will outshine you.

Of course, your environment is most powerful in determining your success. If you're surrounded by people who have a negative outlook, or people who do not support the same kind of success future that you have, it will be disastrous. Associate with people of a similar mindset. You may not be able to avoid some people due to family ties or otherwise. That's fine, just minimize the time you spend with them and share the released time with people who will strengthen your success focus.

Reviewing your progress is critical if you wish to achieve success. Review helps you to keep your focus and it is a means of continuously measuring your results. Do not underestimate the benefits of the review process; it can be on a daily, weekly, monthly, quarterly, or yearly basis. A life worth living is a life worth reviewing.

What is the purpose of achievement if there is no celebration? When you accomplish something it is worthy of celebration. A classic case is the Olympic athlete winner who takes his national flag, runs around the stadium, and later stands on the winner's podium to the playing of his country's national anthem. Celebrate small successes and this will inspire you to work for bigger success.

In conclusion, I would say that if you want greater success in your life and you believe that it is possible, then you can certainly achieve it. The mind is so constructed that it does not let your thoughts surface unless you have the potential and ability to materialize those thoughts. What the mind can see, truly believe, and act on massively and relevantly, will be achieved—to your greater success.

Wright

So what do you consider some of your major accomplishments?

Rochford

At the risk of being considered self-serving, I would say that some of my major accomplishments are:

- Achieving 80 percent of the major goals that I set in my life,
- Giving my six children a voice of their own,
- Honoring my core values,
- Being able to live a life that I enjoy,
- Being a mentor to hundreds of people,
- Providing a sense of self and self-confidence to my peer group,
- Establishing and developing the National Commercial Bank of Trinidad and Tobago; and

- Growing the National Corporation for Gas Stations from 17 to 100 percent of the market.

From the age of seventeen, I began to set goals consciously for my life. This ranged from family life to tertiary education, career development, and esoteric learning. The process of goal-setting helped me to achieve the results I wanted. Notable exceptions were becoming an attorney-at-law, establishing an ashram, and organizing a motivational academy.

My children are all adults and they have lives of their own. They are independent minded and have followed the careers that they wanted. My eldest child, Rory, died at the age of forty-seven. The others, Burt, Mark, Simone, Andrea, and Rachel, followed their own inclinations and are quite satisfied with their lives. I am pleased that I was able to nurture their own voices and, although I do not always agree with their voices, I honor their freedom to make those choices.

My core values are simple and I'm grateful that I have been able to honor them for the most part. These values include honesty, integrity, commitment, discipline, kindness, preparation, and forgiveness. It has not always been easy to live these values 100 percent at all times, but by and large I have honored them. I believe that I was born to be happy, thus I take life as it comes, look on the bright side of things, and practice to be flexible, but not too flexible. My achievement of maintaining balance in the disruptive environment of the world and being able to discern the silver lining in darkened situations have facilitated my having a joyous life. I consider my joyous life to be a great accomplishment.

I've always done my work for the work's sake. You wash a dirty plate in the kitchen sink because it needs to be washed; you do not expect any reward from the plate. Similarly, when I do work, it is done without direct expectation from the work. I do it for the work's sake. Of course I operate from a higher law of what you sow you reap. Therefore, I know that under the iron law of cause and effect, my work will be rewarded—perhaps not in the way that I would like or in its timing. My work has led to hundreds of people electing me as their mentor. I am pleased that I am able to influence others to bring out the brilliance in them, and this has been an accomplishment for me.

One of the reasons for accepting the post of Chief Executive of the National Commercial Bank of Trinidad and Tobago was to establish that there were nationals who could manage the affairs of the country. In 1970, Trinidad and Tobago was still in a state of transition from colonialism to true independence, and individuals needed to put their shoulders to the wheel of service for the country. My efforts have, in some small but important way, reinforced the view that the country had the human resources to become a first world economy. My success encouraged others to step forward and contribute to nation-building. A new sense of self-esteem and self-confidence emerged in the citizenry, and I believe that I played some part in that accomplishment.

My corporate accomplishments, including the growth of the National Commercial Bank and expansion of the market of the National Petroleum Market Company, are testaments to my corporate legacy. But at the end of the day, material accomplishments are transitory. My major accomplishments have been to become more secure in my being and to come to the understanding that I'm an integral part of the greater force that rules the universe.

Wright

So how do you balance your success with your personal and family life?

Rochford

Balancing my success, career, and my family life was a real challenge for me. The dilemma started at age twenty. I wanted to get married, but my girlfriend's father told me that he would not allow his daughter to be married unless her husband could provide her with similar comforts and home furnishings that she was enjoying in his household. I found this at the time to be unfair, as he had worked for many years to obtain his current standard of living. But this taught me a lesson that being able to provide adequately for my family was essential. This added to the driving force that financial success in my career was a necessary condition to meet my family's expectations. Thus, while I was ready at twenty years of age to raise a family from the emotional, social, and physical standpoints, I was not ready financially; I eventually married at twenty-six.

In the early years of marriage, the situation was bearable. The drama started as children were born, requiring greater demands of my time. At the same time, more of my time was needed at work to ensure rapid progress in my career. The situation was further complicated when I grasped the opportunities to pioneer things in

Trinidad and Tobago, as well as striving to make a difference, and a significant contribution.

One of the causalities was my mother. I could only visit her once a fortnight, and I found this unacceptable. I handled this by inviting her to live with my own immediate family. Fortunately for me, Mama was able to rent out her house and came to live with me until her death. My elder brother, Alfred, and my oldest sibling, Valeska, both migrated to the United Kingdom before I launched my career in earnest, so there was no conflict with them.

My wife and children posed different problems. My spouse understood that much of my attention had to be placed on my work obligations in order to provide for the family at a reasonable level. Notwithstanding that, my strategy was to concentrate on providing her with quality time, rather than greater periods of time. This meant that most of the time spent with her would be doing and sharing what she wanted, rather than what pleased me. Another strategy was to engage gardeners and maids to ease her burdens and permit her to do things that gave her happiness. There again, you see, you have to have the money to be able to provide gardeners and maids. I can attest that my success would not have been possible without the solid support of my spouse, Kathleen. Her maternal nurturing of my children was also a key success element.

Perhaps my children suffered most from the demands of my career. At the same time, my drive to be a success was for their benefit. They could not get the best of everything if I were too poor to give it to them. I gave them important spiritual values to balance the material things I provided. The children suffered most in the sense that I was not present at the parent/teacher association meetings, school open days, and I did not attend their sporting activities with any regularity. This was another area that their mother took care of. One way I balanced the scorecard was to take the entire family on special vacations, locally and overseas, from time to time. These occasions helped us to settle outstanding issues, and to get a better understanding of each other.

Over the years I have developed an interesting concept. One of the major intentions of my life was to provide adequately for my family. However, if, in the course of developing my career, I lost my wife or my children became deviant, then the effort was all in vain. This means that you really have to find a way to balance your success and your family life. You are not born with a manual that gives you details of how to operate in relationships. By and large, you operate through trial and error, and by using your parents, guardians, and those in your immediate environment as models. The books and motivational materials I read stopped me from ending my career and family relationships in a complete tragedy. That is the challenge of living—balancing your career with your family life.

Wright

So what is the vision you have for the rest of your life?

Rochford

That's interesting. I have lived for seventy-six years, and I have completed a majority of my major goals. I believe that I made a positive difference in the lives of thousands of people. It is also my view that I made a difference—a small but significant one—to the growth and development of Trinidad and Tobago. Having lived, however, for so long has given me the opportunity, from an individual standpoint, to observe the apparent insignificance of it all. Whatever you do generally pales into insignificance with the passage of time. Given my experience, it stretches my imagination, therefore, to determine what vision I should hold for the rest of my life.

A future vision challenges me to think outside the casket—not the box—but outside the casket. Despite the backdrop of my experience, and the apparent insignificance of our life's journey in relation to the universe, there are five main areas that I would like to pursue for the rest of my life:

- Continue my spiritual journey to get a better understanding of myself and the Creator,
- Deepen the consolidation of my family life,
- Follow the principles of healthy living,
- Be a repository of knowledge, wisdom, and experience that is relatively easily available to others, and
- Establish a movement of motivators to shift the consciousness of society to another level of positive thinking.

In a nutshell, my vision for the rest of my life is to continue to live a life of learning, growing, and being fulfilled. This purpose has been manifested in different ways at different stages of my life. The challenge is to become aware of the underlying and unifying force. It is a learning process, and a work in progress that I have been following from birth and it will continue—at least until the casket. I certainly will continue following my creed. My creed simply is:

I see the brighter side of situations.

I speak the positive side of things.

I communicate with energy.

I listen attentively.

I encourage others.

I keep continuously acclaiming the good in others.

I forgive myself for any limitations.

I forgive others who hurt me.

I am kind to all.

I seek to bring out the best in myself.

I help others to rise to their best potential.

I acknowledge that there is a Supreme Creative Force, and that

I am a spark of it, and that is my life.

Wright

Well, what a great conversation, Philip. I really do appreciate all the time you've taken to answer these questions. I have really been impressed. I've learned a lot and I'm sure our readers will.

Rochford

Thank you, David.

Wright

Today we've been talking with Philip Guy Rochford. He played a key role in Trinidad and Tobago's banking industry after the country's political independence in 1962. We have heard his remarkable story today. He is now a personal growth coach and author of five books, including his autobiography.

Philip, thank you so much for being with us today on *Discover Your Inner Strength*.

Rochford

And David, I thank you for this wonderful opportunity and your insightful questions.

About the Author

Philip Guy Rochford, a top Caribbean Lifestyle Coach, business economist, and former chairman of a bank, airline and petroleum marketing company, lives in Trinidad and Tobago. He has six children and seven grandchildren, and is married to Edlin. He is author of the books *Live a Life of "Virtual" Success, The Executive Speaks, Infinite Possibilities, Glimpses of Greatness: His Autobiography*, and co-author of *A Search for Purpose*. He is also A Reiki Master and an Able Toastmaster Bronze of Toastmasters International. In 1975, he was awarded The Humming Bird Medal (Gold) in the sphere of economics in his country's Civil National Awards.

Philip Guy Rochford

8 Morne Coco Road

Westmoorings

Trinidad

Trinidad and Tobago

868.633.7856

http://www.nurturinglifebooks.com

http://www.nurturinglife.com

philipgrochford@hotmail.com

Chapter Twenty-Two

The Choice of Inner Strength

An Interview With…

Jodi Fraser

Wright (Wright)

Today we're talking with Jodi Fraser, coach, author, and Human Resources Consultant. Jodi's career focus has been in the area of Human Resources for the past fifteen years at various organizations in the San Francisco Bay area. She is also a Business and Life Coach, and has been working with business professionals, executives, and various clients since 2004. Her passion is working with people who are motivated to grow and move to action in their professional and personal lives. Her personal intent is to motivate, encourage, and inspire others to see and embrace their grace, unique beauty, talent, and greatness. Jodi holds a BA in Business Management from the University of Phoenix and is presently completing her master's in Organizational Psychology from Cappella University. Jodi received her coach training from Corporate Coach University and was trained as a Strengths Coach at Gallup University in Omaha, Nebraska. She resides in the San Francisco Bay area and is completing her first book titled *Journey* that will be published in summer 2009.

Jodi, welcome to *Discover Your Inner Strength*.

Jodi Fraser (Fraser)

Thank you, David.

Wright

What inspired you most about this project?

Fraser

The subject itself is fascinating because it is an on-going process based upon where you are and what you may be experiencing in your life. I also found this subject very timely, considering our current economic climate and the amount of life changes that seem to be coming at everyone.

Wright

Tell me more about that.

Fraser

It was a great process for me to become clear on not only what *inner strength* is, but also what the discovery process is as well.

Oprah Winfrey writes an article in each month's issue of her O magazine called "What I know for Sure." This is what I read before any other article in the issue because it always seems to be relevant, insightful, and helps me to see, think, or feel a subject from a different perspective.

As I was prepping for this interview, I had my own "What I know for sure" moment. This experience completely shifted my thoughts around how I was approaching the Discover Your Inner Strength project.

For weeks, I had been writing, rewriting, and editing what I thought would be the right thoughts and words that would help and inspire others to discover their inner strength. Then, a few nights before this interview, I was reviewing it again, feeling that it didn't sound right—that it wasn't flowing.

Wright

What didn't sound right?

Fraser

I didn't sound like me. I sounded as if I were giving a lecture.

Wright

So what happened?

Fraser

Well, using Oprah's term, "What I do know for sure," is that if you are not authentic, it is obvious to others. Dr. Wayne Dyer puts it this way: "If you are overly concerned with how you are going to be perceived by everyone, then you've disconnected yourself from your intention and allowed others' opinions of you to guide you . . ."

In a matter of twelve hours, I had two people very near and dear to me each say something so similar, that I realized I was given a sign, but until I got it, I would be in the midst of this dichotomy of feeling stuck about what I wanted to say.

Wright

What was it that they said to you that shifted your thoughts?

Fraser

My best friend mentioned in passing, "Don't over think the Discover Your Inner Strengths interview. Just let it flow naturally." Then she added, "I don't know why I said it, but for some reason you need to know that."

My partner looked at me the next morning in the mirror, after watching me be frustrated writing and re-writing the questions that would capture what I wanted to say in the interview. He said, "Sweetie, you are over-thinking everything, and sometimes slowing down to feel things, really speeds things up and makes it easier." I looked back in the mirror at him rather perplexed. Then he smiled and told me a story about a driving course that police officers take, and that interestingly enough, the women officers tend to score higher and faster than the men. "Do you want to know why that is?" he asked.

"Sure." I answered.

"Men tend to be more competitive and aggressive when they are driving, while the women are feeling it, perhaps slowing down, but being able to trust that inner knowledge versus having to be thinking competitively."

I pondered that thought a while—thinking versus feeling.

As I drove to work, I suddenly understood why I was struggling with my questions and message. They were not coming from my heart—I was thinking about what would be right. So, thinking versus feeling—what I thought the reader would want to read. What I realized was that if you don't feel this in your heart, believe it in your soul, and in your innate being, then the discovery will not happen. Bottom line, I don't want you to think about discovering your inner strengths, I want you to feel it.

Michael Bernard Beckwith wrote that this is a feeling universe—you can have all the thoughts in the world, but unless you feel it, manifestation or change cannot occur. That is what motivates us. It is that ultimate trust, that complete leap of faith. A leap of faith isn't thought, it is truly felt.

What I had intended as a guide to help people discover their inner strengths was thought and written versus felt and created. I recognized that I cannot tell anyone the exact formula to discover their inner strengths, mainly because of our true uniqueness as individuals. What applies to one, cannot apply to another. This I know from being a human resources (HR) professional, a business coach, a mom, a friend, a partner, and just a human being. One size cannot fit all . . . thank God!

Wright

What else did you discover?

Fraser

What I do know is that people's stories of their experiences inspire us. We either resonate and relate to them or we don't—it has to appeal to each person.

The best example I can give to others about discovering your inner strengths is to tell the story of how this chapter came to be and in the process, how I discovered my inner strength. My intent is to tell my truth, and if my words speak to the readers, then I have done what I intended to do—inspire others to action, to their calling, and discovery.

Because of the beauty of the changes we experience in life, you will continue to discover so many of the inner strengths you have within yourself. The best part is that it's not a one-shot deal, and you will recognize the different strengths carry you at different times.

Life is never easy for anyone. While it may look and feel as if our life challenges are so completely obvious, they can easily go unnoticed, especially to those people who are closest to us. In reality, each of us lives in our own world, completely focused on our life, our challenges, happiness, and dramas. It is only when we stop and remember that every other soul on the face of this planet is also in the midst of their own issues that we become more aware. From that place we can hold their experience with understanding and empathy.

Wright

What is your story on how you discovered your inner strength?

Fraser

The story of discovering my inner strength began about eighteen months ago while I was going through an exorbitant number of life changes, some registering pretty high on the Richter scale of stress. Others were smaller, but still had a profound affect. I wish I were fortunate enough to be able to count them on one hand, but that wasn't the case. In retrospect, I can now choose to view them as great opportunities for growth in my life, as they were catalysts for me to see what I was truly capable of doing and becoming.

Wright

How did you deal with the challenges you faced?

Fraser

I struggled through a divorce, some serious health issues, and job challenges to name a few. Life transitions can be testing and frightening at times. Generally, a first response is to look outside yourself to find the answers. We tend to hyper-focus on how to fix things to make them right again, so that there is an illusion of safety and stability. We want to believe that the tighter we hold on to something, the more we can control life from changing without our consent.

Sometimes, we look to find a person/entity to pin blame on to help us feel better about what has happened. Not to sound harsh, but that really means we are not taking on the responsibility of our own life. Does this sound familiar? Well, if you can say, "Yes, I've done that—" I would also be a person to hold up my hand and say I have done the same thing, numerous times.

My greatest take-away from the challenges I faced was the recognition that when I looked outside of myself for answers, it did not change the circumstances. What I do know for sure is that when I looked inside myself for my answers, it held a different truth for me. What I recognized was that I held the key inside of me, and that was recognizing the ability to choose.

In Neale Donald Walsch's book, *Conversations with God*, he notes that our overall life purpose is to be in a process of creation. He states that "where you are creating yourself anew, seeking to determine 'Who You Want to Be' in every moment you experience. It almost doesn't matter how you label the moment, but the person that you choose to be in that moment." He continues, "Know and understand that there will be challenges and difficult times. Don't try to avoid them. Welcome them. Gratefully. Cultivate the technique of seeing all problems as opportunities to be, and decide, 'Who You Really Are' and who you choose to be in that moment."

Wright

How would you define "inner strength"?

Fraser

I define inner strength as a choice. It is choosing to move forward, choosing to accept, choosing to be strong, or choosing to believe in something that has meaning or purpose for you, even if it isn't the popular decision of others in your life or world. What works for you may not work for others, or vice versa. But, the choice to be true to your core self, your truth, your values, and your dreams is where the discovery starts.

I accepted a job that I thought was my dream job. It seemed to have everything that I wanted: an office with a view, a great opportunity for advancement, a chance to collaborate, contribute, and make an amazing salary to boot. These were so many of the things that I wanted and that I thought would bring me happiness. (Honestly, there is nothing wrong with a great job or making a top salary.) However, as I stepped into this new role, my marriage was in the process of ending, and components of the job included a commute, travel, and at times, long hours, even after I got home. This quickly became my way of life and I bought into the appealing pace, pattern, and lifestyle. In return, the solace it offered me was the opportunity to not have time to face my life issues or to heal from the changes I was in the midst of. Not a good choice, but it is what I did at the time.

The pace didn't lessen, and I didn't do anything to stop it. Instead of being in charge of my life, I allowed my life to take control of me, conscious or unconscious, this was a choice I made at the time. The quality of work that I was more than capable of delivering started to suffer. I didn't have time to devote to friendships, and thus felt very lonely. The time I spent with my son was not quality by any stretch. It appeared that I had so many great blessings in my life, but I really didn't seem to be aware of them. I became very unhappy with myself and my life, and as much as I wanted things to change and be happy, I continued to manifest more of the same. I felt I was in the middle of a vicious circle that seemed to have no way out. I had forgotten that I had the key—the source of my happiness, joy, and bliss was within me. The harder I tried to control things, the more challenges seemed to come at me. My response was to look harder outside of myself to fix things and to find my joy, bliss, contentedness and love.

In mid 2008, the universe provided me with a number of wake-up calls that would become the catalyst for my own growth and change. It would take discovering my own inner strength to shift myself from a place where I felt I had no choice, to a place where I understood that if I wanted things to be different in my life, I would have to choose change and rely on my inner strength to shift my thoughts and behaviors.

Wright

What were the wake-up calls that the universe provided?

Fraser

In late 2007, I had been diagnosed with retinopathy in my right eye, a result of having type I diabetes for almost twenty-nine years (which is a daily challenge and choice in and of itself). By August 2008, I been through four eye surgeries and had lost about a third of the vision of my eye. The possibility of losing my vision was very frightening for me.

In order to prevent it from getting worse, it was my doctors' recommendation to continue to exercise, eat right, get plenty of rest, and keep my stress level to a minimum. However, I continued the breakneck pace I had become accustomed to. It was almost like a drug or an adrenaline rush. The result was additional hemorrhaging in my eye. The next few months that followed would require more intensive and painful laser surgery, with the outcome losing almost half the vision in my right eye. This was a wake-up call to reduce the stress in my life, as well as a sign that I needed to take better care of myself. I was pushing myself very hard, physically.

A few weeks later, I had left the office late to pick up my son, Chris, after school for our week together. However, by the time I reached him, I was heavily engaged on a call from work. "Hey sweetie, I'm on a call—" was my greeting to him. He rolled his eyes at me while he climbed into the car and we proceeded to drive home. I ended the call, only in time for the phone to ring again.

"Mom—" he protested.

"Hang on!" I said back. I finished the call just we rolled up in to the driveway. "Hey there," I looked at him. "How was your day?"

His eyes were full of hurt as he said "Mom, your job is always more important than me." He got out of the car, and went into the house. I felt as though I had been hit in the stomach with a fastball going ninety miles an hour. What was I doing to our relationship? Another sign, one of the most important relationships in my life was truly suffering. I would never get this time back with my son.

The final sign happened two days later. My son and I were driving home from spending a weekend away at a lake, with friends waterskiing. Even though I was exhausted, I drove, struggling to stay alert. For a split second, I closed my eyes. I heard my son scream, "Mom, stop!" right before I hit the car in front of me. Luckily, no one was injured, and while my car sustained some damage, the thought that I had been careless enough to doze at the wheel and get into accident with my son in the car was more than I could handle.

Wright

That must have been frightening. What happened after that?

Fraser

I felt empty inside and, as I sat in my backyard later that evening, I realized I had no idea who I was or what I wanted. I was this person whose only goal appeared to be to live to work while I was forsaking my child, my own well-being, and life to completely focus on a job. I had let it become my identity. I made a great deal of money, but in truth, I was very unhappy. Why did I feel this way? The job did not fulfill me, and I could not connect to the harsh competitive and hierarchal culture. I gave it all my energy, time, and commitment, but there wasn't any way that it could return the level of feeling or satisfaction I was seeking.

I realized I was looking for the job to fulfill that need. I was searching for answers and happiness outside of myself. It was as though I was in a fog and could see, hear, and watch my life happening, but I was not a participant in it. I knew that I could not go on like this. It was the wake-up call to find myself again.

I sat there and tears flowed as I realized a number of things—I was not my job, my coach bags, clothes, status, or car. However, I had let so much of that define me that I had forgotten to be authentic, not only with my outside world, with many of the people I loved and cared about.

The hardest part was the recognition that I had not even been authentic with me. So, if I wasn't authentic with me, who had I become? Not being able to answer that question helped me to see that I had been on a constant search outside of myself to find my source of happiness and joy with the anticipation and hope that it would make me happy. Only I was not out there, I was right here. And right here, I was in a good deal of hurt.

I could choose to stay this way or I could choose to save myself. My ah-ha moment was realizing that I had the power to make changes in my life—only Jodi could save Jodi and only Jodi could change Jodi. But I had to own my power. No one else could do it for me. It was a harsh feeling to see that I was not the woman I thought I had been pretending to be. My world outside was in complete chaos, because my inner self was in chaos. My outer world had become a reflection of my inner world. "As within, so without . . ."—Hermes. Choosing this path would take more inner strength than I was sure I even had. I wondered, how do I do it?

Wright

So how were you able to do it? How did you make the changes you needed to make?

Fraser

That is a great question. One of the best statements about "how to do something" I have ever read was from Bob Proctor in the book, *The Secret*, which is about applying the Law of Attraction. He said that "if you just do a little research, it is going to become evident to you that anyone that ever accomplished anything, did not know how they were going to do it. They only knew they were going to do it."

So, it wasn't worrying about "how" to do it—it was about just moving forward, knowing that I was going to make a conscious choice to change.

And I chose to move forward.

For me, the path to discovering my inner strengths began with the recognition of understanding and knowing myself. I also knew that in order to do this, I would need to shift the mental models that I had been living with and buying into for some time. It was important for me to begin to uncover the hidden assumptions, beliefs, attitudes, points of view, and ways of being that were affecting my life from being the way I wanted it to be, and asking "where am I limiting myself?" Carl Jung said "One does not become enlightened by imagining images of light, but by making the darkness conscious."

Wright

What else did you do?

Fraser

I took time to rest, do yoga, and take time to go within with meditation, breathing, and prayer. I started to be clear about listening to my heart, and what felt right for me, and by doing so, I discovered that I held the key to my own inner happiness and joy. Finding this inside myself, felt sustainable for me, where seeking it outside of myself made it feel very unattainable. This was an amazing inner strength to discover. I decided to start being aware of what was not working for me, then to be very clear on what I did want for me, and for my life.

I took time to write about what was truly important to me—my son and being available for him, being present for him, and really taking the time to enjoy him. I had also deeply missed being with dear friends as well as making time for creativity and spirituality. I was pushing myself very hard physically, and not getting proper rest and down time. I also really wanted to find time to date. I started to read books that resonated with the concept of going within, such as *the Power of Intention* by Wayne Dyer; *A New Earth* by Eckert Tolle; *Harmonic Wealth* by James Arthur Ray; *Zero Limits* by Joe Vitale, and *Conversations with God* by Neal Donald Walsch. Each book guided me to discover different truths about myself, and strengthened the commitment that I was making about choosing my thoughts, listening to my heart, trusting my intuition, living my truth, living in gratitude and knowing that I am the source of my own joy and happiness. All sources for inner strength.

Wright

What were some of the truths you realized?

Fraser

I realized I really loved my career in Human Resources, but my current work environment wasn't a culture of support. The hours required and amount of travel kept me from my son, friends, and even my life at times (perhaps I should say, that I allowed it to do so). I put deep feeling into what was important, what resonated with my heart, what felt right for me. Having been a successful businessperson for so long, it was hard at first to listen to my heart and let the babble in my head go. So, here was an opportunity to discover another inner strength. I held to my choice of wanting to live a conscious life and that my source of happiness and joy came from within me. My priorities were about my son, my well-being, doing a job that I loved and enjoyed, but in an environment that was congruent with my values.

After much contemplation, I chose to step down from my position. I knew I would be able to make a living contracting and continuing to coach clients and take time to expand my writing career.

Stepping down was one of the most difficult choices I faced, but it was also one of the best things I have ever done for myself. I listened to my truth. It was not easy to take a leap of faith that I would be able to make a living by contracting, coaching, and writing. It was my inner strength of choosing what was right for me. It was choosing to move forward, and choosing to believe in something that had great meaning and purpose for me. I held to knowing I was meant to live a life that was aligned with my values, I was available to be the mom I wanted to be for my son, and not let my job always be a priority over him. I knew I needed to have time to take better care of myself, with rest and exercise to allow my body time to heal from the surgeries. With regards to my career, I wanted to draw on my experiences and find ways to be of service and support to others as a coach, a writer, and an HR contractor. It was drawing on the inner strength of trust and faith that what I really wanted in my life could be there. It was the inner strength of realizing that I had the power to make my life what I wanted it to be. This became my life by my design.

I changed the way I looked at things, and life began to change for me.

Wright

That is amazing. How did life change for you?

Fraser

My relationship with my son, Chris, began to renew itself. While it is always challenging communicating with your teenager, we strengthened our love for one another. He knows I love him and am there for him. I have also learned he is there for me as well.

Contract jobs started to show up. Opportunities to write became available and I suddenly had a number of great coaching clients and I was making a sustainable living. I am in the process of completing my first book, and continue to do the things I enjoy with purpose and meaning behind them.

I met a wonderful man, and our dating relationship became the partnership that I had always dreamed of. We continue to learn and grow together each day and have found ways to combine our families and commitment to one another.

Wright

How are things different for you after discovering your inner strength?

Fraser

My life a year later is different in the sense that I continue to seek my joy, happiness, and bliss on the inside. I only can accomplish this by making a conscious choice each day to do this. This is the greatest inner strength I discovered about myself, as well as one I draw upon continually.

The choice to be true to your core self, your truth, your values, and your dreams is where the discovery of your inner strength begins.

Admittedly, I am not perfect. I get off track or things go awry. When I notice this happening, I will draw on that inner strength, making a conscious choice of how I am going to be in the situation. I keep making the choice on this rather than get upset, carried away, or go into a realm of self-doubt.

Wright

So what is your formula on how one does this?

Fraser

While the discovery of your inner strengths is different for each person (as I mentioned earlier), I would begin by asking you how well do you know yourself? What are the things that are important to you? What inspires you? Starting with some basic self-reflection builds a good foundation in knowing yourself. Meditation, prayer, or yoga are other tools that may also help in continuing to build and strengthen this on-going life process. I also continue to read books that inspire me, so a combination of each of these things brings nourishment to my soul.

The next step is that I created some coaching questions for myself. I looked at the situation from the perspective of "How would I approach this with a client or colleague who was in the same type of situation?" I came up with the list below. This list shouldn't be rushed through. I suggest that you take some time and ponder some of the questions. You may want to get a journal and write out your answers and have fun and expand on what you discover.

1. What is it that I really want in my life?
2. If I look at what I really want in my life, and how my life is at the current moment, what no longer serves me?

3. If there are things in my life that no longer serve me, what can I do to let go of them with peace and gratitude?

4. What are the things in my life that work well for me?

5. Of the things that work well for me in my life, how can I embrace them with gratitude to allow more into my life?

6. What is my truth?

7. Am I choosing to live my truth?

8. What would it look like to listen to and live my truth each day?

9. How do I allow myself to be present in the moment?

10. Does my life feel different when I am present? If so, how?

11. How are my words and actions congruent? If not, what are daily choices I can make to ensure that my words and actions are congruent?

12. Are my actions inspired? If so, how?

13. Am I choosing to react or respond to situations in my life? Which takes thought? Which is instantaneous?

14. How am I willing to step out of my comfort zone for what I want and/or believe in for me? If I did, what would that look like?

15. This is my favorite question: If there was something that I wanted to do or accomplish, and absolutely nothing was standing in my way, what would I be willing to risk or try?

As you read what you have written, what will it take for you to consciously choose each day to make these changes in your life?

Wright

This is very interesting. So, where else do you see yourself applying strengths in your life?

Fraser

Right now, finding time for everything in my life takes inner strength to find the balance to do all I need to get done with quality. It is choosing where I need to focus my time and energy wisely. It is choosing to be present with what is important right now. I am in the process of finishing my first book, drafting the next book project, and have my scheduled time with HR clients and coaching clients each week. I make sure I schedule time to exercise, meditate, and get plenty of rest each day. I also have my family life to balance, which includes my son, Chris, my partner, David, and his three children.

We are all learning how to be a family and all the chaos that goes along with four kids, two households, and two careers. Everyone gets along, but, with six different personalities, teenage hormones, work schedules, mood-swings, homework, needs, attitudes, and iPods, things can be a bit crazy. As parents, we work as a team, which involves taking time to listen to everyone's needs, especially when someone is feeling left out. It also means being supportive, reliable, and available for one another, since relationships are never 50/50, and at times one person is carrying more than the other. Making time for everyone in the family as a group as well as taking time to focus on our relationship and friendship is very important. I keep coming back to choice and who I choose to be in each moment. I can choose to be patient with myself and my family, I can choose to be a supportive partner, Mom and friend. I can choose to be mentally and emotionally available for them, as well as for myself. At the end of the day, it feels better to know I made choices to do my best, rather than regret my actions or behavior. You can respond or you can react. Response takes conscious thought.

Wright

I've noted that you have quoted people during our conversation. I'm always fascinated by mentors and the power of having a mentor and being a mentor. My question is, say it's ten years later, you have a son who is twenty-four. Does he get it? Does he know how strong his mother is? Do you think that's going to help him throughout his life?

Fraser

I believe that we always learn from our children and I have learned patience and love from being a Mom. I have re-discovered that role of Mother is my most important job, as we influence how our children how up in the world. Chris is going to be fourteen any moment, and I feel very blessed to have met this wonderful soul that is my son. He is funny, very smart and has a wonderful, warm, loving heart. I want to be the best example I can be as a human-being for him to model.

He has grown up knowing that I have diabetes and that is challenging and scary for a child. He has always been supportive and wants to learn more about what I have. He understood from the time he was two how to dial 911 is Mommy is sick or what to do if my blood glucose drops. He has participated in working the JDRF "Walk for the Cure" here in the San Francisco East Bay Area since he was eight, because it could help his mom. Yes, I think he knows his mom is strong, but I think I have raised a son who has some great inner strength as well.

What I want the most for him is to believe in himself and become the best person he can be, to choose to live his life with integrity and truth, choose to laugh a lot, and enjoy life. I'm very blessed to be his mom and it's a joy getting to watch him grow into an amazing person—even the moments when he drives me nuts.

Wright

This has been a great conversation. I've learned a lot. This topic of inner strength is an interesting one. I think that you bottom-lined it—it's a choice. I really do appreciate the time you've chosen to spend with me answering all these questions.

Fraser

You're welcome. Thank you very much. I appreciate the time getting the opportunity to talk with you as well.

Wright

Today we have been talking with Jodi Fraser, HR consultant and coach. She works with executives, professionals, and various clients who are motivated to grow and move to action in their professions and in their personal lives.

Jodi, thank you so much for being with us today on *Discover Your Inner Strength*.

Fraser

Thank you, David.

About the Author

J odi Fraser's lifelong dream has been to be a writer. At the age of 6, Jodi was writing and illustrating stories to amuse herself and her family. Inspired by her artist Mother, Jodi was encouraged to write and use her imagination. Writing became a life passion, outlet and hobby, which has produced "heaps of journals, poetry, stories, thoughts and adventures... I literally write on anything I can get my hands on, when inspiration hits me."

With a BA in Business Management, Coaching Certifications and a close-to-completed MS in Organizational Psychology, Jodi has been an HR Professional for 14 years, for various companies in the San Francisco Bay Area. After a number of challenging events in 2007 and 2008 shifted her life, she began her quest to discover answers to some very powerful questions about what was truly important for her. Relying on her spirituality and intuitive nature, she stepped into a journey of discovery, self-reflection, enlightenment and listening to and "living" her truth. In September 2008, Jodi left a highly coveted corporate position to "gear her life down and breathe again" and pursue her dream of becoming a published author. The result of journaling through this transformational time became the novel, Journey that is slated for completion in summer of 2009.

Presently the lead writer on her first journal project with Cosmic Cowgirls, Ink, a woman owned publishing company, Jodi is passionately working on Grace & Gratitude ~ a journal for women with Type-1 Diabetes. Also in the works is: Sometimes Chaos, Sometimes Nirvana, the follow up to Journey.

Jodi continues to work as a Freelance Writer, HR Consultant and Life/Business Coach. She resides in the San Francisco Bay area with her teenage son, her partner David, and his three children.

Jodi Fraser
jodi@jodifraser.com
www.JodiFraser.com

Chapter Twenty-Three

Inner Strength: *The Key to Your Career Success*

An Interview With...

Allison Timberlake

David Wright (Wright)

Today we're talking with Allison Timberlake, a professional life and career coach. Allison helps her clients find careers that are a perfect fit for them, and then supports them in creating quantum leaps in career success and fulfillment. Allison believes people are much more effective in the world when they enjoy their work. She teaches clients how to create their own happiness in any situation, which frees them to pursue their inspiration anywhere they choose. Allison spent a decade working in the corporate world where she learned the secrets to career happiness. She went from being deeply unhappy in her work to experiencing joy and fulfillment in a short period of time, and now she teaches others how to do the same in their careers. Her background includes degrees in Biology and Psychology. She is also a graduate of the Integrative Coaching Program at John F. Kennedy University, and was trained and certified by author and life coach Martha Beck.

Allison, welcome to *Discover Your Inner Strength*.

Allison Timberlake (Timberlake)

Thank you, David.

Wright

How do you define inner strength?

Timberlake

I define inner strength as the internal resources that everyone possesses, which can be drawn upon to get whatever you want in life. Inner strength enables you to rise to life's challenges and make it through the tough times that inevitably come up for all of us. Without the ability to tap into your inner strength, it's easy to get tossed around by what happens to you. You'll tend to let external circumstances dictate how you feel about yourself and your goals, and your actions will be determined by how you feel in the moment rather than by your commitment to follow through with your plans.

The most effective people in the world have a deep well of inner strength they can draw upon in any situation where they need an edge—something extra to set them apart from everyone else. It comes in handy when you're trying to get the job or land the big account or ask out someone new.

It can be tempting to attribute the differences between people to luck or opportunities that they're born with. But everyone experiences setbacks and times when things don't go as planned. The difference comes in how you react to those situations. Someone with the ability to draw upon their inner strength has tools to help him or her persevere, while someone without this ability is likely to grow disheartened and give up when troubles arise and the going gets tough.

Wright

What are some of these tools?

Timberlake

Inner strength encompasses many resources that help you succeed, and there are some specific tools that successful people utilize regularly. These tools include faith, passion, conscious creation, and intuition.

A very important one is faith. This includes faith in yourself and faith in a higher power. Faith in yourself is a necessary component to achievement because you must know and trust that you'll follow through with what you set out to accomplish. Without faith, your actions will be half-hearted. Why try your absolute best if you're not sure you'll follow through or if you don't think you're up to the challenge? You must have confidence that if something unexpected comes up, you'll figure out how to handle it or find someone who can help you.

Having faith in God or a higher power can enhance your personal strength. People who live through catastrophic events often credit their survival to the belief that God would see them through. Believing that you're not alone in your struggles, and that there is a benevolent force to assist you, gives you that extra push you need at the time you need it.

Wright

How can one who has lost faith in oneself find it again?

Timberlake

Faith in yourself is created one step at a time. The best way to rebuild it is to keep your promises to yourself, even the little ones. If you say you're going to get to bed thirty minutes earlier from now on, be sure to do it. If you promise yourself you'll exercise three times a week, keep your word to yourself. It may not seem like a big deal if you don't stick to your plans, but little by little, you'll be chipping away at the trust you have in yourself. Would you continue to have faith in a friend who consistently failed to follow through with his or her promises? Probably not, and you won't trust yourself, either. If you can follow through on the little things, you'll find that you become more confident about trusting yourself with the big things.

Wright

You mentioned passion before. How important is it to have passion for what you do?

Timberlake

Passion is another important component of inner strength. Many people come to me for help finding careers they are passionate about because they want to feel happier and more fulfilled at work. When you feel a natural attraction for certain activities, your actions are somehow magnified and you accomplish more with seemingly less effort. Mihaly Csikszentmihalyi found this to be true in his study of flow, or what is sometimes called being "in the zone." People in the zone experience time differently. When you have an extraordinary interest or ability in an area, time can seem to fly by and hours feel like minutes. You are able to stick to the task at hand and not grow weary for long periods of time, making amazing progress quickly. For those who love their jobs, the work day flies by and much is accomplished. For those who don't, the day can seem to crawl at a snail's pace, with little or nothing of importance being accomplished.

When you're passionate about what you do, it's as if the forces of the universe conspire to help you achieve your goals. Your passion and focus attract the perfect conditions you need at the time you need them.

Wright

How does this relate to the Law of Attraction?

Timberlake

The Law of Attraction states that our thoughts are made of energy vibrating at a certain frequency, much like a solid object is actually composed of vibrating atoms. According to this law, you attract back to you experiences that resonate with the vibration of your thoughts. Therefore, you can consciously attract the experiences you'd like to have by changing your thoughts.

What gets in the way of manifesting what you want is resistance. Resistance exists as beliefs and emotions you have that contradict what you want. An example of resistance would be a belief that you don't deserve what you're trying to attract or that there isn't enough of what you want to go around. Any belief that might provide an excuse for your inability to get what you want will tend to keep your desires from showing up in your reality. Having passion for something tends to powerfully focus your thoughts into a strong vibration while at the same time minimizing any resistance. So, you could say that passion is one way to utilize the Law of Attraction to help you get what you want.

I use a simplified formula with my clients to show how thinking leads directly to external results: beliefs create emotions, emotions influence actions, and actions determine results:

Beliefs ➡ Emotions ➡ Actions ➡ Results

A belief is simply a thought you think over and over again until it forms a path like a wheel rut in your brain. The more you think a thought, the more neural connections you form along that pathway, and it becomes easier for electrical impulses to follow that path in the future. To your conscious mind, a well-worn belief pathway feels like a part of you. You feel some ownership in it, which is why beliefs are harder to let go of than mere thoughts. You define yourself by them, and often get a payoff from them, or you would not keep them as beliefs for long.

The next stop on the diagram is emotions. A belief will create a particular emotion in you, positive or negative. Then, these emotions will determine what actions you take. Let's say you are not enjoying your current job and want to look for a new one. If you have positive beliefs, such as "I'm an asset to any company, and I know I can get a great new job," you'll have the energy and optimism to conduct a fruitful job search. However, if you're in the same situation and you believe, "The economy is terrible right now. I bet it will be hard to find a great job," then you will not have much energy or optimism to try to get that new job, and may engage in sabotaging behaviors such as procrastination. That can then create more negative thoughts, leading to more inaction, eventually becoming a vicious cycle. Your results will come from the actions you take and the energy and mindset with which you take them.

Wright

If our beliefs aren't working for us, can we consciously change them, and if so, how?

Timberlake

Yes, people can consciously change their beliefs. In fact, choosing beliefs consciously is how people become the creators of their lives. Going back to the belief diagram, it is possible to work at any point along the path to get different results. For example, you can work at the level of actions, which is where willpower comes in. Willpower is taking action without regard to the emotions you are feeling. It can be a useful strategy in some situations, but people often find it hard to sustain. That's why diet and exercise programs based on willpower often fail. It's hard to go to the gym when you don't feel like exercising, and it's difficult to refuse a piece of chocolate cake when you really want it.

You can also work at the level of emotions. This is where you do what feels good in the moment despite the beliefs you have. Many people do this as a coping mechanism, and it can be very helpful. When you choose to do an activity that brings you joy in order to feel better, you are consciously creating the experience you want to have. This can help you generate the energy and inspiration you need to take action on your goals. However, the strategy can be a problem when you purposely choose activities that cut you off from how you feel. For example, some people watch television to zone out, eat junk food for a temporary high, or surf the Internet for hours following one thrill after another. This differs from joy-inducing activity because it results in less energy and inspiration, and actually keeps you from taking action toward your goals.

I recommend working at the level of your beliefs to create lasting changes in your life. It's the most powerful level at which to work because when a belief changes, the emotions, actions, and results shift spontaneously and naturally. Feeling good and taking action become effortless. To work on the beliefs that are limiting you, it's important to know exactly what they are. You may already be conscious of some of them, but others could be hidden from you.

An easy way to uncover limiting beliefs is to trace the path backward from results to the belief. For example, let's say the result you're experiencing in your life right now is being in a job that you don't like and you're not taking any action to find a better one. Ask yourself, "What actions (or inaction) did I take to get myself into this position?" The answer may be, "I took the first job I was offered even though it wasn't what I really wanted." Then, figure out what emotions you must have felt in order to take that action. You might have felt discouraged, fearful about your finances, or doubtful about your ability to find a better job.

Next, trace those emotions back to the belief you would have had to believe in order to feel those emotions. For example, you may have believed, "I had better take anything I can get because there may not be another opportunity." Now you have the root belief that led to the result of being in a job you don't enjoy.

The next step is to choose the belief you want to have that will lead to a better result. For example, if what you want is a more fulfilling job that pays well, a good belief to adopt would be, "I'm a smart, capable worker, and there are plenty of great opportunities out there for me." Feel the emotions the new belief creates in you. What actions would you be willing to take if you adopted the new belief and felt the new emotions? When you begin to take those actions consistently, you create different external results in your life, which then reinforce the new belief and help you let go of the old one. This is how conscious creation happens.

Wright

Earlier you mentioned intuition. What role does intuition play in the conscious creation of our experience?

Timberlake

You might be surprised at the number of people who credit following their intuition as a huge part of their success. Intuition is a valuable part of your internal guidance system and, if you're tuned in and listening for it, it can help to lead you down the best path toward your goals. The best way I know to describe it is an internal knowing. It's that sixth sense you have about a person or situation that not only keeps you on track, but also can protect you from harm.

Whenever you feel a certain way in a situation, and you cannot explain why, chances are your intuition is speaking to you. It is very important to acknowledge these messages because they can save you from danger and costly mistakes. Victims of crimes often report having a "hair standing on end" sensation shortly beforehand that warned them of danger. Some people report feeling a need to make a drastic life change without being able to articulate why, other than it just feels right. People who act on their intuition regularly report many synchronicities and opportunities showing up in their lives. They'll move to a new city and find the perfect business opportunity. Or they'll start a conversation with a stranger who turns out to be the love of their life.

Wright

How can people who are not very intuitive develop their sixth sense?

Timberlake

Some people are naturally more in touch with their intuition than others, but it can be developed in those who are not. Like a muscle, intuition gets stronger the more you use it. Paying attention to and following it are the very best ways to make it stronger. Set an intention to tap into your sixth sense. When you're in a situation and you're not sure what to do, look within yourself. See if an answer comes to you, and consider acting on whatever it says. The more you practice following that guidance, the better you'll get at recognizing and trusting your intuition.

Wright

Tell us more about the internal guidance system.

Timberlake

I was first introduced to the concept of an internal guidance system in Martha Beck's book, *Finding Your Own North Star*. People have an internal compass that can lead them down the path to their most authentic life. Listening to your internal guidance system is like flying a plane from point A to point B. I've heard it said that an airplane is actually off course 90 percent of the time. The pilot's job is to constantly correct course to keep it on track and get it to its destination. Likewise, your internal guidance system gives you a "yes" or "no" signal when you are engaged in activities or in certain situations that may or may not be best for you. "No" signals mean you're getting off track from the best path, and "yes" signals mean you're on the right track and to keep moving forward.

Besides intuition, one way your guidance system speaks to you is through the amount of energy you have. If a task or a person makes you feel depleted of energy, you're getting a "no" signal. If you feel a surge of renewed energy when doing a task or being around someone, you're getting a strong "yes" signal. For example, if you feel completely drained at work one day, but get a surge of energy when going out with friends that evening, you're getting a signal to continue incorporating social activities into your life.

Another way the internal compass speaks is through your health. If there are times when you habitually feel ill, your body could be telling you you're off course. In times when you feel unusually healthy and vigorous, your body is giving you a signal that you're on track and to do that activity more often.

I'm a singer in a choir, and I used to come down with laryngitis whenever I had a big solo to perform. I recognized the pattern and realized that my compass was giving me a "no" signal—not about performing, but about worrying what others would think of my performance. Once I decided to relax and enjoy myself on stage, I remained healthy for performances.

Another compass signal is memory. In times when you're unusually forgetful, you may be getting a "no" signal. In times or with topics that you have an unusually great memory, you are getting a strong "yes." Occasionally my clients will be horrified that they missed job interviews because they forgot to note them in their calendars. However, upon closer inspection, it is nearly always the case that they didn't really want that particular job, and their internal compass was trying to steer them away from a bad choice.

Another tool of the internal compass is social behavior. Have you ever noticed yourself making a large number of social blunders in a particular group of people? It could be a signal that they aren't a good fit for you. On the other hand, in another group, you may feel completely relaxed and notice yourself being funnier or more interesting than usual—a signal you've found a group that is a better fit for your soul.

The internal compass can also speak to you through your moods. Have you ever found yourself in a mood that made no sense given the circumstances? For example, you may fly somewhere on vacation and be upbeat and excited despite long airport lines and irritable fellow passengers. Conversely, you might feel sad or depressed at a wedding or other happy occasion—a signal from your inner guidance system to look inside and figure out what you need to do to get back on track.

If you pay attention to your internal compass and correct your course accordingly, it will lead you directly to people, experiences, and opportunities that are a perfect fit for you and that will take you further down your right path.

Wright

Can people get so far off-course that they can't get back on the right path?

Timberlake

I believe you can get almost anywhere you want to go from wherever you find yourself at this moment. Your internal guidance system acts like a car's GPS system. When you're driving to a programmed location, and you decide to take a detour from that route, the GPS simply recalculates the best route to your target from your new location. Your internal guidance system does the same thing. If you're traveling down one of life's paths and you get off track, your guidance system will simply determine the new fastest and best course to your destination, and give you signals to help you find the new path.

This is good news for people who don't like making decisions. When you know you can still get where you want to go no matter what choice you make, it's not necessary to agonize over decisions and delay making them until the last minute.

In order for your GPS to work for you, it's important to take action toward your goals. There is a saying that states, "You can't steer a parked car." In other words, unless you're actually traveling in a direction, your guidance system can't tell you if you're off course or not, and it can't steer you back to the right path. Not moving in any direction at all is how people stay stuck. In my opinion, moving in the wrong direction and waiting for a corrective signal from your compass is far better than taking no action at all.

Wright

As a career coach, how important do you think inner strength is to a person's career success?

Timberlake

It is of primary importance to someone's career success. You can bring everything in your inner strength toolbox into your career to produce quantum leaps in success and job satisfaction.

The key to gaining access to your inner strength at work is to take 100 percent responsibility for your experiences there. Work is one area where it is easy for people to give away their power. Anytime you hold someone or something else responsible for how you feel or act, you're giving your power away. It can be very tempting to blame your boss for how unhappy you are, to blame your subordinates for not meeting a deadline, or to blame irate customers for putting you in a bad mood. But to do so can be very harmful to your career success and fulfillment. Your inner strength resources come into play only when you take full responsibility for your own career.

I had a defining moment in my career about ten years ago. I disliked my job so much, I remember feeling like I was going to jail for eight hours every day. I was completely miserable. I began listening to motivational tapes in my car during my commute and every lunch hour hoping that one of them would help me find the perfect new career that would make me happy.

One day I heard something that hit me right between the eyes. It was a quote from legendary basketball coach, John Wooden. He said, "If you're bored at your job, it's your own fault." I thought, "What do you mean it's my fault? My boss doesn't support me, my coworkers are unfriendly, and the projects I have to do are boring. Nobody could like my job!" But his words stuck with me. What if I really was responsible for how I felt about work?

I decided to do everything in my power to improve my situation and see what happened. The results were incredible. In a short amount of time, I not only liked my job, I loved it. I got honest with myself about how I had helped to create every aspect of my unhappy situation and was able to see steps I could take to improve it. I began utilizing my inner strengths. I acted on my intuition when working on projects and interacting with my boss. I found something to be passionate about in every assigned project, even if it was just challenging myself to do an excellent job. I minimized the tasks that drained my energy by getting them over with first, and I had the rest of the day to look forward to the tasks I enjoyed. Taking full responsibility unlocks a storehouse of ideas for improving your situation and gives you access to your inner strength.

Employees who give away their responsibility can be easily identified by their complaining. Conversely, people who take full responsibility ask questions like, "How can I improve this relationship with my coworker? What new skills can I learn to get the recognition I want? What can I do differently on the next project to have greater success?" Then they access their inner reserves of strength, confidence, and ideas to follow through on the answers to those questions. Taking full responsibility is what sets someone apart from the rest of the crowd.

Wright

In closing, what final guidance do you want to give our readers?

Timberlake

Take responsibility for your happiness because nobody else will. Go out and create the life you want! You have all the tools you need inside of you. Once you open your mind to the possibility of a different life, your inner strength will kick in and support you. You don't have to know *how* to do it. All you need to know at any given moment is the next step to take. It's like walking through the woods at night with a flashlight. Once you take a step, the next one will be revealed to you. Lives are created one step at a time—even small steps.

Wright

Thank you for taking the time to speak with me today.

Timberlake

Thank you. It's been a pleasure.

Wright

Today we've been speaking with life and career coach, Allison Timberlake. She helps people make quantum leaps in career success and satisfaction and teaches them to create happiness in any situation. As we've learned today, she believes inner strength is a toolset we can utilize to achieve any goal. By learning to have faith, following our passion, and trusting our intuition, we can create the life we really want.

Allison, thank you so much for being with us today on *Discover Your Inner Strength*.

Timberlake

Thank you, David.

About the Author

As a life and career coach, Allison Timberlake invites us to take full responsibility for our own happiness, looking no further than inside ourselves for the strength and resources to create the career—and life—of our dreams. Allison has coached everyone from corporate executives to entrepreneurs, helping them create careers that bring them fulfillment. An expert in career success and satisfaction, she also helps people discover their passions and life purpose and teaches them how to have better work/life balance.

Allison lives in the Dallas, Texas, area with her husband, dog, and cat.

Allison Timberlake

6009 W. Parker Rd., Suite 149-270
Plano, TX 75093
214-483-3438
allison@careerchangecoaching.com
www.CareerChangeCoaching.com

Chapter Twenty-Four

Discovery Comes with Action!

An Interview With...

Monica J. Griffith

David Wright (Wright)

Today we're talking with Monica Griffith, a life and professional coach. She brings thirty years of corporate leadership experience to her coaching business, Guiding Light Coaching. Monica is a member of the International Coach Federation, Co-Chair of United Way's Women in Philanthropy, and a Chamber of Commerce

Ambassador. She is a licensed seminar leader through the Academy for Coaching Excellence, Sacramento, and a Senn-Delaney Certified Trainer for ImagiNationwide. Monica received her MA in Organizational Leadership from Chapman University, Sacramento. Her volunteer experience includes Sacramento's Suicide Hotline, New Life Community Church, and The United Way. As a life and professional coach, Monica supports her clients through interactive conversation to generate shifts in consciousness, empowering the client to make positive life changes.

Monica, welcome to *Discover Your Inner Strength.*

Monica Griffith (Griffith)

Thank you David, it is my joy to be here today.

Wright

So what does inner strength mean to you?

Griffith

David, inner strength for each of us is very different and unique and personal. We all have it within us and it is what is core to us, yet it is something that we may not normally experience. If we look at the meaning of inner strength as referenced in the Encarta Dictionary, we find it is "located near or closer to the center of something; located or happening on the inside of something; a quiet exterior that hides an inner confidence."

Inner strength can be seen as the amount of energy transmitted and the power to induce taking a course of action or embracing a point of view. Inner strength is something that we may either consciously or unconsciously push aside in order to do something that is easier or more familiar or seemingly safer. What is interesting is that our inner strength is truly our nucleus; it is our primary spirit. Often others see it for us and try to point it out, but until we see and experience it for ourselves, it remains a mystery. Once it is discovered and experienced, though, this strength becomes a familiar friend and we welcome it to all our actions and interactions.

I believe that to discover your inner strength, one must go to the well and allow the cup to fill with what you have not experienced previously. David, have you ever taken a walk and dipped a tin cup into water from a spring and taken a long slow drink? That water is so fresh and crisp and cold and refreshing! Now, I see myself and others as a container, a well if you will, that is continually being filled from that spring. Each time I dip that tin cup deep into that freshly filled well, fill my cup to the brim, and take a long, slow drink, I experience something that is so fresh and exhilarating! How often, David, have we watched an Olympian achieve the unimaginable or a hero who summons up incredible strength to save another person? Have you known someone who did something so out of character that it just made you sit back and question, "Gosh, where the heck did *that* come from?" Well, I believe it has always been there, just waiting to be drawn to the surface to be experienced. That to me is inner strength.

Wright

So do we all have that inner strength hiding somewhere inside us—something that has not yet been tapped? And if so, how do we find it?

Griffith

I believe that we all have inner strength; however, it is an essence that has not yet been tapped by all of us. I recall a quote from Mark Twain, "Twenty years from now you will be more disappointed by the things that you didn't do than by the ones you did. So throw off the bowlines. Sail away from safe harbor. Catch the trade winds in your sail. Explore. Dream. Discover."

As to how we find it, there are several criteria that will help you discover your inner strength. First, we must be awake to the possibilities. Many of us are on autopilot—we do what we have always done, and we get what we have always gotten, we behave as we have always behaved. Then we wonder and we grouse that we can't or we won't or something is getting in the way; someone is always an obstacle for us! We immediately go to that negative place where, unfortunately, we find comfort because it is familiar to us. We do not see the possibilities of "what if?" When we turn off the autopilot and wake up to what is before us, we will be amazed by the possibilities.

Next, we need to tap into new experiences. What I see here is a willingness to have the experience—to be open to what may be if we just take that first step. I mean, how often do we say no or quickly discount something that is a different experience for us? What would it be like to say "Yes!" to what is before you no matter what! What would it be like to dip your cup into the well, not sure of what will come up, yet willing to say "Yes!" to that experience?

David, so many times we can see what is in front of us and yet we remain in autopilot. We often do not realize that what we can do is to say "Yes!" to what is before us and take action. We lean forward and flip the autopilot switch off, take a step, and do what is there to be done. The action may be a small step, such as picking up the phone to make a call or cleaning off the exercise equipment to be ready for your workout in the morning. When we see what it is that can be done, and then we take the small physical action of dipping the tin cup into the well-spring and taking that long, slow drink, we have then tapped into what lies before us and have begun to stir our inner strength.

Third, the support system is crucial. So many people ask, "How can I do this all alone?" And yet, are we really all alone in this? Some of us feel that there is nobody who can possibly understand or know what we are going through. I just ask that we let this be one of our greatest lessons in discovering our inner strength—we are not alone in this universe. To accept; no, not to accept, but to welcome the support of others is one of the most precious gifts one can receive. I see that as such an energizing experience. Without the support of others, we may remain on autopilot, unsatisfied with what has always been and the way it has always happened for or to us. Yet, when we enlist the support of others, and when we listen to what we are saying to them, we then have the opportunity to see what is right in front of us.

Finally, celebrate the success of the experience! Take another look to see the truth that you did what you said you would do and revel in the experience of that action. We are so quick to chastise ourselves and others, but we rarely allow ourselves to celebrate or commemorate or even honor the experience. When we do consciously invite recognition of our success into our lives, we find delight and peace in our discovery. That simple act continues to strengthen the experience. This allows the well to continue to fill from the spring, ready for our next discovery in our journey.

It is important to know that this is a journey, not a "one and done" act. We continue to discover different facets of our inner strength and each may bring us to another level of experience, often times in various areas of our lives. It could be physical, emotional, or spiritual. How each journey progresses and the learning along the way are fascinating!

Wright

Will you share a personal example? What started your journey and what was the turning point for you?

Griffith

David, my autopilot was on and I was one who was always coasting along and letting what will be, well, just be. I was pretty much a qué-sera-sera kind of gal! Several years ago, I had an opportunity to apply for a position within my organization as a facilitator in a program that was designed to shift our corporate culture—our sense of who we are. At that time, David, I had a very demanding full-time job that was in the process of transition and yet, I wanted to have this facilitator experience. I believed in the program; it was something I had been dreaming about for some time, I just never pursued it. This opportunity presented itself and I applied for the position. I feel blessed to have been selected to join a team of about twenty-four other facilitators. I would add the role of facilitator for the ImagiNationwide program to my already very full-time job. Needless to say, I was thrilled and very proud of what I was about to do.

Shortly before the training was to take place, my job became more involved, as our transition kicked into gear. I then received word that my younger sister, Lori, was diagnosed with pancreatic cancer. This was the most devastating news our family had ever experienced. I felt so alone. I was ready to resign from the program and go back to my comfort zone of letting what is going to happen, happen. But instead, one of my greatest supporters, my sister, Lori, had me take a look at what was right in front of me, to see clearly the possibilities. I had spoken to her about the program. She understood the essence of it, and she could see the affect it already had on me, just thinking about the possibility of doing this. She encouraged and supported me to continue with the training. She could see the possibilities, not only to the organization and to me, but also to our family. Lori was wise beyond her years. So, I said "Yes!" to the training and I welcomed the support of my family, friends, coworkers, and fellow trainees.

In the training and sessions that followed, I was faced with the task of sharing personal stories to illustrate a particular topic. I asked Lori's permission to share her story of her illness and the challenges that she and the family faced. She was very willing for me to do this and continually encouraged me to practice with her. The time we spent in our discussions was such a precious gift for me; it was a true celebration of the woman she had become.

I look back on that experience and realize I was continually dipping into my well and drinking the water. In taking another look, I celebrate the truth about what I did and that experience and how it allowed me to share Lori's story and courage. I see how it profoundly affected my life and brought such great peace to me. I consciously recognize the simple act of being willing to be open to the possibilities of what could be as I chip away at the things that are getting in my way—things that do not seem to be the right fit for me. I find myself embracing the challenge of going beyond my comfort zone to realize new experiences, thus crafting another set of tools to go deeper into that well.

This is one example of a turning point in my journey. I have seen the affect of being awake to the possibilities, saying "Yes!" to what is before you no matter what, welcoming the support of others, and celebrating the success of the experience. This can have a profound effect on your life as well as those with whom you come in contact.

Wright

So how do we deal with, or as you said, chip away the things that we notice about ourselves that don't seem acceptable?

Griffith

That is a good question. Really looking at what is important to you is the best way to begin; it is one thing to know it and quite another to really see it, realizing that we will uncover layer upon layer of comfort to get to where we need to be. The questions are, "Am I seeing the truth? Am I seeing what is really more interesting? Do I always have to do what I have always done?"

Many of us are great dreamers—we can visualize what it would be like, we can meditate on it and pray on it, and beg for it to come to be. These are all good things to do, yet there is a difference in dreaming about what could be and discovering that dream in reality. Chipping away at what is between our dreams and reality can be the biggest obstacle because it requires focused energy that culminates in action to effect the change. Discovery comes with action.

Action is the product of exerting energy for the duration of an event. In what we are discussing here, action is the process of moving from autopilot to taking control. This does not happen by simply willing changes, but by identifying and taking physical action toward what you have envisioned. It is more than noticing or becoming aware of what we want for ourselves or what "could be, if only." It is about shifting to what can be done to bring those dreams to reality. This is the time when we begin to hear the negative self-talk about how impossible or unrealistic or hard it will be to make this happen.

Sometimes, our visions seem very big and it is much easier to keep dreaming and listening to the excuses of how it could never be. Those who create a plan with small steps of action and continually focus their energy in achieving each step will see their dream become reality and discover the sweet beauty of what was there, inside, all along!

David, let me give you an example of how I have experienced this. I have been in the workforce for many years and had the good fortune to continually advance in my career. In many discussions with my managers, I was advised to go back to school— go to college and get a higher education. As a child, I was not very interested in the educational process of school. I was an average student and enjoyed the social aspect of school; average was good enough to keep me out of trouble so that I could enjoy the clubs and outings. I planned to get married and raise a family and be a good parent; being well-educated was not on my radar. As a young adult, I could see that college would be a great advantage to my career, but that would take time and money and energy. I was only an average student in high school and the kids are so much smarter today. My negative self-talk was very loud. Yet, there was something missing for me, something inside was aching to be discovered. But college? As a single parent, thirty-seven years old with a full-time job, I certainly could not see the possibility of a college degree. I had all the excuses. Then, in a new town with a new job, I thought about what would it be like if I just took one class. If I could survive one class, then maybe . . .

My first action was to simply go to the college campus and talk to someone. Surely, someone would tell me this was impossible and I would be off the hook! No, the counselor was very happy to see me and after talking with me for a short time, she suggested just one class she thought I might enjoy.

Action two was to sign up for the class and buy the books.

Action three was to actually attend and complete that first class. After I started this first class, I went back to the counselor and suggested we put together a plan for my AA degree. It is simply amazing—when I look back to that first class, I now see that by planning and taking the action of small, simple steps of one class (sometimes two) at a time, I received my master's degree in Organizational Leadership. Yes, it was thirteen years in the making, but what a sweet success it is. I discovered so much about myself and others in that journey.

The truth is, I really was always interested in a higher education, that dream was always there. I knew that it was the first step in finding something that was more interesting. I simply needed to come out of autopilot, to do something I had never done before. In that action of shifting out of autopilot and putting myself in the driver's seat, I took control of bringing my dream to reality. In chipping away at the negative self-talk, I discovered an inner strength that has taken me on the ride of my life. I celebrate it and savor it every day.

Wright

Monica, that is a great example! But, how can I be sure I'm on the right track?

Griffith

Well, there is something really interesting about being on the right track. I often ask myself, if I did it right, or if I'm about to do something, what if something goes wrong, maybe I should, maybe I shouldn't, and that is where all the negative self-talk comes into play.

I was thinking about this the other day and I recalled the quote that Neil Armstrong made at the moon landing, "That's one small step for man, one giant leap for mankind." What I discovered, through some research, is he actually misquoted the intended message. Apparently, there was much discussion about it and he did misstate the comment NASA intended. The quote was supposed to be: "That's one small step for *a* man, one giant leap for mankind." David, my point is that we do not always get it right, do we? What is the right track? A more interesting series of questions and places to focus our energy is am I continuing to move on and am I awake to what I am experiencing? Am I finding joy and fulfillment in what I am doing and am I bringing that experience to others? This brings us to who we really are and what we have to offer.

You know, by looking at who we intend to be and how we intend to contribute, we continually learn something about ourselves. We can see the path and that it is up to us to take a small step, whether it is the right step or a wrong step, it is, nevertheless, a step in a forward direction—forward, not moving back to our comfort zone where we do not see what really is possible.

It is important to realize that creating a goal or plan and developing small, sweet steps toward realizing that goal in the reality of today is where one discovers the inner strength we are talking about. It is outside that familiar comfort zone and it is outside the negative self-talk with which we are so familiar. As you continue to move toward that goal, there may be many missteps. In fact, you may find an entirely new direction, just by saying yes to what you have previously said no. Being awake to the steps you are taking and simply realizing the path is different from one on which you have been before is, in itself, an experience to celebrate. It is much more interesting than questioning if it is the right path!

Neil Armstrong's goal was to walk on the moon. That is quite a lofty goal and to get there he had to chunk it down into small steps. So much led up to the historic landing and the quote that we will long remember; but, it did not just happen overnight and he likely made mistakes along the way, as do we. You know you are on the right path as you realize you are moving forward. Your journey may not be straight and there may be many obstacles; however, it becomes very interesting when you see that you are building skills. The path becomes easier once you realize how far those small steps have taken you. If you are willing to savor the experience and share the learning with your support system, you will continue to fill that well and draw from it as you forge new paths on your journey forward.

Wright

You talk about support; what or who is support?

Griffith

Support is so important. Webster describes support as someone who encourages a plan. When Lori was going through her cancer stages, we were all in the midst of doing many things, yet we all felt so alone. We did not realize that there were so many supporters around us. Every person who came to visit Lori and her children, as well as those who sent cards or made calls, were part of our support system. During my ImagiNationwide interview and my training, I had the support of Senn-Delaney coaches and instructors as well as the support of other trainers, my parents, sisters and my coworkers. A supporter is someone who is in your corner—someone who does not give up on you, even when you give up on yourself.

We all have goals and dreams, but it is easier and we are much more familiar with talking about our doubts and worries. We are familiar with the conversation that begins with "if only," and we so quickly see the negative in a situation. How many times do we begin with a positive and then add that famous three-letter word "but"? When we have the right support system in place, we can direct our doubts and worries to actions, which lead us to realizing our goals and dreams. It requires us to dip into the well. Our support will continually encourage us and help us to see clearly the possibilities of what is truly important to us and transform those dreams into reality. Our support will help us shift from the "but" to "and," which will help direct us to what is really important. Remember, earlier I said that often someone else can see that inner strength before we can? Our supporter can see that and help us to continually pull away at the dirt and sludge and obstacles that are getting in our way.

Wright

Let's talk about support for a second. Where do I go, what qualifications should I be looking for? How do I know if I have the right support?

Griffith

Where do I go? That is a big question. The simple answer is: everywhere. Support is all around us, we simply need to be awake to all the resources surrounding us in our daily walk. For example, "where" can be a simple act of making your needs known to family and intimate friends. Many companies offer employee assistance programs, a confidential resource that we may not fully utilize. You can also enlist the support of a trusted coworker. Another possible direction is seeking the help of professionals such as clergy, medical professionals, teachers, counselors, and coaches. Not everybody realizes that he or she has many opportunities to receive support. How often do we fail to ask for assistance because we do not know where to go or we think someone else will not be interested in where we are headed or what we have to do? It is a very precious gift to have someone who holds your goals and dreams with you.

Realize there are places to go and people who really want you to be successful and want you to share what you have. Who are they? They are people who see that you have much to contribute. They can identify with your values and your strengths, and challenge you to delve deep within. You know what your values are, but have you actually expressed them? Has someone asked you to put them into words and then helped you to see how you demonstrate them in your everyday life? A supporter is someone who can identify the small steps toward your goal and is willing to support you as you take those steps to see your dreams become a reality. A supporter is someone who is a real partner with you on your journey, who is nonjudgmental, who has as much at stake as you do, for you. He or she is someone who can help you see the truth and someone who is in the game for you, not for herself.

At times, my support system has been someone who knows me very well, perhaps a family member or dear friend. When I was focused on a loftier goal, such as getting my degree, I sought continual support from those who could partner with me on that journey and help me maintain focus on the small steps of one class or even one assignment at a time. These were teachers, counselors, fellow students, and the like who were truly partners with me in my success. They celebrated each and every accomplishment with me.

When Lori was so ill, I thought my support system was very limited to extremely close friends and family. It was not until much later that I realized the clergy, hospice, coworkers, and even the people who ran the hotel my family called home for so long were also my support system. They all were there for me and the family, encouraging, helping, and easing us along this journey. With their support, each of us dug deeper into our primary spirit—to our core—and pulled up a strength we did not realize existed.

Another support system can be found in a professional life coach. Life coaching is a method of supporting people, with the aim to clearly design and achieve some goal or develop specific skills. You and your coach create a partnership where the coaching relationship continually gives all the control back to you, the client. After all, you are the expert in your life and the only one who makes your life choices.

Choosing a life coach may be one of the first steps you take in discovering your inner strength. Be selective. At this time, coaching is self-regulated. I suggest you interview your potential coach for his or her training, and check if the person is a member of the International Coach Federation. The coach should be able to provide references. I also suggest a complimentary coaching session so you can feel comfortable with the personal chemistry and trust. I have a life coach who asks powerful questions, helps me focus on what is important right now, and continually supports me as I progress on my life's journey.

Now, how will you know if you have the right support? You will know when you are no longer on autopilot, when you are taking each obstacle and seeing the possibilities of the experience, and when you are continuing to move toward making your dream a reality. Your support will change throughout your journey. At times, one person may provide the support you need and at other times, you may be surrounded by it. You will know this as you wake up to your surroundings and are open to receiving the gift.

Whether your goal is to graduate college, find satisfaction in your job, improve parenting skills, walk on the moon, create a savings plan, recover from an addiction, or thrive in the midst of one of the many life events you encounter, the journey is much easier when you willingly accept support. An effective supporter challenges you to see choices you had not previously noticed, and then encourages you to act. By engaging in enlightening conversations, he or she facilitates tapping into your inner strengths and gently guides you through the obstacles to make your dreams become reality!

Wright

So how will I know when I've tapped into my inner strength?

Griffith

David, do you see that you are restricted only by what you are not willing to experience? When you are aware of what is going on, and really awake to it, you are looking at it from outside your normal makeup. You realize that you have so much more to offer, and that offering may be to yourself or to others. It is something that has been hidden or covered that you have not even experienced. Once you have taken action to put that strength into play, you will know you have tapped into something very special. It was always there, you have just not taken the chance to set it free and become aware of the experience.

This experience may be different for each of us. Let me share with you a few examples of moments I experienced personally as well as those I have experienced being a supporter of others. The best way I can describe this is a cool freshness that just explodes from me when I actually stop and look and take it all in. While in pursuit of my degree, I did realize joy and satisfaction with the completion of each assignment and each class; however, when I was walking across that stage in my graduate cap and gown, well, that was an explosion of realization. When one of my coaching clients becomes very quiet and then says with simple surprise, "I see it!" this is a moment of discovery.

Often, when we accomplish something, we tend to dismiss our role in that experience. We may momentarily give ourselves a pat on the back and then we are off to our next task. It has become a check-the-box type of behavior and we do not truly savor the experience of what we have just accomplished. I do not mean this in an egotistical sort of way; but rather, simply recognizing that hey I did it! You will know you have tapped into an inner strength only when you take time to truly recognize grace and gratitude for the risks that you took in coming out of your comfort zone. You must not only be awake to taking the steps out of autopilot, you must also be awake to celebrating that you are the one who had the experience. Allow yourself the joy of the accomplishment and knowing that you have brought something very special from just a vision into your reality.

Wright

So let's say that I see I have discovered my inner strength, now what?

Griffith

And this again is a step we often overlook. We do not celebrate our successes—all the successes—especially the small ones. We are so busy in our day-to-day activities that we may see only how overwhelmed we are with what is going on in the world around us. We do not often take the time to just be joyful and savor what we have discovered and recognize what we have to contribute.

Let me first share with you a story about savoring and how it may look to delight in something. My sister, Carole, and I took a road trip from Southern California up the coast to the small town of Solvang. We enjoyed the coastline and had wonderful conversations along the route. We were both looking forward to investigating this hamlet and planned to spend a full day exploring its nuances. Throughout the day, we delighted in the quaint shops and breathed in the fresh scents of the European aromas of the restaurants and bakeries. Now, I must share with you that Carole is quite a chocolate lover! This little village had a chocolate shop about every other store and Carole felt called to sample something in every one of them. I am not a chocolate lover and yet she was really enjoying this trip, so we stopped and we would have a bite of chocolate or a piece of candy or a chocolate sundae or something of that nature. At about the fifth shop I had had enough, so I simply watched as Carole bit into her order. This time, I truly observed the transformation that came over her as she experienced the explosion of chocolate and sugar in her mouth. She breathed deeply and closed her eyes. She was completely intoxicated in the moment. She savored and celebrated each morsel. She was truly awake to the experience.

Once we have made the discovery and savored the experience for ourselves, it is important that we see the contribution we can offer to others and act upon that gift. I look to Robert Greenleaf who is a model leader of servant leadership. The figure of servant leader is the contribution one makes as one demonstrates the presence of being so that others may see the model and engage in their own experience.

Let's look back to Carole, and the contribution she made to me in that moment. The intent of this trip was to let go of the stress and pressure of daily life, if just for a short weekend. Until I noticed the change in Carole during her chocolate moments, I had not realized how to let go. My journey back to Southern California was filled with new discoveries. For example, as we stopped to take in the ocean, my experience was one of awe and wonder at the massive expanse that lay before me. I was being in the moment with nature. I followed Carole's lead and closed my eyes and breathed in the life around me. I became aware of the crisp air filling my lungs, the breeze tossing my hair and the salt water spray on my face. I was out of autopilot and in the moment. I felt it to my core.

David, you asked, now what? Now that we have discovered what we have to offer, we become the model. We live our experience for ourselves and others to see. In that, we share with others and become a supporter. "Now what" is to simply relish, savor, and live the experience so that it becomes more familiar and more comfortable. The delight in discovering your inner strength is knowing there is still more to discover, savor, celebrate, and share. The next time you go to the well and you dip your cup, you know that something fresh and joyful will come of it, and it will not be nearly so difficult the next time around.

Wright

So what is the most important learning that you can give us?

Griffith

I believe that within each of us we have the ability to create and contribute incredible gifts—to give what we have not yet even conceived is ours to give, to do the seemingly impossible with clarity and ease. The smallest gift we have to give may be the most important gift another can receive. To discover and to give freely, with grace and gratitude of being able to give is most important.

David, I would like to share one more story of how this lesson recently touched me. I received a call about three o'clock one morning that my youngest son, Jason, had been seriously injured in a fire. I was needed there immediately. Family and friends came to my support as I spent a very traumatic day of making travel arrangements and flying through four time zones and various flights in unfamiliar airports, not knowing anyone. My family and friends made themselves available by phone, no matter what the hour, should I need to call on them. I did not know Jason's friends who volunteered to pick me up from the airport and take me to the hospital. I had no idea what I would find when I arrived or what I would do once I knew. I was just exhausted mentally and emotionally. I barely remember the drive to the airport to pick up a rental car once I was in Alabama. I know I was not taking in much of the surroundings—I was truly lost in my thoughts and just trying to gather up some energy for what I was to face.

At one point, I looked out the window and I saw a billboard that said, "For God so loved the world that He gave." That was it. Now, I knew there was more to this scripture found in John 3:16. I wondered about the reason why the rest of the scripture was not included. And then, I shifted to something more interesting—what it would be like if I simply focused on what was there, rather than what was missing? I recall becoming aware of the gift of giving and how that has carried me through. Do you see it? For God so loved the world that He gave? The most important learning is that He gave.

We too have so much to give—so many things that we have not yet tapped into and the benefits that giving will reap for others will in turn bring such joy and grace to our lives. I think the most important learning of discovering your inner strength is *discover what you have yet to give to others and you will see that what comes back to you is exponentially greater.*

Wright

Well, what a great conversation. I think I'll write your telephone number and every time I get down, I'm going to call you and see if I can tap into your inner strength.

Griffith

Oh, I would love to support you as you tap into your inner strength. David, you know it is there and that is just what is so delightful about it. We do not even realize it until one day it is awakened and you say, "Oh my goodness, where did that come from?" Then, you look in the mirror and realize it was from within you!

Wright

I really appreciate all this time you've taken with me today to answer these questions. This is really going to be informative for our readers; I know that because I got a lot from it.

Griffith

David, thank you for inviting me. It has been a delight to share my thoughts and stories with you today.

Wright

Today we've been talking with Monica Griffith. Monica is a life and professional coach. She supports her clients through interactive conversation to generate shifts in consciousness, empowering her clients to make positive life changes.

Monica, thank you so much for being with us today on *Discover Your Inner Strength.*

Griffith

Thank you David it has been a pleasure.

About the Author

onica Griffith is a life and professional coach. Through her business, Guiding Light Coaching, she offers one-on-one coaching and facilitates small support group discussions, book-study workshops, and skill-building seminars. Monica brings thirty years of corporate leadership experience and holds a Master of Arts degree in Organizational Leadership from Chapman University, Sacramento. Monica is a member of the International Coach Federation.

Monica J. Griffith

Guiding Light Coaching
8389 Old Ranch Rd
Orangevale, CA 95662
916-847-7537
mgriffith@guidinglightcoaching.com
www.guidinglightcoaching.com

Chapter Twenty-Five

Practical Health and Wellness: Creating Balance

An Interview With…

Luanne Pennesi

David Wright (Wright)

Today we're talking with Luanne Pennesi. Luanne is a registered nurse practicing for over thirty years in both conventional and integrative medicine. She has dedicated her life to sharing information that motivates people to take back their personal power and lead happier, healthier, and more productive lives at any age. With a master's degree in Natural Health and a certification in Chinese medicine, including an extensive clinical and administrative background in adult medicine and oncology nursing, Luanne clearly has the experience and the credentials to help people reach their highest health potential. Her dynamic energy and humor makes understanding and actualizing new information easy.

Luanne, welcome to *Discover Your Inner Strength.*

Luanne Pennesi (Pennesi)

Thank you.

Wright

So will you give us some practical definitions of health and wellness?

Pennesi

Understanding the definition of health, I believe, is really paramount to becoming healthy, and there are so many angles from which you can define health.

Politically, our systems define health as an absence of disease measured by illness, acuity, and an episode. Quite frankly, any illness that we have is the body's way of begging for our attention and saying, "Pay attention to me, there's something that you're doing that is not for my highest good." So unfortunately, our political definition of health, which governs our present healthcare system, might not be the most accurate definition.

Philosophically, health is a value between opposite states of illness and wellness, ability and disability, or fitness and non-fitness, so it's like a dynamic somewhere in between.

Holistically, it's really about balance or harmony, of subtle energy fields in and around one's body and it encompasses the mind, the body, and the spirit, all interconnected.

Now, on a practical level, health really is all about the consequences of how we choose to live. It's about our choices—what we pick up and put in our mouth every day (our diet), if we exercise or not, and the use of things like recreational drugs or alcohol or cigarettes. It's how much happiness and joy we have every day—every thought you think affects every cell in your body and every cellular reaction in the body. It's also about how much fun you have; it's the kind of work you do, how much time you spend in relaxation or hobbies, or how you manage stress or not, and how much time you spend on improving yourself. All those things play into how healthy you are.

So my definition of health is that it's an evolving consciousness about one's potential, not only physically but also mentally, emotionally, and spiritually. And a lot of it has to do with our belief systems. My work involves helping people to be optimally healthy on every single level.

Wright

Most people associate a good diet with health. How important is a healthy diet and what, in your opinion, does a healthy diet look like?

Pennesi

The diet is meant to fuel the body. Some people put better fuel in their cars than they do in their bodies. We've been conditioned to desire things that are sweet, salty, and crunchy. Many of us have been indoctrinated to eat to fill an emotional void or just to take away the feeling of hunger, when what we really need are some basic nutrients; and of course, we need water.

1. Water: One of the things I have noticed is that if people just got a little more hydrated with healthy fluids, they'd do great. Water alone is a wonderful detoxifier; it keeps the cells nice and healthy.
2. Complex carbohydrates: The carbohydrates that are healthy for you are complex carbohydrates like grains—amaranth, wild rice, brown rice, millet, etc.,—and squash, potatoes, and sprouted whole-grain breads.
3. Proteins: There are some healthy proteins that we can put into our bodies like beans, nuts, and seeds. One thing that most people don't realize is that seaweeds like dulse, kelp, arame, and hijiki are higher in protein than meat. It's amazing, and not only that, but there are also minerals that the body needs that alkalize the body, so seaweeds are a great protein to have. There are also other proteins, such as low mercury fish and soy proteins. Now, there has been some controversy about soy and I'll tell you that if you have a well-made,

organic, non-genetically modified soy as a part of a balanced diet, it's really quite good for you. Be careful about soy if you have thyroid problems or allergies to it. We certainly don't want to have too much soy, but certainly, soy as part of a balanced diet is, in my professional opinion, healthy. Pumpkin seeds are high in zinc and it's very good for male hormone health. If you mix beans (think of all the different beans there are) and all the different grains, they create a complete protein. Then there are protein shakes made from powders out of rice protein, soy protein, whey protein, egg white protein, hemp protein, and even pea protein. Who knew that there were so many different sources of healthy protein shakes?

4. Healthy fats. It is very important to have healthy fats in our diet. One of the best fats we can put in the body are fish oils, coconut oil, nut and seed oils, and avocado oil. So this is not about having a low fat diet! Low fat diets are not healthy for the body. Our brain and many of our hormones and our nerves are all made of proteins and fats; they get their energy from carbohydrates. If people want to lose weight or they want to be as healthy as they can be, they need a good balance of protein, carbohydrates, and fats, but it doesn't end there.

5. Vitamins. I encourage people who live in industrialized societies to take vitamin supplements.

   a. One of the vitamins that we don't make is vitamin C. Humans, guinea pigs, and primates do not synthesize vitamin C, so we need take a supplementation form of it. The question is how much? Well, if you knew how many different functions vitamin C played in the body, you'd take a lot of vitamin C—anywhere between 1,000 and 10,000 milligrams a day depending on your height, your weight, your activity, and what kind of environment you're living in. So vitamin C is wonderful.

   b. Antioxidants, omega-3 fish oils, a good multivitamin, and B-complex are just some of the basic ones. There are many, many more that I discuss with people when I individualize protocols for them.

    c.   Then there are the minerals that you find in your green leafy vegetables and seaweeds or in supplements. We need to have lots and lots of those.

6.   Green chlorophyll. People tend to not eat enough green chlorophyll. Green chlorophyll is what detoxifies our bodies naturally, so have a salad, or better yet make a green vegetable juice. Take vegetables like cucumbers and celery and parsley and then throw in some lemons and apples into a juicer. You will get a delicious, fresh green juice that cleanses all of the toxins out of the body. So if you're breathing in toxins, if you're exposed to electromagnetic pollution (we all are), and even if you're under a lot of stress, the green vegetable juices flush all that out through urine.

7.   Red chlorophylls. The red chlorophylls are so very important for your body. Those are found in berries—strawberries, raspberries, blueberries, cherries, pomegranates, and cranberries. All of these red/orange/pink colored foods are very important, like the red skin of the apple. It's the red chlorophyll that heals our damaged cells. People who tend to look so well in their fifties, sixties, and seventies are usually the people who eat lots, and lots of red chlorophylls. You can get concentrated red chlorophyll pills and you can get red berry concentrates. Put the concentrates in a nice protein shake every day for your breakfast and you'll be loading your body up with all the phytonutrients that it needs.

8.   Enzymes. You can get enzymes from papaya or pineapple, which are most important for biochemical reactions in the body.

These are just some of the basics of a healthy diet.

Wright

So what else affects health?

Pennesi

Well, there are six major areas I look at that really influence one's health:

1. Certainly your genetics—the genetics you get from each parent—play a role. But having a gene that may give you a propensity for a disease does not mean you will get the disease; it just means you need to put more attention into keeping yourself well fortified in regard to the "weaker" gene expression.

2. Peace of mind and bliss—knowing who you are, loving who you are, and living your life consistent with that. So many of us are living our lives adapting to other people's expectations of us. We lack self-discipline, we lose our playfulness, our ability to laugh out loud, and be spontaneous. These are the elements of what I call the spirit—peace of mind and bliss is really what our spirit is about. The practice of self-discipline is your capacity for unconditional love. Look into the eyes of a child, an animal— one of your pets—or a bird and you will see unconditional love. You know the look—they look at you as though you're just the greatest thing on the planet. That's part of your peace of mind and bliss, too. It's also your ability to laugh out loud and engage in activities and hobbies that make you lose track of time. It's a conscious choice of being happy and of course, most of all, it's your ability to express gratitude and appreciation.

3. The next area is managing your emotions. Many of us believe that when we have a negative emotion, we've got to hold onto it, stuff it into our bodies, and create a drama with it. But that is unnecessary. Negative emotions are there for us to get our attention; they are motivators for us to make change and if we see them as such—whether it's anxiety or fear or anger or depression or worry—they are there to get our attention. Negative emotions indicate that your spirit is broken; pay attention, something's not right. And it's usually something that we can't control. So when you're feeling an emotion, feel it; get into it, experience it, and then ask yourself what you need to mobilize—what do you need to do to learn from this event? You learn and you take your lesson. You can leave the negative emotions behind and march forward with your new lesson. It's a wonderful way of living of your life without holding on to that emotion and carrying grudges and holding on to old pain from the past. When you have permission to let these things go, your whole

physiology changes. Part of that is having nurturing, healthy relationships in your life on every different level.

4. The next area is managing your physiology, which has to do with your diet, taking supplements, exercising your body daily, including having a healthy sex life. It's also about the quality of your breathing and how well you are eliminating (moving your bowels). We ingest food and liquid into our bodies and these substances are processed. Remember, we've got twenty-eight feet of intestines and three to four more feet of large intestines in addition to the small intestines, so we need to make sure that we're moving our waste out on a regular basis. So making sure that you're moving your bowels every day, at least once a day is important.

    How about posture and alignment? Chiropractic adjustments help to make sure that our spines are aligned. Walking and sitting using good posture is imperative because when the spine is out of line (remember, the spine is your lifeline!) it feeds every organ in your body and every muscle. When the spine is aligned, our body functions much more efficiently.

5. Here's another area: rest and sleep. So many of us aren't getting enough sleep! We're living such busy lives that we lack the proper sleep. When we're sleeping, that's when our body is detoxifying—it's like recharging your battery. So we need to have a good solid sleep, anywhere from six to eight hours.

    As we age we also have to keep our hormones in balance, and there are many ways to do it naturally. We don't have to use synthetic drugs. One of the most important things I've learned since I've studied holistic medicine is that there is a plant out there on the planet that can rebalance any imbalance in the human body, whether it's a mental imbalance or physiological imbalance. When you understand that and you open yourself to the information, you'll see that plants don't have the side effects that many of our drugs have, when used correctly. I always start with a natural approach, then, if people need synthetic drugs to help them with an imbalance, by all means we'll work with a physician and bring it right into their protocol. There are two more areas that affect your health:

6. One is your physical environment—the climate of your home, your workplace, your car, or public transportation; personal hygiene, environmental hygiene, and attacks by microbes in your environment. Then a very important piece that is the root of many of our chronic illnesses is heavy metal toxicity that we get from the strangest places, like silver fillings in teeth and aluminum in deodorants and aluminum pots and pans, just to name a few.

7. The last thing that affects our health is our energy—the fields of energy in and around us. We have to look at our internal energy and the energy around us, receiving the intentions of other people, and cleaning ourselves on the cellular level. That includes releasing old pain and being able to ground your energy every day.

So a lot of things are in play when you look at what influences your health.

Wright

There's been a lot of research on the affect that exercise has on long-term health. How important is it and what's the best type?

Pennesi

Exercise is so very important. We have hundreds of muscles and we need to use them. I encourage people to find an exercise that works for them. Not everyone likes to go to a gym, so some people work out on their own. Other people like being with groups, some people like sports, and other people enjoy a nice long walk or a hike, so I encourage an exercise that works for each person.

There are people who say, "Well, I'm sitting at a computer all day, I don't have the time to exercise." Well yeah, you do. You can do exercises sitting right in the chair. There are things you can do sitting right in your chair at work. You can put your right elbow to your left knee and then switch your left elbow to your right knee and just sit there. Then just do opposition crunches and you'll have a beautiful waistline. You can do seated squats, what I call "butt cheek squeezes," waist bends . . . there are so many things that you can do while sitting.

So why exercise? Well number one it increases the oxygenation of your body, and oxygen increases your energy. Virus, parasites, yeast, cancers, and anaerobic bacteria cannot grow where there is a lot of oxygen. So we encourage people to do a lot of breath work while they're doing their exercises. And just as a little side bar, your green vegetable juices also provide loads of oxygen for your body.

The other thing that exercise does is it increases your metabolism, so it helps you burn fat. In addition, you end up with more endurance, you have more strength, and even better than that, when you're exercising and moving your circulation, you're removing toxins from all of your organs, especially your liver, and lymphatic system. It also helps your colon with elimination, it benefits the lungs, the skin, and the bladder, that's why sweating is so great for you.

Also, when you exercise, you increase your endorphin levels and you balance serotonin levels. Those are the elements that help you maintain a happy mood. So when people work out regularly they seem to be in better moods; best of all, they like the way they look. In Chinese medicine practitioners understand that the tone of the skeletal muscle is a reflection of the efficiency of your digestion. So the more toned your muscles are, the more efficient your digestion is. That's a great motivation right there, if you have any issues with your digestion.

Exercising is a manifestation of focus, attention, and discipline. Those are the three hallmarks of functioning from a higher, more self-actualized place. So yes, exercise is very, very important. Do what works for you. Always stretch before and after to prevent injury and to stabilize the body. I encourage people to do something cardiovascular or aerobic like stationary bike-riding, dancing, swimming, and so on, and then combine that with some kind of resistance workout like circuit training or free weights or calisthenics. A fun thing to do is to get a little rebounder and do some bouncing! Bouncing is far and away one of the best exercises you can do. So combine them, figure out what works out best for you and work out five to six days a week.

Wright

So what is the role of genetics, or your constitution on your health?

Pennesi

Well, I think genetics has received a lot of attention in terms of how it influences our health. The term "constitution" is used to describe the physical, emotional, and mental inheritance that we receive from our parents. In one sense, it's our genetic makeup, which is determined at the moment of conception. Traditional Chinese

Medicine teaches that the energy from both parents is stored in the child's kidneys because that's where the life energy sits—it's our life force and is responsible for our growth, development, and reproduction. It also determines our lifespan. So even though we all have the same biological template, our propensities from each parent are expressed differently with each conception.

Determinate factors in your genetics include health issues such as if either of your parents used cigarettes or recreational drugs, if either of them had a medical problem(s), their nutritional status, if they have weak constitutions, the quality of their sleep/rest cycles. In other words, their state of health at the time of your conception affects your health at birth. So clearly the healthier both parents are, the healthier the child will be. Also, remember that we each have innate strengths and weaknesses.

For instance, I had the same exact diet and lifestyle as my siblings, and yet each of us grew up very differently in terms of our propensities for illness. I had severe acne and my siblings did not. So you really appreciate this when you see that there are certain differences and yet there are other areas in which we are all the same. Again, it comes from your genetics.

While it's important to understand, it doesn't dictate whether you're going to be healthy or not, and one of the things that I oppose is if a woman is told that she has some kind of genetic propensity for breast cancer, she is told to have bilateral mastectomies. In my opinion as a licensed health professional, I would encourage her to examine her lifestyle and fortify her immune system before having cancer-free breasts removed preventively. Just because you have a gene that may form a propensity for illness, it doesn't necessarily mean that you're going to get the illness. What it does give you, though, is a heads up that you have to overcompensate for the weaker areas in your genetics, and that's a big part of my work with people.

It's so exciting to see that when people use these tools, oh my goodness, their health just skyrockets.

Wright

So what other aspects of our biology are important for optimal health?

Pennesi

Well, let's take a look. We talked about nutrition and I mentioned juicing, and supplements. As I said, these are very, very important.

One of the most important things we need to do is to detoxify. We have to look at what in our life is adding toxins to our body. It could be our emotions, our environment; it could be smoking cigarettes or regular use of alcohol or caffeine. Caffeine is not a healthy substance to ingest at all. Caffeine affects our physiology amazingly. It depletes and dehydrates you and it removes many of your vitamins, especially your B vitamins and folic acid, which are so important. So I encourage use of substitutes for caffeine.

We also need to eliminate dairy products. We don't look like cows, we don't have the same physiology as they do, and we don't have their immune system, so when we put dairy products in our body, we create phlegm throughout the body; we become Petri dishes for infections. There are many dairy alternatives. Coconut milk is one of my favorites, then there is rice milk, soy milk, nut milks (like almond milk) and all of those are great.

Sugar and artificial sweeteners are far and away the worst things we can put in our bodies. There are healthy sugars like stevia and agave nectar, and xylitol. These are natural sugars that are far better for the body that don't increase blood sugar.

Carbonated drinks like sodas and seltzer are injected with gases that wear away our bones. I see many men now even getting osteoporosis when they don't have to; they just need to let go of all that soda.

Even whole wheat is not healthy for us. As a society, we've grown to become allergic to whole wheat flour. But there are many other alternatives, like spelt, and sprouted whole grain products. Before the grain actually blooms, you've got the sprout where concentrated energy and concentrated nutrition are. So sprouted whole grain bread is the best choice. Also available is sprouted whole grain pasta. So there are many alternatives to whole wheat flour.

I also encourage people to eat organic produce as much as possible, mostly because they're grown in mineral rich soil and there are no pesticides on them. Depleted soil, pesticides, rodenticides, and herbicides get into our bodies through non-organic produce and wreak havoc on our cells. So healthy produce like organic potatoes, squash, sweet potatoes, yams, fruits and vegetables, and beans and grains is an essential part of a diet that is healthy for us.

When you start eating healthy, your body is going to eliminate better, it's going to detoxify better, and age very slowly. Then we have to repair the damage done to the cells, and that's of course what those red fruit phytonutrients, your healthy essential fatty acids, and healthy proteins do.

And of course, we also need to include emotional repair. You've got to learn to forgive people. Forgiving is far and away one of the best things we do for our bodies because it stops the production of internal stress hormones that we hold onto subconsciously.

Finally, there's rejuvenation, and that's when you challenge your body on every level. I went from just exercising so that I didn't gain weight to exercising to really tone and trim my body. Finally, I moved on to becoming a world class athlete. I went into rejuvenation by challenging my body, and now I can see what my body is capable of doing. I never imagined that I could be this fit at my age. As we age, we think that we've got to slow down, but I don't agree with that at all. I've done the New York City Marathon with seventy-, eighty-, and ninety-year-olds, and if they can do it, you know, what's my excuse? So those are some of the things that affect the body.

Wright

So what is the role of self-esteem in regard to our health?

Pennesi

Self-esteem is everything. I can give people all the information they want, and they can manipulate their physiology with vitamins, but, if they have low self-esteem they're not going to have the incentive—that passion, that drive—to be self-disciplined and to do whatever it takes to get themselves to live at their highest level. As a holistic nurse, I would say that most often, the cause of many diseases is low self-esteem. So when I work with people, I often start with just building their self-esteem up. I familiarize them with those six pillars that Nathaniel Branden speaks of:

1. The first one is living consciously, understanding that events happen; life happens. Two things happen when there is a life event: you can either be a victim of your life circumstances or you can build your character from them. There is a choice. Most of us don't think there's a choice. And in life, pain is inevitable but suffering is an option. We are a society that's

built on the drama of suffering. But suffering is dumb. If you're in pain, that's your body's way of telling you to pay attention and help. So if you pay attention and help, you'll see that the pain usually goes away. Keep your self-esteem strong by understanding that in life there is really no stress; there are two things: there is good information to which you need to respond, and the rest is free live entertainment.

2. The second principle is the practice of self-acceptance. I ask people to look at their thoughts, actions, and emotions without self-repudiation. Experience them without having to slash away at yourself because it doesn't meet someone's expectations of you. Love you for who you are and what you've got. Every single one of us is unique. We all have greatness and we all have something to contribute to make this planet better because we were here.

3. The next one is the practice of self-responsibility. Understand that you're the author of your choices and actions and that no one is coming to save you. You've got to direct your own life.

4. Next is the practice of self-assertiveness. This, in my opinion, is about just being authentically you, not hiding your feelings, and not worrying if people disapprove of you. It's being respectful of people around you without needing them to accept you. When you suppress or deny your feelings it's usually out of fear, and that's when self-esteem goes right down.

5. Then I encourage people to live purposely. In other words, do whatever you need to do to get whatever you want. Each of us deserves that.

6. And finally, practice personal integrity. Be real, be truthful, and keep your promises.

Wright

So how significant is management of our physical environment on our health?

Pennesi

Well, our physical environment plays a huge role, so I encourage people to look at the basics. Number one, look at the air you're breathing. You can purchase little mini air purifiers that you can hang around your neck. I have an air purifier that plugs into the cigarette lighter of my car, too. These things are wonderful to help you only breathe in healthy air. Then there are larger units you can put into your home. When you have clean, pure, healthy air, you're protecting your lungs from damage.

Next, look at water. Most of our water, whether it's from a well or it's municipal water, has some kind of treatment done to it. So I encourage people to get good water filtration units for their homes. You can get one for the whole house or you can get something for the kitchen and then something for your shower. Make sure you have good clean water coming into your home.

Then examine the chemicals in your home. There are natural, planet friendly products for cleaning. You can use something as simple as peroxide. Take a little brown bottle of peroxide, put a spritzer top on it, and spray your shower curtain or shower door, tiles, and fixtures. It kills everything, and you don't even have to wipe it away. Same thing is true with rubbing alcohol. Put a spritzer top on a bottle of rubbing alcohol, spray your surfaces, and wipe it off (alcohol requires friction).

The other thing to use is very, very, very diluted bleach to clean floors (1:10), and vinegar for mirrors and glass. These are very inexpensive. There are even laundry magnets and papaya bleach so you don't have spend money on laundry detergents.

There are so many wonderful things to bring into your home—there's a whole other world out there when you learn about natural approaches to living.

I encourage people to get rid of wall-to-wall carpets, and consider the materials of the pillow you're sleeping on. Look at how much time we spend on our pillows. Make sure you have a good hypoallergenic cover for it.

There is full spectrum lighting that is much better than regular lighting. One of the greatest things we can do in our environment is to get rid of microwave ovens. They are so dangerous. They denature the food and fluids; and remember, the whole purpose of putting food in our body is to put energy into it. When you put any food in a microwave oven, even if you're heating up water, it denatures it, taking the energy right out of it. Not only that but the microwaves are very harmful to human cells, so stay away from microwaves altogether—get rid of them. Toaster ovens, stovetops, and convections ovens are all fine to use.

Make sure no one wears shoes inside your home. Think of it, it's just reasonable. Look at all the microbes and parasites, the garbage out there and the dirt that is coming from the outside into your home when people wear shoes inside your home. I encourage people to have people take their shoes off. You can get those little thin shoe covers that people can wear instead. This practice keeps your house clean, keeps the microbe population down, and prevents infections. Remember, infections are one of the top sources of chronic illness in our population.

Even our cell phones are dangerous. You have to make sure that you have a cell phone shield where the sound comes out of your cell phone. This is especially applicable to your cordless phones as well because you want to protect your brain from all that electromagnetic toxicity. I've been seeing more and more young people with acoustic neuromas. Neuromas are the tumors that form right beyond the ear from chronic electromagnetic and radiation exposure from cell phones.

And of course, everyone should have a carbon monoxide detector in the house as well as smoke detectors.

Always reuse bags when you go to the grocery store, use cloth bags so that we're not polluting the planet with all kinds of plastic. There is even natural pest control.

Make sure, before you eat all your fruits and vegetables, that you're cleaning them off thoroughly. There are commercial veggie washes available.

I think one of the most important things people can do is to declutter their physical environment. Go through all of your "stuff" and give it away, sell it, or throw it away—use it or get rid of it. We need to understand that our physical environment is a reflection of what's going on in our head and what's going on our bodies. This is similar to the art of Feng shui. So when you have a lot of clutter and junk and stuff that you're holding onto, it usually means you're holding on to junk and clutter in your emotions and junk and clutter in your body. Remember how good it felt when you collected a bag full of old clothes and gave it away? You just feel lighter, and you travel farther with a lighter load. So I encourage people to really, really declutter their physical environment and keep it clean using all natural products.

Wright

So what about day-to-day rituals concerning personal hygiene?

Pennesi

I encourage people to start out with natural shampoos, cosmetics, and bath and shower products—things that are planet friendly and much safer to put on our bodies. Remember, your skin is a semi-permeable membrane, so it absorbs the things that we put on it. Consider using natural face washes and avoid cake soaps because they harbor bacteria. The pump dispensers are a better choice.

In terms of oral care, I encourage people to use toothpastes that are made with peroxide, baking soda, sea salt, or natural toothpaste, without fluoride or saccharin. There has never ever been a scientific study that proved that fluoride has any effect on the development of cavities. In fact, it's toxic to the body. I discourage any child from having fluoride treatments on their teeth. If they're eating a healthy diet and they're maintaining good oral hygiene, there is no need for them to have fluoride in their mouth.

Another thing that I really discourage people from getting is silver or mercury fillings. It is one of the chief causes of heavy metal toxicity in our society today. There has also never ever been any proof that showed that mercury fillings were safe; they're not.

I remember when I was a nurse in the hospital; if our blood pressure machine fell over and the mercury fell out, you had to go through a whole ritual with special gloves to handle the toxic mercury. And that's the mercury that is going into tooth fillings! It's a contradiction. I discourage people from having silver fillings placed in their mouths. There are beautiful biocompatible composites that holistic dentists can put in now.

I also encourage people to soak their toothbrushes in peroxide at least three times a week to disinfect them. Store your toothbrush and cups inside of a cabinet. Most of us keep our toothbrushes in the vicinity of toilet bowl. When the toilet is flushed and the lid is left up, microbes from the toilet will now settle on the toothbrush.

These little things make such a big difference.

There are also natural deodorants that use baking soda. They are made with Thai crystals and enzyme deodorants that are far better for the body than the standard deodorants with aluminum in them. Remember, it's aluminum that's causing a lot of the symptoms of diseases like Alzheimer's.

Heavy metal toxicity is a huge factor in disease today.

Wright

Many of us are in high stress jobs and then we're running home and raising our children. What are some of the ways to manage stress?

Pennesi

The first thing I would encourage people to do is take time out every single day to relax and reflect, or better yet, to meditate. And there is no right time of day to do it. Now, when most of us think of meditation we think of someone dressed in a toga closing their eyes going, "ohmm . . ." Well, it doesn't necessarily have to be that way. I encourage people to use their senses when they're meditating—have something that you can see, have something that you can listen to, whether it's through a headset or on a music system, but have sound or have something that you can watch.

Take time out every day and sit for at least a half an hour and learn to ground your energy. Most people have wonderful energy but they just don't know how to manage it. We try so hard to manage all the important things in our life. Yet there are things out there that you just can't control, and when you can't control something or someone, that's what we call "stress." Stress is actually the frustration we feel when we are trying to control an uncontrollable situation. So when you pull back and you ground your energy, you're able to use your intuition to problem-solve better and to manage the conflict more effectively.

Here are some great ways to meditate: First of all, know that there is no outcome to meditation, the only outcome really is a deep sense of relaxation and bliss. Meditation strengthens the breath. And again, you're increasing oxygenation of the body.

In Chinese Medicine, the lungs rule the part of the immune system that wards off externally induced infections, so when you have a strong breath—a strong lung energy—you tend to not pick up microbes in your environment. Plus it grounds your energy, so it helps you sleep better.

I encourage people to do their meditation before they go to bed if they have trouble sleeping. And it can be as simple as taking a hot bath with a couple of cups of Epsom salts, a bottle of peroxide, and maybe a couple drops of lavender oil. Put some beautiful music on and just lie back and relax. So many people don't give themselves permission to feel that kind of relaxation. We've been conditioned to feel that if we are not busy doing something that we are not worthy. Well, let me tell you, only the people who take really good care of themselves first will be better able to be more helpful to other people. So this is one of the hallmarks of health—learning to sit down and ground your energy.

There are progressive relaxation tapes out there. There are yoga, or Tai Chi, or Chi-Gong classes. Just getting a therapeutic facial sometimes is wonderful. You can get a healing touch treatment like Reiki or Hands on Healing treatments from healing touch practitioners.

There are affirmation tapes by wonderful people like Louise Hay and Alan Cohen. When you listen to positive statements that apply to you and you replace the junk in your head with positive statements, you will see that your life indeed changes for the better. Remember that 99 percent of your life is in your head so if you take out the junk—just like you declutter your physical environment and keep moving your bowels—and you put the good stuff in your head/body/environment, it changes your life!

There are other things like guided meditation tapes, alpha induction tapes, and alpha waves. Alpha sounds are the ones that relax you as though you're listening to a harp or some other soothing sound.

Then there are group meditations. Sometimes you can sit in nature or enjoy special time with your pets or do some gardening. People love to garden because it's so relaxing. There's also guided imagery and visualization. You can get these tools right out of the library.

Then there are flotation tanks. These induce controlled sensory deprivation. Try this if you're really ready to do some advanced meditation. Sometimes having a good message is wonderful. Then there are meditation videos.

I have something that I plug in to my computer called "Sacred Geometry." It's a special CD-ROM that you put on your computer, so for those of you who have to sit at computers all day, here is a way to meditate at work! The colors and the graphics are magnificent, as is the sound. You can just sit there and meditate right at your desk.

Creative minds always find a way to make things work for themselves and these are just some suggestions to help you ground your energy and deal with stress.

Wright

So what are the root causes of chronic illnesses and premature aging?

Pennesi

There is not only one thing that accelerates your aging and creates chronic illness, but there are certainly specific things that we can consider. Number one is chronic inflammation. So many of us are allergic—we've had delayed reaction allergies to foods or to things in our environment. Chronic allergens and environmental toxins add to illness.

If you're taking public transportation every day or if you're in an automobile every day, you're breathing in exhaust and toxins. We have so much air pollution on our planet; hopefully we're at a time now where we're going to turn that around. There are chronic toxins that come into the body that create inflammation.

Over time, the inflammation confuses your immune system and you become prone to what we call autoimmune illnesses. Those are illnesses like fibromyalgia, multiple sclerosis, Alzheimer's, diabetes, Parkinson's disease, cardiovascular disease, and arthritis. So when you're eating foods that are full of toxins and you're breathing in air that's full of toxins, when you're getting electromagnetic toxicity, and you're holding on to negative emotions and stressing out over things unnecessarily, all these things create inflammation in the body. That alone can certainly add to aging you prematurely and creating autoimmune illnesses.

The other element affecting our health is chronic infections. This includes viruses (e.g., herpes, hepatitis, and chronic fatigue syndrome), bacteria (e.g., pneumonia, urinary tract infections, cellulitis), Lyme's disease (caused by a spirochete), and yeast infections.

If we get an infection, we're given antibiotics and the physician doesn't suggest that you take probiotics. Probiotics are the healthy bacteria that are killed in our bowels when we take antibiotics, which then causes diarrhea. There are natural antibiotics to use like garlic, oil of oregano, and grapefruit seed extract. There are number of them that are very, very good for the body that don't have the terrible side effects that our synthetic drugs have—killing off our healthy bacteria in the bowel. Chronic infections really drain the body and they accelerate the aging process as well.

Life events also create inflammation in the body. Death, loss of a job, loss of a pet, ending relationships, weather disasters, accidents, and the like are perfect examples. Life events sometimes can really take their toll on us, so that's why it's so important to see your life events as opportunities to build your character and then pull back and make sure you spend the time to take good care of yourself after you've experienced it.

We need to also consider the affect of hormone imbalances. For example, we need to make sure that we don't have high sugar diets because then our internal insulin pump ends up turning on us and we develop insulin resistance, which leads to hypoglycemia and diabetes.

People who aren't sleeping well enough at night don't make enough melatonin. Keeping the room dark and supplementing with melatonin can be very helpful.

Also, as we age our sex hormones decline. Thankfully, there are "bio-identical hormones" that are made by taking plant hormones (plants have estrogen and progesterone just as we do) and we bio-electrically turn them into human hormones! They're very natural, they don't cause cancer, and they help you to maintain a healthy body even as you're aging. So hormone balance is a very, very important.

And of course, as I mentioned before, heavy metal toxicity is a huge contributor to poor health and chronic illness. There are so many things in our environment and in our diets that add heavy metals to the body. You really want to make sure that you get them out of your body. Green vegetable juices help to take those out rapidly, as does healthy algae, like chlorella and spirulina. So when you're eating consciously and you're staying away from these things in your environment, it really makes a huge, huge difference.

As we age, the body takes calcium from our bones and deposits it in our organs. Over time, the organs get more and more rigid, therefore they work less efficiently, and eventually we're supposed to die in our sleep. But that doesn't have to happen if you have healthy hormones in the body, you're exercising, and you're giving your body what it needs to work for you.

We could live up to one hundred and fifty or one hundred and sixty if we would only give our body what it needs to work for us!

Wright

How effective is having healthy, supported relationships to our health versus having strained, unsupportive ones?

Pennesi

I ask people to make a list of the supportive people in their life and then the dysfunctional people. Usually the dysfunctional list is pretty long. Healthy relationships are just so very important. Louise Hay said it so well, "All relationships are important because they reflect how you feel about yourself. If you are constantly beating yourself up thinking that everything that goes wrong is your fault, or that you are always a victim, then you are going to attract the type of relationship that reinforces those beliefs in you." I ask people to take a good hard look at the kinds of people they have in their life. She goes on to say, "Likewise, if you believe that a higher power has surrounded you with truly loving people . . . then those are the types of relationships you will ultimately draw to yourself." You need healthy relationships in your life if you're going to be healthy for sure.

One of the things we need to realize is that there are no perfect matches for us—people are not going to be in our lives to fill in our gaps. The healthiest relationships are those where each person perceives himself or herself as great, whole, and complete and when their energies merge together they are both even more of who they imagined they could be because each is in the other's life. That's a healthy relationship. It is based on mutual respect, admiration, and candor.

Most people lose their whole identities to their relationships. And not only their relationships with their partners, but also with their kids. Sometimes we lose our identity to our jobs. I encourage people to maintain their own identity and maintain their jobs and their relationships as an extension of who they are—to help them to be more of who they are and vice versa.

There are actually six things that I encourage people to do in order to really keep their relationships strong. I learned these from one of my most respected mentors (and coauthor of this book!), Brian Tracy. One of the first things is to be agreeable. People feel valuable and important when you come from a place of love. So there's a difference between criticizing someone and offering constructive counsel. Sometimes it's just the words you use. Instead of saying things like, "You know what's wrong with you," you could try saying something like, "Have you ever considered—" and offer your suggestion.

The next thing is to be accepting. We're so busy trying to make everybody be like us, but that will never happen because there is no one just like each one of us. So accept people for who they are. Sometimes just a smile is just enough.

The next is appreciation—always have gratitude. Even if you're in a marriage, make sure you're still saying please and thank you and being courteous to the other person. Appreciation is so very important. We all want approval, and one of the great motivators is being approved of by other people. Praiseworthiness is one of the best measures of high self-esteem. Praise people when it's deserved and be very specific.

The other thing is admiration. Compliment people sincerely. When you find the good in people, they're going to find the good in you.

Then of course, the most amazing thing that keeps relationships strong is attention; this is what life is—the study of attention. It reflects interest, and you feel that a person is important if you're giving him or her your undivided attention.

Another thing I encourage people to consider is that we all come into this life with different life energies. I got this information from health and nutrition expert, Gary Null, and it has had an amazing affect on my life. There are three different types of energies:

1. Dynamic energies: People who have dynamic energy are very charismatic. They love to create change and they love getting out there and making big changes. They always see the big picture and are born leaders.

2. Adaptives: Adaptives are not charismatic and they don't like change. You give them a set of rules to live by and they will adapt to it. They are the hard workers of society—the glue that makes the community successful.

3. Creatives: Creatives are actors and musicians, muses and artists. They are people who dedicate their lives to art. They're a different breed of people who tend to work best with each other versus the other life energies.

So many of us are trying to make other people our energy. For example, if I'm a dynamic energy and you're a creative energy it's a waste of time to have me to expect you to become a dynamic energy so I can have a better relationship with you. There are some relationships that are better left alone. With this understanding, you can enjoy relationships on different levels. I have friends who are very, very creative but I couldn't imagine living in a house with them because I couldn't imagine living the way a creative person lives. It's just their way of connecting to their worlds. But it doesn't mean I can't enjoy a wonderful relationship with them.

So I encourage people to look at the relationships in their lives and see which ones are there to help them with their self-esteem or to appreciate something that they're not or to discern if there is someone they have lost their identity to. The greatest gift you can give yourself is permission to let go of toxic relationships with love. If people are constantly putting you down to make themselves feel good, these are not healthy relationships. Look for someone who shares your same temperament and has the same values and the same life energy so that you can live more in harmony. And have other relationships that compliment what you're doing so that your relationships are nurturing instead of destructive and condescending.

Wright

Well, what a great conversation. I really have learned a lot today. I'm going to have to take this back and study it. You've covered so much information; I'm sure that our readers are really going to be glad to read this chapter.

Pennesi

I encourage people to be self-informed and not indoctrinated. It's only through reason that the truth is revealed and the information I've shared is all based in universal truth; it applies to everyone.

Wright

Today we've been talking with Luanne Pennesi, a registered nurse. She has dedicated her life to sharing information, as she has done today, that motivates people to take back their personal power and lead happier, healthier, and more productive lives—as she states—at any age.

Luanne, thank you so much for being with us today on *Discover Your Inner Strength*.

Pennesi

It is an absolute pleasure to be here.

About the Author

Luanne Pennesi, a registered nurse practicing for over 30 years in both conventional and integrative medicine, shares information that motivates people to take back their personal power and lead happier more productive lives at ANY age.

Her work is the missing link between the confusing, overwhelming and conflicting information about "new age" or "alternative" approaches to health and anti-aging and the practical application of real-time, commonsense, scientifically based information to help you take full control over your health and longevity and often save your own life naturally. She makes learning fun as she presents wholistic health concepts in a manner that is easy to understand and to integrate.

Luanne Pennesi, RN, MS

Professional speaker, trainer, and consultant

631-504-6198 or 973.766.2214

www.metropolitanwellness.com

whnn@aol.com